H3

THE YOUNG MAN
FROM
DENVER

THE YOUNG MAN FROM DENVER

WILL FOWLER

Doubleday & Company, Inc.
Garden City, New York
1962

To Mother
and
To Beverly

FOR GENE

Well I remember how your letters, Gene,
Fresh from your pen, alive with love and laughter,
Spanned the three thousand miles that lay between
Your home and mine. Reading them through years after,
I feel your living presence still, old friend,
Though now our homes are more than miles apart,
And speak the words with which your letters end:
"Love to you always!" sure that they reach your heart.

Robert Hillyer

Note: This was the last verse Robert Hillyer would write. He died that night, Christmas Eve, 1961.

ACKNOWLEDGMENT

First I would like to offer my deepest gratitude to my mother who has been generous, understanding, frank, and broad-minded regarding the writing of this work.

Thanks to Richard O'Connor for his continuous encouragement when my doubts were mountains. And to Luther Nichols, my editor; I appreciate his directions and his getting more out of me than I thought I had.

Ilka Chase unwittingly allowed me to use her retort to a Hollywood actor who said: "I hear you're doing a book . . . Who's writing it for you?" Her rejoinder was: "No one . . . Who is going to read it to you? . . ."

My wife and four children were most patient during the nearly two years it took to complete this book. Not once did they suggest that I seek other quarters.

While the income was nil, Ralph Trejo, whom Pop called "The Calexico Clipper," gave the male members of my house free haircuts, and his wife, Angie, brought us fine Mexican food she had prepared (also free).

Raconteurs Al Hesseltine and Rickey Biagi, composer Joseph J. Lilley, Art Jackson and Bill Hipple of American Airlines, Gene Sherman, Bill Kennedy, Mike Jackson, Art Ryon, Howard Bishop, Frank Russell, Bill Elmendorf, and Earl and Gen Hannah were all kind not to insist that I mention their names in this biography.

A special thanks to the one person I have forgotten to thank, and who will remind me of this oversight the day after he reads the book.

Al Birch, Martin Dunn, Robert Hillyer, Ben Hecht, H. Allen Smith, and Arthur Robinson supplied me with much material and fresher viewpoints which a son is unable to collect singly.

And thanks to the few who have not forgotten Mother and continue to visit and call her. Those such as Zasu Pitts, Harry Brand, Dr. Barney Kully, Jack Dempsey, Paul J. Howard, Jimmy Durante, and Red Skelton.

Lastly, I wish to thank my father for the exciting privilege of having been his son.

PREFACE

It was a long time ago that I decided to write a book about Gene Fowler.

I talked to him about this in 1951. Nearly a year later, while compiling notes for his next to last book, *Minutes of the Last Meeting*, Pop made a tape recording on the subject while sitting in his workroom on April 25, 1952. He said:

"Sometime in the future, Will intends to set down some reminiscences and things that he knew about me. That seems to be in his mind. About a year ago, he spoke to me about this. I advised him, from the so-called wealth of my experience, not to jump at these things and write about a living man, but to wait. Wait until the inevitable happens, as it must to everyone. And then put things down fairly, and honestly, and without pulling punches (unless of course it hurts someone living) and say what he really thinks.

"Put in the faults, the eccentricities, and those things which some unthinking persons blush to recall, but which are the very essence of true biography.

"I hold that a man's estimate of his own life is the least dependable, and his account thereof the least credible. He exaggerates his virtues to his fellow men, and before God would minimize his sins. The truth of this is apparent in the great bragging hieroglyphics of the Pharaohs and in the deathbed repentances of Tammany politicians.

"Today it seems that we are creatures of terror. What other persons think of us, say of us, becomes our lodestone and our star. A lovely and decent nature, of which we all partake, succumbs to the rancid whispers of some moronic neighbor. The hissing ignorance of an in-law becomes the dictum of the Supreme Court.

"I, personally, would like to be well remembered, of course, and kindly. But I would chuckle over any idiosyncrasy that you might recall.

"One time you said to me spontaneously, Will, that 'I was always afraid to grab the brass ring because I thought my finger might be taken off.' That is almost my own life. I like that . . . I wish to hell I had written that myself. . . .

"I feel that I should bring this reel to a close because one feels that he is getting a little maudlin—or at least mechanical—when he writes a letter to his child by means of a tape recording.

"I have nothing more to say that makes too much sense, except that I love you very much, and I wish you every success in the world, and I know damned well you're going to write the book."

Will Fowler
Encino, California.

Chapter One

MAN IS AN ACCIDENT
BORN OF AN INCIDENT.

GENE FOWLER

It is nine o'clock in the evening. My often irreverent, but seldom irrelevant father, Gene Fowler, died just five hours ago, concluding the three score and ten years he prophesied he would live . . . seventy years during which he became the youngest, most unpredictable top editor for William Randolph Hearst in the heyday of journalistic sensationalism; rose to be the highest paid screen writer in Hollywood; was the close friend of such headline artists, athletes, and nonconformists as John Barrymore, W. C. Fields, Jack Dempsey, Red Skelton, Dr. Frank Baxter, Ben Hecht, Grantland Rice, "Bugs" Baer, Lucius Beebe, H. Allen Smith, James P. Mitchell, Erle Stanley Gardner, Jimmy Durante, Babe Ruth, and many more, and wrote books that have endeared him to all who like their prose rich, their nostalgia deep, and their laughter uncontrollable.

When the end came, he was alone with my mother, Agnes, on the patio of his Brentwood, California, home pursuing his favorite leisure: looking down over his hillside rock garden which is splashed with brilliant early summer colors sometimes seen in a Van Gogh canvas.

Sitting now at Pop's desk in a modest building I built for him ten years ago, I listen to sporadic fireworks explosions and whistles, these from impatient youths trying on Independence Day for size. No objecting barks come from the usually active dogs along Tiger Tail Road across the gully below.

Pop once told me that the late Broadway musical comedy star and writer of patriotic songs, George M. Cohan, was actually born on July 3. He said, "Cohan always claimed to have been born on the Fourth of July. Remember his *Yankee Doodle Dandy?*" There was the question of moving our national holiday up twenty-four hours, or having George destroy his red, white, and blue birth certificate. Generously he yielded to our Founding Fathers . . .

Pop had awakened this day at four A.M., brewed his coffee, then traveled halfway down the garden steps to this sanctuary to write. He had been struggling for four months with the final pages of the nineteenth chapter of his last book, *Skyline,* a delightfully rambling biography of the twenties round and about New York's Park Row.

When Pop came upstairs from his hillside office he found Mother sitting on the living-room divan reading the morning papers. He paced the floor in his gray necktie-silk bathrobe. Mother could instantly identify any of his moods. She knew what to say at the right time. She knew when and how to be silent. She continued reading the papers, sipping her coffee and waiting for him to get it off his chest. After about six laps, he finally spoke.

"I think I finished the last chapter. Now I'm going to get dressed and visit all my children."

This meant my sister, Mrs. Jane Morrison of Glendale; Gene, Jr., who lives in Beverly Hills, and myself. My home is in Encino, a district of the San Fernando Valley. The ones with whom he would spend the most time, though, would be his seven grandchildren and my brother's German shepherd, Anna.

"That's a good idea," said Mother. "Why don't you hop in the car and see them all?"

Official approval had been granted. Pop headed through the hall and bedroom to his dressing room. He put on a white shirt and gray necktie, gray slacks and a black salt-and-pepper, loosely woven wool sport coat with red silk lining and bone buttons. Mother had made it for him.

Looking around this small room, one could tell that, with the exception of the sport shirts he wore around the house, Pop was a conservative dresser. A few of the sport shirts, though, looked like mutations from an exploded paint factory. Below the Crucifix I had given him when he was baptized a Catholic in 1950 was a wide shelf with more than a hundred bottles of pills, salves, and elixirs. Pop was a dedicated hypochondriac. If one answered anything but "just fine" when he inquired about one's health, one was in for a lengthy diagnosis and would be sent packing with a variety of medications.

Pop's single disappointment of the day was that he was unable to reach my sister on the phone. He called Gene, then me, and told us he would drop by our respective houses "if you're not too busy."

"It's a hell of a hot day," I said. "Don't overtax yourself. You're a bit overweight."

He said goodbye to Mother. "I'll be home early. Beverly has some fresh corn and strawberries Willie picked for me. That's all I'll want for dinner."

First, he dropped in to visit with the actor Thomas Mitchell, then headed for my brother's home.

He found Gene in his backyard, looking over what the workers had done the day before on his new swimming pool. My father offered constructive criticism regarding the steel reinforcement. Pop would have been in his glory working alongside the architects of the pyramids of Egypt. He had a native talent for these things.

My brother's thirteen-year-old son, Gene Nunnally, and daughter Kim, six, followed their dog Anna into the yard. This was their time for play with Grandpa.

Concluding his recess with the children, Pop told Gene he was going to deliver the last seven pages of his nineteenth chapter to Lee Stitch, the girl who typed his manuscripts, then head over to my place. None of us ever knew just how long Pop would stay anywhere. He seemed always so restless with nervous energy that he usually started the process of departing directly following his "hello."

Shortly after he had delivered the material to Lee Stitch, his five-year-old Ford pulled up in our circular driveway. A cordon of waist-high juveniles giggled various greetings. Among them was my fourth child, five-year-old Jenny Gene. Pop distributed easy-tounwrap hard candy and the children followed him to the front door like a comet's tail. It was one o'clock in the afternoon.

When I greeted Pop at the front door and kissed him, I was wearing bathing trunks. We children always kissed Pop in private or in public.

As usual, Pop bore gifts. He had two packages for my wife Beverly, and a book for me. The book was Boethius' *De Consolatione Philosophiae,* the Latin edition printed ten years before Columbus discovered America. I had purchased an English translation the year before and was studying this last of the pagan philosopher's work.

"Boethius wrote this book while awaiting his execution by torture in 524 A.D.," Pop told me when I first became interested in Boethius. "I wish you could read the Latin, son. It loses somewhat in translation."

Pop pulled off his sport coat and sat down in the leather governor's chair we called "his." The children draped themselves around his neck and filled his lap. He had the gift of never speaking down to anyone. Perhaps this is the reason he was always so popular with children.

Beverly made her entrance with a package of fresh corn and two boxes of ripe strawberries. She said, "I'll put them in the refrigerator until you're ready to leave." She reproved the children for mussing up Grandpa, and sent them outside for a swim in the pool. Everyone has a swimming pool in the San Fernando Valley. The heat makes it a necessity beyond snobbery.

I told Pop I had just put the finishing touches to a song Jack Tenney and I were writing called *Cold Is the Wind.*

"That's one way of cooling off in this heat," he said. "Didn't Tenney write *Mexicali Rose?*"

"The same," I said.

"Let's listen to the new song," he said.

I played the piece on the piano and sang the lyric.

Criticizing the lyric line: "Steel is the moon; lead is the sky," Pop said, "It's too inventive. Do what the public understands. Say: 'Pale is the moon; gloomy the sky.' The general thought of the lyric is fine, though."

Beverly opened her presents. The first package contained four green marble ash trays Pop had purchased at a bargain price from an odds-and-ends store he had recently discovered. The second package held three abalone shells. "They're ash trays for your patio," he said. "You can polish them on an emery wheel and they'll reflect purple and pearl colors."

He lit his third cigarette and took a short puff. About five more puffs and he would grind out the ember. His snipes were always long. He was a tobacconist's dream.

"I'll fix you a salami sandwich, and you boys can sit and talk," said Beverly.

Pop swallowed all but the last inch of milk in his glass. "Well, all right," he said. "I'm rather tired anyway. And I do have a few things to say to Will." He never did finish a drink of anything to the bottom of the glass. "When I was a boy in the Rocky Mountains," he once explained, "there was always some sort of bug-surprise at the bottom."

We listened to some Tchaikovsky, then to Beethoven's Fifth Symphony on the phonograph. The latter was his favorite. I turned the music low so we might talk, yet stop our conversation to appreciate the finer moments of the music. While we listened, Pop, who appeared tired and drawn, said, "I have the strangest feeling that this might be the day."

I pursed my lips and tried to speak matter-of-factly. I wondered if he might be a seventy-year-old man seeking sympathy, and said, "Just because you told Mother there would be an earthquake last week, and there *was* one, doesn't mean you could be right about this, Pop. You've had these feelings before."

I spoke too swiftly, as one does when that sick, fearful feeling begins to surge from within. I sat on the arm of his chair.

He reassured me. "There's no cause for alarm, Will. I just want to give you a few directions."

It was ten minutes to three, and I was hoping Beverly would come in from the garden to change the subject.

"You've been trying to start your book about me for months now," he said, "but you have the wrong perspective."

"I never wanted to write it," I said. "I have so many fears about whatever writing talent I might possess."

"Barney Oldfield got scared. He used to urinate on the floor of his auto just before the flagman signaled the start of a race in which he was driving. If you can, I'd like you to come over to the house later and start your book in the room you built for me. Just make it simple; report what you saw; give your opinions; be kind to Mother."

"When that day comes," I said, "will it be easy? Will I be able to do my book the way it should be done? I might be out of style."

"You've been composing good music for more than twenty years. Keep writing it the way you want. The age of melody is bound to return one day."

"I'm talking about my book," I said.

"I'll admit this is a 'father is a sonofabitch' era, in regard to the writing of biographies," he said.

"How should I do mine?"

"Do it the way you feel it," Pop said. "In any event, I promise it will be easy, and it will be right."

Naked, shivering children burst into the living room. They were hugging puffy white towels and looked like gay balls of cotton as they bounced onto Grandpa's lap once again. Beverly ran in and pulled them away. "Now leave Grandpa alone," said my blonde wife. "He's tired."

This man had fought more valiantly to be called "Grandpa" than he had to be named "Pop" by Gene and Jane and me. He was even happier when my brother's daughter, Martha Warme, made him a great-grandfather by presenting her husband, John, with a daughter.

Pop picked up the phone and dialed Mother. She answered and he said, "Mother? I have a wonderful lap-full of girls."

"That's not surprising," said Mother from the other end.

"I'm coming home now." He hung up the receiver after I left the room to get some color snapshots I had taken of Jenny, my sixteen-year-old Will, fourteen-year-old Michael, and thirteen-year-old Claudia.

Beverly took the fresh corn and strawberries from the refrigerator as Mike and Claudia arrived in time to say goodbye to Grandpa. Pop got into his car. He said he was sorry my son Will was not there to visit with him. Will was working at a vegetable stand five days a week during the summer months to earn money enough to buy an automobile.

Pop started the motor, then expressed the wish that two of his close acquaintances who had been at odds might "get together as friends."

He mentioned he would like to go to confession, but said he was too tired, and "anyway, I have nothing on my conscience to interest even a young priest." He thanked me for the photographs of the kids.

As he turned the Ford onto the street, the neighborhood children shouted, "Goodbye, Grandpa!" from the yard next door.

It was a few minutes after three o'clock.

I wandered into the house and sat at my desk. I began to mull over ten years of notes I had made from time to time about my father. I ran across an old newspaper clipping Pop had offered me as an idea for a television play. The sub-headline contained the story idea. It read: *"Monk, Once General, Dies with Uniform under Robe."*

Beverly reminded me that the Olympic Games track trials were on television. I tuned in in time to see the fifteen-hundred meter run, the one-hundred meter high hurdles, and the pole vault.

Just as the station was signing off at four P.M., Don Bragg went up and over the standard to establish a new world's record, less than an inch under sixteen feet.

I turned off the television set and chuckled, recalling what Pop had said about this entertainment medium. "It's a glass furnace. It burns up material and talent swiftly. Why, a comedian is a has-been while he's taking a second bow—except for Red Skelton."

The phone rang. I picked up the receiver. It was Mother. Her "hello" was nearly uncontrolled. It was a few minutes after four o'clock.

"Is Pop all right?" I asked.

"I don't know!" She was at the highest pitch of emotion I had ever known her to be. "Come right away!"

I hurried into the bedroom, beginning to shake as I put on a zippered jump suit, searched for socks and loafers and my identification card holder. I ran toward the backyard where my car was parked, then had to rush back into the bedroom to put on my shoes. Just as I was getting into the car, Beverly came up and asked, "What's wrong?"

"I think Pop is dead."

I had to hold back on speed as I was breaking in a new sports car, and consequently drove through only three red lights. I wondered why there were never any motorcycle officers around during an emergency. As I traveled over Sepulveda Pass, I prayed that Pop's end had come without pain. Then I wondered: Why all the rush to get to someone who is beyond all human help. But I couldn't be sure, actually, that Pop was gone. Perhaps it was just another attack, and my mother had become unduly alarmed.

A few minutes later I was pulling up to a stop in the forecourt of my parents' home, I leaped out of the bucket seat and hurried to the front entrance. The door stood ajar. Inside I saw Father Murray, rector of St. Martin of Tours, which was Pop's parish. My mother was standing near him in an attitude of complete helplessness and despair. Father Murray held up his hands in a cautionary manner. "Now, Billy," he said. "Stop." He sounded calm enough. And he called me "Billy." This is what Mother calls me. "It's all over," he said. "Your father is gone." Mother had told him how to break it to me. Where the hell *is* gone?

I noticed the sadness and weariness in my mother's face. I don't recall her words, but I remember she appeared more worried about me than she was about her own feelings. That is the way she is.

"Now, Billy," she kept saying as I began to walk into the front reception room of their home. I stole a glance to the right to see if Pop was in his bed. He was not there. I thought, "Damn it, Pop. I told you you'd drop dead in your garden heaving around those big rocks."

Mother put her arm in mine. "He's right where he said he'd be."

Father Murray followed me through the living room. I heard someone say Pop was in the patio, on his chaise longue. I walked outside.

Before I looked at him full on, I noticed two quiet Mexican boys who had been building the cement block wall at the bottom of his garden so Pop might fence in the yard for a dog his boyhood friend Jack Dempsey was going to get for him. There was an uncorked brandy bottle and a crudely sliced Bermuda onion resting on the glass-top patio table. The Mexican boys, who spoke no English, had found the onion in the kitchen and put it under Pop's nose to see if they could revive him. It was this moment that I suddenly realized I had already begun to write my book.

I took in everything, including a tenacious fly rubbing its fore-legs together like a miniature Scrooge before attacking a shiny bead of brandy on the glass-top table nearby.

Now I turned and looked at Pop.

I grabbed him in my arms and said, "Pop, I love you."

About a minute later, I tried to communicate with the Mexican boys in the few Spanish words I knew. I wanted them to help me put a chair under Pop's legs so they would be straight up. There was a sort of quiet beauty in their stoical faces.

I placed a pillow beneath Pop's right elbow, then was able to cross his strong arms. I turned to Mother to ask, "Did you call Jane and Gene?" She told me that she had. But first of all, my agnostic mother had followed Pop's directions and called a priest. This was a typical selfless gesture on her part. Only about once every two years would Mother sit up defiantly and say, "Now for once, I'm going to do something *I* want to do." This statement would direct us all to get into line, ask no more questions, and give Mother one of her few moments. The following day, she would be back making clothes for the grandchildren and doing everything else she could for her family.

The second phone call Mother made was to a doctor who had never before treated Pop. The medical man, a neighbor, told her only what an impersonal physician would tell anyone under these circumstances, then disappeared before I had arrived on the scene.

As I waited for my brother and sister to arrive, I called local television newscaster George Putnam. George was one of Pop's two "adopted sons." Next I called Sybil Brand to have her get in touch with her husband, Harry Brand, publicity director of 20th Century-Fox motion picture studios and the man to whom Pop had dedicated his last book. Then I called Frank Nolan, Pop's close doctor friend who would eventually sign the death certificate.

My brother was the next to arrive. I was sitting with Pop when Gene came out to the patio. When I saw him open the door, I stood up. We grabbed each other fiercely and buried the hatchet some of us must bury following many years of competition for a father's affection. "We've had many dress rehearsals for this day, Bill," he said. This was the first time I felt I really had a brother. Pop had said: "It makes me sad that you boys can't get together."

George Putnam arrived next on the patio. After he went back into the living room, I found myself alone once again with Pop. I held his hand as I began to search for an answer to why one should take death with forbearance. Here now, I thought, is flesh which no longer contains the counterpart of personality. Here is the body of a man who less than a few hours ago was receptive to his children's and friends' braggings, who was handy to untangle confusion, who was available to comfort bruised egos. Had his body been taken away before I arrived at the house, I could have gone along with Nature's little sleight-of-hand game of Now You See Him, Now You Don't. But here he lies before me, yet he is not.

Now I remembered what Pop had asked me to do. I went into his dressing room and from the wall above his collection of medicines, I took down the Crucifix with which he wished to be buried. I went to the patio again and placed it in his hands. As I did so, I began to rotate the knuckles and fingers of his right hand so they would not become rigid. He had worked hard for many years with this hand, wielding a pen so he could make a living for his family as a writer. This great, full-muscled hand, which one would have associated with that of a day laborer rather than an author, was now noticeably cold.

My sister Jane's quiet voice was in the living room now. She preferred not to come out to the patio. I went into the living room to greet her.

Sybil Brand had arrived. She was taking care of everyone. A cup of coffee here, a glass of water there, and a kind word all around.

There was my brown-haired, handsome sister sitting calmly on the couch, holding Mother's hand. Jane, twenty months older than myself, was Pop's great joy as a little girl. I had worried that her grief might shatter Mother's composure. But then, Jane is always unpredictable, somehow able to find shelter within herself.

When Mother got up to answer the telephone, I followed her. I did not know who it was, but before she hung up the receiver she paid a touchingly casual tribute to the man who had been her husband a few weeks short of forty-four years. She said quietly, "Well, he was a lot of fun, wasn't he?"

The well-dressed gentlemen of the black wagon arrived. Their expressions were professionally blank. I showed them, with their rubber-tired litter, around the back way to the patio.

Gene and I helped fill out papers which seem necessary these days before one is recognized as being truly out of this world. I am afraid some of our answers were bluntly sarcastic. When one of the gentlemen in black asked the silly question: "Sex?" I offered the equally silly answer: "More than occasionally."

Gene and I went back into the living room, closing the outside door behind us so the professionals could get on with their chore. How often I had seen their expensive wagons on the highway and thought nothing of their presence. Now they would always be reminders of this day.

The telephone rang endlessly as the news of Gene Fowler's death got around. After I answered a call from Jim Bacon of Associated Press, I knew that other phones would be ringing. Friend would call friend to say: "Didn't you know? Gene Fowler just died."

When Dr. Frank Nolan arrived with Thomas Mitchell, Mother smiled gallantly as she opened the front door wide. "Come on in, boys," she said. "Gene just left."

My brother, George Putnam, and I went to the mortuary with Pop's black suit, the one he always joked about, "the one I'm going to be buried in." Checking the clothing down to the handstitched Irish linen handkerchief for the breast pocket, the funeral director said, "There are no stockings." Gene took off his shoes, then his socks, and offered the latter to the gentleman.

We entered the show room. Gene muttered to me, "Speak low. This joint is probably wired." In any event, we chose a solid walnut casket. Pop was a nature lover, and this choice seemed appropriate.

As Putnam and I started out the front door, Gene took the mortician aside and slipped something into his hand. I thought this was a hell of a place to give someone a tip. Pop never seemed to have any money no matter where he went. I discovered later that Gene had requested that the burying men stuff a dollar bill in Pop's pocket in case there were toll charges.

Now I see by my father's work-room clock that it is nearly midnight. My brother is rapping on the door, calling for me to let him in. So I shall knock off my writing for tonight and settle down with him. We have much to talk about.

Chapter Two

As far as Pop could remember, it all started with an Irishman named John Parrott. He was born in a town called Bandon in Queenstown, Ireland. His birth date was March 1, 1794. At the time of the War of 1812, John, a Protestant Orangeman, had grown his hair to fall down both sides of his neck and hide the cauliflower ears the Catholic boys had given him. He traveled by clipper ship to Canada, opened a tavern in New Brunswick, then gave that up to become a circuit preacher after he discovered one of his children, Matthew, age four, daily downing the dregs of wayfarers' drinks. His daughter, Lorinda, wrote poems, the only ancestor who showed a talent for writing until my own father was born.

John, Jr., when he grew up, traveled to Montana and discovered a copper mine which he sold to Marcus Daly for $10,000. While John, Jr., spent two years drinking up his profits, Mr. Daly made this mine the greatest copper producer in the United States. John, Jr.'s sister, Elizabeth, married a man named Norman Wheeler after their wagon train, with which they intended to go all the way to California, bogged down at Leavenworth, Kansas. Along the way Norman had been shot in the backside by an Indian arrow. It was decided to avoid further perils and settle in Leavenworth.

When John Parrott, Esquire, was ninety-two, he was put to bed for the last time in 1886. Unable to recall one of his own verses, he dramatically recited a couplet from the hymn of John Wesley:

> *In age and feebleness extreme,*
> *Who shall a sinful worm redeem?*

Norman and Elizabeth Wheeler migrated to the city of Denver, Colorado, shortly thereafter with their only child, a daughter named Dora, who had been born in 1873.

In 1889, the fifteen-year-old Dora married a locomotive pattern maker named Charles Francis Devlan, Jr. He earned $1.20 a day.

Elizabeth Wheeler despised Devlan, and before my father was born, she had shamed her son-in-law out of the house. Devlan disappeared into the Rocky Mountains and became a hermit for thirty years, never actually to meet his own son until he was a grown man.

On the night of March 8, 1890, my father, Eugene Parrott Devlan, was born. He was delivered at the family home, a modest red brick house liberally endowed with Victorian scrollwork. A thunderstorm was flashing in the mountains surrounding Denver. Dr. J. S. Hayes, who hated both thunder and late calls, showed up a bit worse for drink as the threatening black clouds burst open. The good physician charged ten dollars per birth. Pop being a high forceps baby, the doctor charged fifteen dollars. Dora's first child weighed twelve pounds, three ounces.

Dora eventually remarried. Her new husband's name was Frank D. Fowler. Elizabeth, whom Pop called "Granny," resented the intrusion of the name Fowler for a short time, but capitulated at length. By the time he was six, Pop had possessed three names: Devlan, Wheeler, then Fowler. This mixup confused the boy's entire outlook. He developed an aversion to names, to labels of all kinds. So deep-rooted was this distaste that he was unable all his life to remember the names of many friends. One day when his stepfather reprimanded Pop for doing something wrong, Frank Fowler said, "I gave you my name. I want you to wear it proudly."

Pop stared at him and said, "Would you like it back?"

Dora and Frank Fowler had two children. One was Jack. The other was a daughter named Normadine. Pop loved to carry Jack around on his shoulders. He liked being close to his younger brother. He took great pleasure, too, in making little presents for Normadine.

But he could only regard his stepfather as an intruder. "I didn't see him in bed with my mother," Pop told me, "but I saw him the next morning. He was wearing an old nightgown, and he stood on his head. I'd never seen such a demonstration because men were modest in those days."

Fowler continued these setting-up exercises in view of his resentful stepson while the family lived in a clearing in the Rockies called Red Mountain and later when they returned to Denver and lived in a house near Granny's. One Sunday morning in Denver Pop witnessed this exhibition for the last time. The night before Fowler had taken his stepson to a boxing exhibition, but he couldn't make a pal out of the boy. Dora, noting the rage on her son's face as her husband nakedly upended himself, hurriedly handed the boy a bowl and told him, "Run over to Granny's and ask if she can spare some sugar." Before she could prevent it, however, Pop kicked his stepfather in the head and dashed out the door, seething with resentments which might have interested a Viennese doctor named Freud.

"Granny," he said a few minutes later at the house up the street, "Dodie wants some sugar." Then he blurted out, "I don't want to go back there any more."

From then on he lived at his grandmother's house.

Deprived of what latter-day oracles would call the father image, Pop wistfully idolized two men he often saw on the streets. One was a dashing attorney named Wright who was said to own a library costing $1000. Mr. Wright, however, ignored the boy. His other hero was the aptly named Wild Bill Lyons, the sergeant at arms of the Colorado State Senate. The husky Mr. Lyons wore a revolver strapped to his side. Enthralled by Wild Bill's don't-give-a-damn attitude, Pop would, on occasion, say, "Bill, break me a window!" Without mulling it over, Lyons would pick up a stone and hurl it. When the citizen stormed out to protest having his window broken, Lyons would draw his gun and say, "Well? What you gonna do about it?" Upon seeing Lyons with his pistol, the citizen would turn tail, and Pop would beam at all the fun he and Wild Bill were having.

Eugene Parrott Fowler landed his first paying job when he was ten. He became apprentice to a taxidermist. The back room and dark corners of this establishment would remain in the nostrils and mind's-eye of this introspective child for the rest of his days. The dismemberment of dead animals, the entrails, the discolored, decaying flesh, the brown, opaque staring eyes and other macabre sights and smells caused the boy to virtually turn vegetarian from then on. So powerful were the impressions made on him during his short-lived position at the taxidermist shop that he found himself unable to hunt game with his young friends in the Rockies.

Children have wonderful ways of expressing themselves. When he was thirteen, Pop loved the prairie because he could run on it. "I was not the greatest runner in the world, but I could run long distances. When you go a certain speed, a great loping speed, and you have a little form, you hit a spot where you don't seem to have to exert yourself too much. It's like the thumping of a gold beater's hammer—the bounce carries the hammer. I liked to run. I guess I have always been running, either to or from something. Never walking, always running; running from myself most of the time. I loved the feeling of flight. The thin, cool, dry air."

The love Pop had for his mother was of a different texture from that he had for his Granny. The visits shared between these two were stolen moments of delight. Dodie Fowler was truly a child when her son was born. She was not quite seventeen. She was his very own possession now when they removed their shoes and stockings to wade in the waters of Mullen's Mill Ditch. She would sing to him in her soft soprano, with that rare, sweet quality which needed no instrumental accompaniment. Dodie would wrap her arms about him, but he was afraid to show his overwhelming affection for her for fear he might do something wrong to stop the flow of love.

"Once Dodie slapped me, not too hard, for something I didn't do," Pop told me, "but I didn't mind because I loved her. I never called her 'Mother.' I was afraid to. I never quite felt I could take that liberty for some reason. But I wanted to all the time. Maybe that's the reason I like to call my own wife 'Mother.' Perhaps many of us have a sissy side to us that secretly likes to have a mother substitute."

The boy yearned for affection, felt unwanted to begin with. He thought he was a peculiar child. He did not believe he was very bright, although he could not recall when he could not read.

"Possibly, if Dodie had lived, I would not have appreciated her," he said. "Maybe I would have grown tired of her. But at any rate, she never grew old."

Dodie took ill in 1903, and on March 1, she died in St. Joseph's Hospital of peritonitis. The following day she lay in a white coffin in her house, a white lace canopy overhead. The cream-colored satin dress made for the Spring Festival was her shroud. Friends and relatives gathered at the Fifth Avenue Methodist Church the next morning as the organist played *Abide with Me* over and over again.

During his junior year at West Denver High School in 1908, Pop became editor-in-chief of the school's monthly magazine *The Heraldo*. Since a fractured collarbone suffered in the previous season's last game was still healing and he couldn't go out for football, he took a course in public speaking. And he won an oratorical contest with his speech on "What Constitutes the State" despite the fact that, just as he stood up to speak, the seat of his trousers split open. Those seated on the platform behind Pop got an intriguing glimpse of his home-made, flour-sack underwear showing through with the trademark "Pride of the Rockies" clearly visible.

While in high school Pop had formed a friendship with a news-boy five years younger than himself named William Harrison Dempsey. The boy, who would become the most spectacular of all heavyweight champions as Jack Dempsey, sold papers on the streets of Denver only when there were no ruggeder and better paying jobs available to help support his hard-pressed family. Usually he worked in the La Plata County mines, and on Sundays, both for sport and profit, would catch wild horses on foot. Studying the habits of the wild herd, he noted that every third day it halted at a certain spring. When their bellies were filled, young Dempsey would single out a horse to run down. The horse, unused to being chased, would wind easily. When it could run no farther, Dempsey would grab the horse's neck, put a hackamore over its nose, then jump on its back and find out who was the master.

The meeting of Pop and young Dempsey was the beginning of a friendship which would last half a century.

Pop's intention was to enter the University of Colorado at Boulder as a pre-medical student. It was my impression that he wished only to pursue journalism there. My mother, however, told me it was Pop's strongest desire to become a physician.

It was 1910 when the twenty-year-old Gene Fowler faced the problem of raising enough money to get to the university to register. A philanthropic English teacher at West Denver High gave Pop one hundred dollars to make his way to Boulder and advanced learning. Pop sent on twenty dollars for the required matriculation fee, then set out to say goodbye to his pals.

There was a magic about having money in his pocket, and Pop found it impossible to walk past George Wilke's pawnshop. He purchased a leather valise and a set of practice boxing gloves which were supposed to have belonged to retired heavyweight champion James J. Jeffries.

Pop bought drinks for everyone he could find in Tom Holland's Saloon, then suddenly remembered he must catch the interurban trolley for Boulder. He missed it. The sensible thing now was to return to Holland's and continue to buy drinks for the house.

Pop woke up next morning in the saloon. He had a half hour to kill before the next interurban would depart for Boulder. Walking off his hangover, he found himself hypnotized by a pair of yellow and white, two-toned, high-buttoned shoes in the window of Weiner's haberdashery store. He had to have them. The shoes were the largest Weiner's carried in stock, but were a size too small for Pop, who took an eleven D. The salesman assured him the shoes would be broken in to "the softness of chamois in just a few hours." And they were such a bright yellow. Pop was sold.

His final stop before boarding the interurban was at Fonda's Drugstore, where he parted with his last nickel to pay for a small package of gumdrops.

Broke, lonely, and hungover, Pop now began worrying over how he could manage to work his way through pre-med, medical school, and two years of a hospital internship. He registered in Jim Lockhart's journalism class in the basement of Old Main, the first large building erected on the Colorado campus.

Pop's first job at the university was washing dishes in a sorority house. The cook was an outwardly stern but generous lady of middle age. She saw to it that my father had the best of everything in her kitchen to eat, and all he wanted. Actually, when the coeds discovered Pop's talent as a writer he never had to risk dishwater hands again; instead he wrote essays for the girls and tutored them for examinations. Before writing their essays, Pop, a ghost who took his duties seriously, studied each girl's earlier grades, then wrote just a little better than what was expected of them by their professors. If the girl was a "C" student, he would write a "C plus" paper. If she was a "B plus" student, he would give the paper all he had.

As a member of the Alpha Tau Omega fraternity, he made close friends with a fellow named George Shaw, who afterwards became a prominent corporation lawyer. Following a gay evening on the campus, George and Pop were hauled into the Dean of Men's office where the two revelers received a severe lecture. During the reprimand, the Dean asked why the two young men could not pattern their behavior after other industrious students such as Floyd Odlum, "Deke" Aylesworth, Ralph Carr, and Pete Rathvon. The Dean also predicted that Shaw and Fowler either would land in prison or be hanged. Afterwards, Shaw and my father decided to nominate privately the three Boulder students least likely to succeed. They had several candidates, all of whom they liked personally. The three who won out were Odlum, who today is head of the Atlas Corporation (and one of the richest men in the world); Aylesworth, who founded the National Broadcasting Company, and Carr, who went on to become Governor of Colorado.

Although the food was good, his chores at the sorority house did not pay enough to sustain him, so Pop looked about for another job.

The supplemental college job Pop had been seeking finally presented itself. Floyd Odlum managed a laundry route in partnership with "Bull" Sterritt, a great quarterback on the football team.

When Odlum and Sterritt were graduated, Pop's friend, Eddie Sullivan, persuaded them to bequeath their successful laundry business to my father.

Pop failed in this business venture within six weeks because he was taken in by his customers' hard luck stories and continued to give them unlimited credit.*

Although the luxury of college athletics were out of the question for Pop, he found time to make use of James J. Jeffries' boxing gloves. Money being of the utmost importance, he had thought of an angle. His ATO fraternity brother, Kenneth "Cac" Kennedy, was a skilled amateur boxer. Following many long sparring sessions to sharpen up Cac's reflexes, Pop began to promote bouts for the husky, always smiling lad at nearby coal-mining camps. The last match was arranged in a camp near the town of Marshall. Kid Eggert, a professional pugilist, beat Cac's ears back, cut his brows, broke a rib, but could not rub out Cac's game smile. The three-dollar purse, on the loser's side, went to the doctor who dressed Cac's wounds.

Years afterward, Kennedy became vice president of an airline. The last letter Pop received from this stouthearted fellow referred to a large brass spittoon which Pop had appropriated as a souvenir at the Elks' Club the night of Cac's defeat. The reason Cac Kennedy mentioned the spittoon was that when Fowler collected the three dollars for the fight, Kid Eggert and his manager made slurring remarks to the effect that "the punk made a lousy show" and did not deserve a cent from the purse. At this, Pop grabbed the nearest object, which happened to be the spittoon. He tossed the contents into Kid Eggert's eyes, then bounced the spittoon off the manager's head. The two college boys then took to their heels, outdistancing several enraged coal miners. Pop then noticed that he was still carrying the dented cuspidor.

In telling me about this, Pop added, "I read in the papers the morning after I received Cac's letter that he had disappeared during a transoceanic flight. I am sure he went down smiling."

By the end of his first year at Boulder, Pop knew he had to come

---

* When I requested permission to use the above story, Floyd Odlum wrote back, "Use anything you wish, Will. But remember that your father and I also had another mutual friend: Buffalo Bill."

to a decision. He had been earning straight A's in Jim Lockhart's journalism class and Professor L. E. Cole's psychology course, but no money, above his current expenses, to send home to his grandparents. There was nothing to do, he decided, but get a job and abandon his education. The first place he applied was the Boulder *Camera,* a daily newspaper with 1200 circulation. The editor offered him a chance to try out as a reporter.

His first assignment—and his last in Boulder—turned out badly. Pop was sent to cover a fire, at which a fireman fell through the roof and fractured his leg. Somehow the novice thought, with a humor the editor considered misplaced, that the story had its comic aspects. He sat down and wrote his story in that vein, concluding with a few cautionary paragraphs to the local fire fighters suggesting that they refrain from executing ballet steps on burning roofs "unless they are equipped with bedspring inner soles."

Pop departed Boulder that night. He said goodbye to no one before boarding the interurban for the thirty-mile ride back to Denver.

Along the way, the motorman took out a meatloaf and raw onion sandwich. He offered half of his sandwich to my father, who gladly accepted it. As they ate, the benevolent motorman studied the hungry youth. "You come a long way, son?"

"Not yet, sir," said Pop, "but I expect to." He swallowed some more of the sandwich. "I came back to Denver to make thirty dollars a week. There has been a position offered me, and I am traveling back home to consider it."

Pop stepped off near his Granny's home and thanked the man for the half-sandwich. Then the passengerless trolley clanged away into the fog as though it expected another trolley to answer it from somewhere in that all-too-lonely night.

Chapter Three

EVEN AS WE GAZE UPON IT,
THE STONE WEARS AWAY.

GENE FOWLER

Pop's first job back in Denver paid him ten dollars a week. He spent each night in the basement of the Telephone Company Building, where he worked as a signal clerk for the American District Telegraph Company. It was his monotonous business to record on charts the many bells that banged out numbers whenever night watchmen rang signal boxes during their isolated rounds in warehouses, banks, factories, lumberyards, and amusement parks. Twelve hours each night, with a half-hour intermission for lunch and beer at Tom Holland's Saloon, Pop and five other clerks in the basement listened to the clanging bells.

After several months in the Telephone Company basement, Pop received a two-dollar raise, but his ambitions ran higher than sitting in a basement and listening to bells. He wrote Jim Lockhart a letter asking how to go about getting a job as a newspaper reporter.

A week later, Pop received an answer. The journalism teacher suggested he look around City Hall. "You're bound to come in contact there with some helpful gentlemen of the press."

Some days later, Pop was surprised when Lockhart looked him up and told him, "I've talked to James R. Noland. He's city editor of *The Denver Republican*. And he's promised to interview you for a job as cub reporter. But you'll have to start out at six dollars a week."

The Denver Republican was Eugene Field's old paper. Cronies of the beloved poet still worked there and drank an occasional toast to Field's memory. Josiah M. Ward, regarded by certain students of the newspaper craft as one of the men who showed Mr. William Randolph Hearst how to capitalize on the trend toward sensationalism, was editor-in-chief of that lively sheet. He was an austere and impersonal taskmaster who demanded much, said little and handed out assignment memorandums to his vassals at the end of a long pair of shears.

There were four other daily newspapers in Denver at the time, whose owners all hated each other or pretended to. If a reporter got fired from one, he had little trouble getting a job on another. George Creel's blistering editorials for the *Rocky Mountain News* had brought about the fall of the Speer administration and attracted the attention of Presidential Candidate Woodrow Wilson, who later made Creel one of his principal advisers. Jack "The Great" Carbery was swinging his reportorial ax in the *Express.* Eddie Day was starting his career as guide and counselor to newspapermen on the *Times.* And there was the *Denver Post,* a most unusual newspaper published by promoter Frederick Gilmer Bonfils and former bartender Harry Heye Tammen from executive quarters aptly called "The Bucket of Blood."

Whiskey was ten cents a drink—two for a quarter at the more fashionable places—and anyone who paid more than eighteen dollars for a suit was considered a dude. The only wars they knew about then were the Spanish-American, whose Denver veterans seemed to have suffered more from their own bullets than the enemy's, and the Civil War, in the form of reminiscences by their grandpas. The schottische was the popular dance. It was a pleasant era, on the surface, anyway.

The following day, Pop stood in front of the old graystone *Republican* building feeding an apple to a horse as he rehearsed the speech he would give to City Editor Noland. He stopped rehearsing when he noticed passersby staring at him. Until that moment, Pop was under the impression that he had known everyone in town, but suddenly all who passed now seemed to be utter strangers.

Pop looked at the clock across the street. The *Republican's* first deadline had passed and it was time for his interview. Just as he started in the front door, a large scruffy dog nuzzled up against him. Pop scratched the flea-ridden creature, and when he turned again to enter the building, he found his new friend was still with him. The dog followed the prospective reporter upstairs to the city room and sat next to him on a scarred pine bench inside the reception pen.

Pop was about to meet the first of the many characters he would come to know in the hurly-burly of Western journalism. It was not City Editor Noland, but a soldierly old gent with gray goatee. He carried a black walking stick with a silver handle and wore a square-crown derby hat. A rosette, the size and color of a Brussels sprout, occupied one lapel of his Prince Albert coat. The man was Colonel W. A. Jamieson, who had served as a corporal in the Union Army, but afterward promoted himself from year to year. He was the fabulous blade once known among the entertaining ladies of Market Street as "Bouquet Jimmy." Coming to Denver in the 1890s after a relative left him two thousand dollars, he had changed his money into two one-thousand dollar bills and fashioned his bequest into a rosette which he wore as a boutonniere. When circumstances induced him to change the banknotes into bills of smaller denominations, he made new rosettes of hundred-dollar bills. By now, he was wearing a single five-dollar note for his posy.

Colonel Jamieson began to unravel delightful and heroic tales about himself which were about as valid as his brevet commission in the Union Army. Nearly two hours had passed when Pop interrupted the colonel to tell him he had an appointment with Mr. Noland. Just then, a tall man with a green eyeshade pulled over his brow, appeared in the doorway and almost fell over the mongrel dog which was scratching itself on the threshold.

"There's your man," said the colonel.

As Mr. Noland passed by the bench, Pop rose to speak, but his speech stuck in his throat. The colonel stopped the editor and said: "Jimmy, this young man has been waiting nearly two hours to see you."

Noland hurried along, shouting back, "Tell it to MacLennan!"

Colonel Jamieson turned Pop in the direction of Assistant City Editor Art MacLennan's desk and told him: "Take opportunity by the horns, young man."

MacLennan was occupied with looking at a photograph of a young lady clad in nothing but her earrings. "Mr. MacLennan?" Pop said as the man lifted his eyes from the photograph, "I want a job."

MacLennan put on his hat and slouched out of the city room. Pop followed at his heels. "I studied with James Lockhart of the School of Journalism at Boulder—"

"Good Lord!" said MacLennan. "Not another one of *those!*"

On the way downstairs, MacLennan stopped to talk briefly with a dumpy, red-faced man who was on his way up. "Colonel Jamieson's upstairs, Mr. Ward," said MacLennan.

"The hell you say!" Mr. Ward exclaimed in a high-pitched voice as he turned and started back down again. "I'll be at Tortoni's. Telephone the office to inform Colonel Jamieson that I just had a stroke and was taken to St. Anthony's Hospital." Pop was so impressed by seeing the celebrated editor, Josiah M. Ward, in person, that he paused at the saloon door to watch the little firebrand of Western journalism belly up to the bar.

"I had a year in the School of Journalism," Pop said, reopening the subject of his getting a job on the *Republican*.

"In that case," said MacLennan with sulphuric sarcasm, "we'll put you in charge of the paper."

"Didn't *you* start at the bottom?" asked Pop.

"It's all bottom and no top," said MacLennan, "like the fat lady in the sideshow."

"Then there's no job for me as a reporter?"

"You'll be kicked around, hooted at, and I personally will try to break your heart. Then, if you can stand a year of it without cracking up, hating everyone including yourself and murdering your family in their beds, you can consider yourself on your way to being a newspaperman."

Pop's excitement made his voice rise to falsetto. "You're putting me to work?"

"I'm recommending you to Mr. Noland," he said. "He does the hiring. I make it possible for you to get fired."

"When do I report to work?" asked Pop. "And may I buy you a drink?"

"No, you can't buy me a drink," said MacLennan sharply. "Re-

port in tomorrow afternoon at one. Meantime, I'll speak to Noland.
And after tomorrow you and I are strangers."

Pop's first assignment on the *Republican* was to report the dedication of Denver's Catholic Cathedral of the Immaculate Conception on October 27, 1912. He was deeply impressed by the solemn
ceremony as the cross-bearer and acolytes slowly came down the
long steps that lead from the bishop's home, where stood a full
company of Knights of St. John. One hundred choir boys and men,
cassocked in purple and red and surpliced in white, were followed
by as many black-cassocked priests. Following them came the pur-
ple-clad bishops—fifteen of them—each accompanied by two chap-
lains surpliced in white. These were followed by Archbishop John
B. Pitaval, who was to celebrate the Mass, his flowing train supported by two pages in suits of white satin and purple capes.

Then came the panoplied figure of His Eminence John Cardinal
Farley of New York in golden cope and jeweled miter, his long
court train of vivid red upheld by two more small pages dressed
in white satin, with cloaks of cardinal velvet. As he passed, his hand
lifted in blessing, the fifteen bells in the high tower began to sing
their thunderous praise as the procession circled the church. Then
when the cathedral's pastor, the Rt. Rev. Hugh L. McMenamin,
LL.D., entered the place of worship, the huge bells ceased to ring,
the full-toned peal of the organ sounded and the great choir burst
into triumphal hymn.

Later, as Father McMenamin received guests in the rectory, Pop
sped off to write his first newspaper story for the *Republican*.
He was amazed that the paper allowed him so much space. In Jim
Lockhart's class, the rule was to make your story as concise as
could be, but City Editor Noland said: "Open up all the stops like
the great cathedral organ and select words as velvet as Cardinal
Farley's vestments!"

Toward the end of his story, Pop described the parade: "Ten
thousand of them led by their pastors marched the streets that day
to the music of seven bands to show their gratitude for the comple-
tion of the cathedral, and their appreciation of the efforts of
Bishop Nicholas C. Matz, Rev. Hugh L. McMenamin, and the laity
who made the building possible, and their reverence for John Cardi-

nal Farley and other church dignitaries who came for the dedication of this magnificent edifice."

The following day, Father Mac (as his parishioners called him) summoned Eugene Fowler for a personal interview. He wished to congratulate the young man on his story. The two exchanged opinions nearly through the night until Father Mac said he must retire in order to say Mass at six o'clock. "I am not a young man, Eugene," he said, "therefore, I must get at least three hours sleep every night."

As Pop left the rectory, Father Mac said to him, "It is only a question of time until you become one of us."

The following week Pop received his pay envelope containing a five-dollar gold piece and one silver dollar.

MacLennan had put him to writing weather forecasts, a dreary chore. Then one day the editor called Pop to his desk. He said, "You've bragged about knowing Scout Wiggins ever since you came to the paper, so go out to Larimer Street and get a deathbed statement from him."

Ninety-year-old Scout Oliver P. Wiggins, who had been the protégé of Kit Carson, lay dying, the result of a diabetic gangrene of the leg, complicated by a secondary infection caused by a rifle ball wound inflicted sixty years before in a battle with Indians.

While interviewing the Scout, Pop mentioned the name "Buffalo Bill." Wiggins raised up on his elbows and shouted, "Don't *ever* mention that faker's name in the same breath with Kit Carson!"

As the doctor shooed the young reporter from the premises, Pop asked a parting question, "What kind of weather will we have, Scout?"

Studying his gangrenous leg, Scout Wiggins answered: "I got this old wound here that never fails as a barometer!" He flexed his leg carefully as Pop inched back toward the door, then hollered: "It will be fair tomorrow, cloudy next day, and the day after that we're gonna have the damnedest cloudburst in years! And you can tell all the citizens for me, except Cody [Buffalo Bill], to keep out of the way of Cherry Creek!"

The old man died the day before all hell broke loose on schedule at Cherry Creek.

When Pop discovered that the owners of the *Republican* had been persuaded to merge their journal with the *Rocky Mountain News* under the latter's logotype, he decided to join in the wake with which newspapermen traditionally bid farewell to a newspaper shot out from under them. The death of a newspaper is seldom a matter for mourning by its readers, but to its editorial workers it is a disaster— not merely the loss of a job but an institution for which they have risked their necks, worked long hours for low wages and invested with the only kind of reverence most of them know. For the next several days the Denver Press Club was the scene of desperate wassail.

When Pop was suddenly stricken by sobriety, he found himself sitting in front of a typewriter and turning out a story about a little girl who would have no Christmas. As the fog dissipated, he became aware of a man standing behind him and reading the story in his typewriter.

"More speed, Fowler," the man said. "You'll have to respect the deadlines on the *News*."

Pop blinked. The *News?* What was he doing here? He swiveled around to find Henry D. Carbery, editor of the *News,* standing behind him. Later it developed that Mr. Carbery, although a strict teetotaler, had hired Pop during the revels at the Press Club.

Somewhat shaken, Pop finished writing his sob story. When the edition came up from the pressroom, he learned that he had not only been given a job but his first professional accolade. The story he had foggily turned out was headed BY GENE FOWLER—his first by-line.

Chapter Four

TALENT NEVER QUESTIONS ITS MEDIUM,
NOR ART ITS SOURCE.

GENE FOWLER

A hangover at the age of twenty-two—especially in 1912 when most whiskey was good whiskey—was half-licked when a young man got out of bed, took a cold shower, and dressed. A hearty lunch completed his rehabilitation. Pop was ready for whatever challenges his new job offered.

Whatever the *Republican* was to Pop, the *Rocky Mountain News* was that tenfold. "Although I possessed a nearly unrestrained nature," Pop told me, "I felt I had an editor in Carbery, a man who understood my unpredictable whims."

This was to be his year of recognition, a year which would bring him to the attention of Alfred Damon Runyon and the entire city of Denver, but Pop was animated more by a sense of fun than a sense of destiny.

The old Denver Press Club was in the Kittredge Building. This Christmas Eve, the boys were playing cards and drinking a little, and losing as usual to Colonel Gideon McFall. The Colonel was a Southern gentleman, had long silver hair and possessed a remarkable talent as a poker player. He also carried a gold-topped walking stick.

My father told me the reporters were always in debt to the Colonel. "However, he was very gentlemanly, and if you happened to be in a winning streak and had owed the Colonel for a long time, he would reach for your stack, fingering it courteously, of course, to ask, 'Do you mind?' and pinch off exactly the amount you owed him. He never made a mistake.

"Well, the Colonel was taking us to the cleaners this day before Christmas," Pop continued, "when Dud Humphries, a retired newspaperman, entered the club. Humphries declined to join the game and the Colonel thought it time to break it up because nobody but himself and the heavy losers were playing. As was his custom upon folding a game, the Colonel ordered a round of drinks for everyone."

Humphries remarked over his grog that he had put in a call to his sister who lived on Capitol Hill, then the exclusive residential section of the city. He learned that she had been called out of town for Christmas Day. Humphries explained to the Colonel, within Pop's hearing, that he had expected to take Christmas dinner with his sister. Humphries wistfully hinted that he did not wish to eat alone.

Colonel McFall found some excuse for not inviting Dud to his home, and the rest of the reporters were so deeply in debt to the Colonel and to the club that they could not invite Humphries. In fact, most of the boys would have to go without Christmas dinner because of their carelessness in drinking and in matching their gambling skill against the Colonel's.

My resourceful father asked for some copy paper and a pencil. He then wrote in Dud Humphries' behalf the following ad:

Wanted: An invitation to Christmas Dinner. I am a bachelor, gentle and refined; no relatives on earth; have not sat down to a home dinner for years. Am lonely, and seek home company on this day.

Pop left the club, hailed a horse cab, and was driven to the business office of the *Denver Post*. He had his ad inserted there and it appeared in the five-thirty edition that day. He then returned to the club where he found the Colonel's conscience had been troubling him. Colonel McFall said, "Never mind that ad, Fowler," and proceeded to invite Humphries to his hotel for Christmas dinner. But Humphries turned down the invitation because of Pop's ad, stayed around the club for a while, had a few drinks, and then concluded he would not get an answer to the ad.

Pop suggested that he and Humphries go over to the new *Rocky Mountain News* office and tell City Editor Jim Noland about his ad in the rival newspaper. Noland was quick to perceive the "human interest" in this situation and assigned Dick Milton, a former *Kansas City Star* reporter, to write a story about the lonely bachelor.

Christmas morning the *News* ran a front-page story on Humphries, but without using his name. About ten o'clock Pop called the *Post* ad department to see if there had been any answers. He summoned a barfly to pick up the mail. Shortly thereafter, the barfly returned with one hundred-odd letters. Pop opened a few and knew at once that Humphries was in for a good dinner in almost any part of the town, and in almost any grade of society.

"Now a great many of us had spent the night at the club sleeping on the sofas, the chairs, the pool table and the floor," Pop told me. "The commotion caused by Humphries and the club steward, Jim Wong, as they opened the letters and cheered, roused up all. Everyone wanted to pinch-hit for Humphries and pose as lonely bachelors. Humphries said no, that the night before we had not been any too sympathetic with him."

Humphries took his bundle of letters and went to Tortoni's Restaurant, where the *News* morning shift was having eye-openers. Josiah Ward and Jim Noland heard of Humphries' windfall and prided themselves on the results of the story they had ordered, not giving the ad in the *Post* any credit whatsoever. Together they opened the letters and Ward made a speech about the spirit that had made the Old West come once again to the surface. Noland also made a speech on the revived spirit of Christmas, on which they congratulated themselves.

There was a letter from four bachelor girls who described themselves in loving detail, the dinner they would provide, the musical program they had in mind, and an indication of even greater pleasures. This letter had such strong appeal to Humphries that he was all for accepting it.

"However," Pop recounted, "Joe Ward had just finished reading a letter from a small boy who wanted Mr. Humphries to be with him, not only for a good dinner but to meet his kindly father.

Ward now was having his sixth drink and said: 'Humphries, this is the goddamnedest human interest story I ever came in contact with in all my newspaper experience and I'll be damned if it's going to be spoiled by any frivolity.' "

Ward was called to the telephone and after a time came back to announce: "I have just talked to a sweet little old lady who read Milton's story!" Ward brushed all the letters into a nearby basket and announced to Humphries: "You're going out and see that old lady whose sweet voice I have just heard!"

"By this time," Pop continued, "the swaying group had journeyed en masse to the *News* city room. I started to write a follow-up story for the next edition. Ward put in a telephone call to the old lady and insisted that Humphries talk to her personally and accept the invitation. Humphries was a bit disappointed and said he still would like to go see the four bachelor girls, but when Joe Ward promised to send the lasses four dozen of the best roses 'to pave the way for future reference,' Humphries consented to go to the little old lady's home.

"Humphries demanded that Ward provide him with a carriage. I queried the *New York Herald* on the wire, and that paper took thirty-five hundred words for thirty-five dollars, which I put in the pot for drinks afterwards."

Arthur MacLennan had the good sense to retrieve from the basket the letters Joe Ward had brushed aside. Half the staff accompanied Humphries to the Glenarm Turkish Baths where he refreshed himself so that he could meet the little old lady without falling over her threshold.

"Humphries rolled up to a small bungalow out on Park Hill at six o'clock, there to meet a handsome female with snowy white hair," said Pop. "MacLennan and I accompanied him, but we stayed in the carriage waiting for him to get us invited inside for a meal. When the door opened, an old lady appeared in the light. We heard Humphries announce himself as the 'Lonely Bachelor' and watched the woman place her hands on his shoulders, then heard her say: 'The Master sent you.'

"Mac and I remained out in the cold for two hours. The long wait was insufferable in that we had forgotten to bring a bottle of the 'craytur' with us."

Pop learned afterwards that the old lady and her husband met Humphries inside; that they were deeply religious people who tried to convert the Lonely Bachelor to the ways of the Christian life as he toyed with an undercooked turkey thigh.

"After we had waited for what seemed a millennium," said Pop, "I mentioned: 'What the hell are we waiting for?' and brought out some letters. I held lighted matches while we looked them over. We found the missive with the address we wanted most of all. Then I ordered Humphries' carriage driver to carry us to the place where the four bachelor girls lived.

Arriving at the front porch, Pop represented himself as the Lonely Bachelor and asked if the girls minded if he brought along a friend. The four extremely attractive girls, all seductively attired in transparent negligees, squealed with delight as they bade Pop to bring his friend inside.

Completing his recollection of this gay night, Pop philoso- phized, "It seems that Christmas is the slowest day of the year for 'ladies of the evening.' I suppose this is because it is a time for straying husbands to remember their duties at home. But then, I was unhitched, and certainly not lonely that night."

Humphries was infuriated when he learned that my father had taken credit for the roses sent the four girls. He was somewhat en- couraged, however, when he called at the *Post* next day to find more than five hundred invitations to dinner, twelve proposals of marriage, and one chance to make a loan of a thousand dollars.

Pop was handed his envelope at the end of his first week's work with the *News*. Inside were a twenty- and a ten-dollar gold piece. He had reached his goal in life. Thirty dollars a week. All this money just for writing words on a piece of white paper. All this money for a service he would have offered free of charge.

Editor Carbery of the *Rocky Mountain News* had a capacity for filling journalistic hearts with fear. His forgiveness of Pop's numerous pranks caused endless wonderment in the city room. Not only that but Pop was promoted to city editor within six months after his employment. On taking command of the city room, Pop brought a cap-and-ball Civil War pistol to work with him every day. When reporters showed up late for work, Pop would fire the pistol in the direction of the sleepy or hungover journalists. A lead ball would tear a hole in the already scuffed pine flooring.

When Carbery was informed of Pop's Billy the Kid tactics by a plaintive reporter, he nodded and said it was "the only sensible way to discipline the men."

On another occasion, Carbery returned to the office unexpectedly one evening to find Pop throwing apples the length of the city room at a typewriter. The apples had been the governor's gift to Carbery for which he had returned to the office. Everyone expected Pop to be demoted from his post as city editor, if not fired. Instead, the non-drinking Carbery amazed the staff by removing his coat and joining Pop in the game at five cents a side.

Shortly thereafter, Carbery needed an Easter poem to fill a purple-ink box on page one. He called for Pop, who that moment was calling for bourbon at the Black Cat Saloon across Welton Street. Carbery found my father wrestling on the sawdust floor with a powerfully built bartender. He escorted Pop back to the office, sat beside him and watched the young man compose a verse entitled, "Risen Is the Christ." After finishing eight stanzas, Pop turned from his typewriter and said, "Would you please sign it for me, Mr. Carbery?" He then collapsed on the bullet-riddled floor.

There is something to be said in favor of the companionship between two males over that of a male and a female. The major asset of such a relationship is that the law frowns on a legal marriage between the two.

If these two fast friends eventually have a violent difference of opinion, there are no estates to carve up, no alimony to pay, no redress to be made except that of taking back all the good things one has said of the other. So when a man discovers a fellow who possesses his own general tastes, habits, and viewpoints, there are no posting of the banns. The two merely become sounding boards for each other's discoveries, joys, irks, woman troubles and/or small victories.

Pop's first great friendship was with Lee T. Casey, a reporter who had joined the *News* staff shortly before him. Casey was a few months older than Pop, thin as a slat, with a mop of blond hair and penetrating gray eyes. Tennessee-born, he came to Denver via the University of the South at Sewanee, Chicago, and Kansas City. Falling victim to tuberculosis, then the dreaded and all but incurable "poor man's disease," Casey arrived in Denver on a stretcher. The dry cool mountain air brought him around in a hurry, and he soon rose from his sickbed, ready to tackle the newspaper business again. Thus he began a forty-year career on the *News,* with a brief time out for teaching the history of ancient Rome at the University of Colorado, during which he became one of the most widely read columnists in the West and eventually editor of the *News.*

He and Pop romped through the carefree, pre-war years together. Soon enough Pop was relieved of his administrative duties, for which he was not exactly suited by temperament, and shifted from the city desk to what was then known as the Sporting Department. Perhaps it was inevitable, with his fierce love of sports, both as a participant and a spectator, that he would wind up writing about them.

Baseball and boxing were then the major sports. Pop brought new techniques to covering these fields. In writing about a fight, for instance, it was standard practice to devote most of the story to the winner and how he won. Pop reversed this procedure and wrote his account from the standpoint of the loser—possibly a demonstration of his sympathy for the underdog. He would devote most of his story to how the fight was lost. And he followed the same pattern in handling the story of a ball game. When the home-town team was defeated, ardent fans found solace in his clinical way of reporting that defeat without once offering an excuse for the loss.

When the coldest spot in the nation is reported by today's television weather experts, the odds are four-to-five they will mention Aspen, Colorado. When I hear of Colorado, and sub-zero weather, I always remember the story Pop told me about the late autumn in 1913 when nimbus clouds began to stockpile above North America's watershed tighter than sheep's wool. This payday found Pop and Lee Casey putting the last edition of the *News* to bed.

The lead story speculated on the size of the impending storm. The two changed their twenty- and ten-dollar gold pieces into silver at Holland's Saloon, then looked around for Colonel McFall. The bartender informed them that the veteran gambler had glanced at the clouded sky which appeared to him like "a million cow's udders from the viewpoint of a prairie chip," and repaired to his lodgings with two decks of cards and a case of Wilson's best bourbon whiskey.

That seemed like a good idea to Pop, Casey, and Jack Carbery, who had joined them at the bar.

As prospective guests of the Colonel, Pop, Casey, and Carbery matched his prospective hospitality by purchasing another case of Wilson's for eight dollars and sixty-four cents (ten per cent off by the case, otherwise, eighty cents the quart) and two more decks of cards.

Protected against the cold weather with topcoats, long scarfs, fedoras and ear muffs, the triumvirate hauled their case of liquor aboard a horse-drawn carriage and demanded that the driver head toward Colonel McFall's residence. Snowflakes the size of potato chips began to curtsy around the black carriage like a thousand ballet dancers.

The Colonel chuckled as Pop carried the whiskey over the threshold. "Expecting a storm, gentlemen?"

"Inform Noah that it is time he began constructing his ark," said Pop as Casey and Carbery shook the snowflakes from their topcoats.

Casey glanced at the twenty small logs stacked against the fireplace wall and said: "I see you also think we're in for a bit of weather. Damn it, I'm cold."

"Quoting one of your Roman philosophers," the good Colonel said to Casey, "Nectar warms only from within."

"Also," said Casey, *"In vino veritas."*

Carbery broke the first deck of cards. Pop uncorked a bottle of Wilson's best. Colonel McFall placed four shot glasses around the green cover hugging the oak table in the center of the room and started to count out chips, ten at a time. All but Casey removed their suit coats.

They drew for deal. Colonel McFall won the honor. "Remember, gentlemen, I will show no mercy. No jokers. Stud and draw."

After the first twenty-four hours of play had passed, Colonel McFall had won all the money. He allowed his friends unlimited credit. As Pop recalled it to me: "Casey held his own. He was only short twenty dollars. Carbery had lost his pay check plus eighty-five dollars. As for me, well, I had six weeks' worth of earnings on the black side of Colonel McFall's ledger."

The second day Pop opened one of the two windows in McFall's room, complaining that it was getting stuffy. Casey cried out bitterly that too much sub-zero air was entering the room. The Colonel studied his dwindling supply of logs and continued to deal. Pop closed the window, then suggested that he telephone the paper to let them know where he could be reached in case he was late for work the following morning. "In case you gentlemen don't know it," he said, "we're having a hell of a blizzard."

The Colonel pointed out that there was no telephone.

The middle of the third day saw the end of the log supply. The card players had gone through one case and three quarts of Wilson's. It was too cold to sleep. Pop outdrew McFall's straight with a full house in a big pot. With his changing luck for the past seven hours, he had climbed back to where he was only a week's pay in the Colonel's debt.

Now Casey found it difficult to move his arms to deal while wearing two topcoats. The snow line was up over the window and Pop headed once again to open one of the two snowed-up casements. "If you do, Fowler," shouted Casey, "I swear I'll kill you! I don't know what with, but I'll kill you if you open it!"

"I just wanted to see if it's day or night," said Pop.

Casey stood up and threatened to call an end to the game. "I came to Denver to be cured of tuberculosis," he roared, "and not to be buried because I froze to death! We need more logs!"

"Impossible," said the Colonel.

"We might show ingenuity," said Pop. He stood up and embraced two hard chairs against the opposite wall like a long-lost pair of brothers, broke them to sticks with his powerful arms and threw them on the fire. The room began to warm up again.

"This also means that you drinkers must start rationing the whiskey if we are in for a long winter," said Carbery.

The men resumed their card playing and sipping from their respective bottles. There were only three for each remaining.

On the fourth day, Colonel McFall began to show the strain of this prolonged game. Much older than his adversaries, he commenced to catnap at the table. His judgment faltered. This offered the newspapermen renewed courage, and soon they were nearly even.

The men had broken up the furniture with the exception of the oak table and four chairs in the center of the room where the game was in progress.

Pop and Carbery had long since rolled down their sleeves and donned suit and topcoats. Now Casey was decked out with two of Colonel McFall's bed blankets hooding his balding pate.

The card players cracked the tops from their captain's chairs to make these seats into stools. Then the stools went into the fire. Then the oak table legs were snapped off. Now the poker players sat cross-legged on the floor, transacting their card business on the top of what had become a pre-modern coffee table.

Halfway through the night, the Colonel began to lose with regularity. He prayed that the storm would cease.

By then they were on their bellies, playing on the wooden floor with the last frayed deck of cards. The rug had gone up and offered more smoke than heat. At last, when the oak table top went, the newsmen were winning consistently from McFall. They were into the Colonel for the collective total of about one hundred dollars. Casey warmed his backside against the hearth after kindling a few books and old newspapers he had not noticed in the room until this time. The Colonel relinquished his last bottle of booze so that he might recover sufficiently to begin winning again. This last bottle was passed around, but for "sips."

During the fifth afternoon there was a knocking on the door. Members of the Denver Fire Department were helping to dig out local residents. Colonel McFall's shack was one of the first to be reached. Now that the poker enthusiasts knew deliverance was at hand, they reckoned up to discover that McFall had been taken for a fat sum of money. Never a good loser, McFall deflated the winners by penciling an account on an overlooked piece of paper. He deducted from the winnings a modest price he set on his burned-up furniture, rug, and books. "Although I was keeping them for future reference," the Colonel said, "the newspapers are outdated, so I will not charge you for them." From Casey, he collected fifty cents; from Pop, seventy-five cents, and from Carbery, an even dollar.

Upon departing Casey berated the firemen for not being earlier to the rescue. But all this commotion was meaningless to Colonel McFall. He was already sound asleep on his coverless bed.

Recalling that epic poker game and his days on the *Rocky Mountain News,* Pop said: "It seems that I never could have lived anywhere else in my youth than in this untamed town. I have to laugh at my own naïveté, for I had thought that the mass behavior of Denver shortly after the century dawned was the norm for the entire world. Both my great joys and supposedly great sorrows came from this child-like credo when I finally pranced along the avenues of New York and the Left Bank."

He added: "In a sense, I have waged a mighty battle of Fowler versus sophistication, but I may say that I am losing the war loudly and with at least vocal defiance. Of course, I now know that a man who dares laugh or pursues his own simplicities is bound to be kicked to death. But this does not deter me."

He also recalled how he ached for sleep following the protracted poker game. Returning to the *News* city room, he placed his trousers between heavy bound volumes of the paper so they would be pressed when he woke up. Then he picked up a stack of old newspapers from the floor and retired to a corner of the sports department near a pot-bellied stove. The newspapers served both as blankets and mattress for the weary journalist. It was not until ten hours later that he opened his eyes again, ready for work as the city room stirred back to life.

"In a newspaper office," he told me, "I always felt at home."

Chapter Five

FOREVER IS A WOMAN'S WORD.

GENE FOWLER

Where the Fowler legend really started was on the liveliest sheet west of the Mississippi, the *Denver Post*. In those days a newspaperman changed his job almost as frequently as he changed his shirt. Pop was happy enough on the *News,* but he allowed himself to be lured over to the more prosperous and less inhibited *Post,* which was prepared to hire him as a general assignment reporter and rewriteman on the recommendation of staff member Nick Carter and promoter Jack Kanner. The understanding was that Pop would work on the city side, but he had other ideas. Reporting for duty at the *Post,* he strolled unbidden into the sports department, sat down and began to write an analytic account of the Denver Grizzlies' losing streak on the diamond.

Sporting Editor Otto C. Floto, a blimp of a man with a sizable temper (he had once feuded with Bat Masterson when that retired gunfighter was a Denver sporting figure), arrived at noon and looked over Pop's shoulder. "One thing I can't stand," Pop said, "is someone looking over my shoulder while I'm writing."

"What the flaming hell are you doing in my sporting pen?" Floto demanded.

"I came to work for you, Mr. Floto." Pop went back to work.

Next day Floto informed him that he'd been officially assigned to sports. From then on, they were the closest of friends. Although Floto was hard on his underlings, Pop generally escaped his wrath. When Fowler did not show up for work, Floto sent scouts to various Turkish baths. It was usually reported that he was in a horizontal position. The invariable procedure then was to have bathhouse attendants prop him up on a rubbing slab and direct a stream of water from a fire hose at the reporter. Then he would be delivered to his desk.

Pop also became a favorite of co-publisher Harry Tammen, who would borrow him from the sporting department for a major city-side assignment. Tammen was less patient than Floto with Fowler's wayward tendencies. As an added deterrent to puckish behavior, Tammen appointed Pop editor of the *Post's* weekly magazine, *The Great Divide,* one of the nation's first insert sheets. This one was devoted to mining and farming. Although he had lived among miners in Cripple Creek, Pop knew little about the ores that men wrested from the earth. He had also lived on farms in Kansas and the western slope of Colorado, but he had paid more attention to the people than to their weedings and their plowings. He realized if he tried to get technical in print about mining and farming, subscribers would quit the paper. He believed farmers and miners liked to read about women (and look at their pictures) after the drudging at the shaft and furrow. Instead of farming and mining data, Pop printed *women* data. The idea took hold immediately. Farmers and miners *did* like women! Veteran editors who had warned Tammen about this young wild man were dumfounded. Tammen glowed as circulation began to boom on *The Great Divide.*

Bonfils and Tammen owned a good-sized traveling circus which started as a dog and pony show. It gradually built up and was called the Sells-Floto Circus. Although Otto Floto had no financial interest in this circus, Tammen could not resist putting that name he so loved in lights, coupled with that of the former owner.

At the time, Colonel William F. Cody was financially and literally on his uppers. He was about to suffer foreclosure of his small remaining interest in the Buffalo Bill Wild West Show. Bon and Tam picked up Cody's interest and added the aged Indian fighter to the circus as a special attraction. Mounted on horseback, he would ride about the center ring and shatter glass balls with his

Winchester rifle as they were tossed into the air. Oddly enough, no spectators were killed.

The circus winter-quartered in Denver. During this layoff period, the *Post* would publicize Cody's presence and he would hold court in a great oaken chair at the top of the stairs just outside the editorial rooms each Saturday morning. Cody would lift children on his lap and have others crowded about him as he related tall tales of his early days fighting Indians and killing buffalo around the unsettled frontier lands. Although the *Post* publishers paid Cody whiskey money, the attraction for the kiddies was free.

Following one of Buffalo Bill's Saturday appearances, City Editor Al Birch assigned Fowler to interview the silver-locked Indian scout. Pop went into the hall and sat cross-legged on the floor at Cody's feet. Pop's opening question was: "Well, Colonel, how are all the girls?" Buffalo Bill's reputation as a womanizer was better founded than his fame as an Indian fighter.

Cody was so taken aback by this question he missed the nearby spittoon by a foot. He began to reprimand Pop, who cupped his hand to his ear and pretended to be hard of hearing.

Then Pop asked, "Well, Colonel, do you really believe the girls of forty years ago were better in the hay than the girls of today?"

Cody stood up and shouted: "An older man demands respect, sir! My hair is hoary!"

"But not with years, Colonel," said Pop. "Did you have to work as hard then as a fellow does today to get a gal in bed?"

Buffalo Bill's face turned white with rage. He shouted: "Sir! you are insulting a trail blazer!"

Pop cupped his ear once again. "Eh? How's that? I can't hear you, Colonel."

Cody stalked into the city room and snapped at Al Birch, "Give me another reporter! That sonofabitch Fowler is *deaf!*"

The news got back to Tammen the following day, but it was another week before he began to see the humorous side of the interview. It took a month before Cody laughed; then over a tall glass of whiskey he told Pop: "Seducing an unwed Indian wench in my younger days was child's play," adding, "But the practice was not advisable for a white man unless he had the hearing of a coyote and the quick take-off of a jack rabbit. Those young braves were most possessive, son."

Aside from such antics as baiting his elders, Pop was a busy man. He was refereeing boxing bouts at the old Baker Street Theatre, reporting on city side for Tammen, writing for Otto Floto in the sporting department, and putting out *The Great Divide* once a week. Pop had little time to cut loose until Saturday afternoon. Often these were solitary binges. His favorite place to take his liquor aboard was in the small office of Frances Wayne, the *Post's* sob sister.

"Gene would start drinking until he was good and plastered," Al Birch told me. "When sleepy, he'd lie down on one end of the green carpet and, placing an extra bottle handy on the floor, he'd grab the end of the rug and roll over and over until he was wrapped up like a mummy. He often wound up at one end of the room with his nose pressed against the baseboard."

On Monday morning, Frances Wayne would get Birch to go with her to see if Fowler was still there. If he was, Birch would put him into a carriage and have him headed home to be cleaned up in time to report back to work.

"Being star reporter on the sheet," Birch said, "Gene was often called upon by Mr. Tammen to cover one of his policy stories. If this order came through on a late Saturday afternoon, I'd say, 'But boss, I just sent Gene up to Boulder to cover a student gathering,' or 'He's gone to Greeley to cover a political story.'

"Suspicious of Gene's continuous absence on Saturday afternoons," Birch went on, "Mr. Tammen sneaked into the building and had the superintendent unlock every office door.

"When they opened up Miss Wayne's room, they found Tutankhamen mummied up in the green carpet, sound asleep."

Tammen phoned the Albany Hotel manager, Harry Dutton, to report that Pop was on his way. "See that he's put to bed, and take good care of him until Monday morning," he instructed.

"This time Mr. Tammen had saved his temper for me," Birch said. "He gave me holy hell for lying about Gene's phony Saturday assignments. All I could do was grin and say, 'Well, boss, Gene Fowler is a real genius. We'll never get another one like him on this paper. I've been trying to go easy on him so he'll stay with

us.' Mr. Tammen said, 'I'm not mad at Fowler. I'm mad at *you!*'
Then Tam said, 'I guess we have been working that guy too hard.
Maybe we'd better ease up on him.' "

Later, as city editor on the *Denver Post,* Pop demonstrated that
he possessed a strong sense of intuition. It was November 1916.
His hunch was that the California electoral vote might swing
the Presidency over to Woodrow Wilson. Republican candidate
Charles Evans Hughes, confident of victory, had already gone to
bed.

During his lonely wait, Pop was making up a headline with three
columns open below for a lead-all. The headline read:

WILSON! THAT'S ALL!

Pop ordered five thousand copies run off. He had members of
the circulation department call out all available newsboys to report
three hours early to be ready for the extra edition.

The waiting was hard on Pop; because it would cost the *Post*
heavily if his gamble failed.

Then the wires came alive with the bulletin, *"Wilson Elected!"*
Circulation men spread the word to newsboys who now awakened
Denver with the California electoral vote result. The *Post* had
scooped the Middle West and the East.

Pop celebrated his lucky guess in the saloon across the street
from the *Post*. When Mr. Tammen found him the following morning, he asked Pop, "Just how did you know?"

Pop pushed a bottle of whiskey respectfully towards the publisher. The label read: *Wilson's—That's All.*

Tammen chuckled, bought a drink for the house, then told
Fowler to take the afternoon off.

Pop returned to the sporting department to find Otto Floto
thumbing through his Thesaurus, seeking a phrase for the second
paragraph of his friend Bill Naughton's obituary. Naughton was
the foremost boxing commentator of California at the time. And
Floto thought "foremost" people should have their accolades sprinkled generously with polysyllabic words. Floto's lead to Naughton's
obituary read:

As we stand upon the threshold of grief this melancholy morn, there is an increased secretion of our lachrymal glands.

With great effort, Pop sidetracked Otto in favor of a simpler approach. Floto then wrote one of the finest tributes a sportsman ever composed in memory of another.

Floto afterwards began to call my father "son," and wrote to him throughout the remainder of his life, even long after Pop traveled to New York and fame. When he was dying thirty years ago following a severe stroke and had lost his ability to speak—and knew none around him—Otto Floto would not allow a photographic portrait of my father to be removed from him. When he was found dead in his hospital bed by a nurse, he was still clutching this picture of my father he had hidden beneath his pillow.

Floto was one of a breed of men that typified those great days of the West when the frontier spirit had not died and people still seemed to be trying to live up to the grandeur of the country they had seized and transformed. As my father's friend Al Birch wrote me a few years ago: "The times were different. The people were different. The nature of the whole town was different. People would be put in jail instantly today if they tried to do the things Tammen and Bonfils and Gene Fowler did in the heyday of this paper [the *Post*]. It took BIG men, men with guts and understanding, to do what they did . . . When I look around me at this joint—at the cut-and-dried, straitlaced, timid bastards who are afraid to let a single line go into the paper that hasn't been approved of by some insipid School of Journalism boy—I almost give up my innards! I'm almost seventy-five now, but I still believe I can out-work any five of these milksops; and I wouldn't surrender my memories of the more robust days for anything anyone could offer me."

Robust was the word for some of Pop's experiences as a free-wheeling reporter and young-man-about-Denver. Such as the day he went over to the District Court Building on a most innocuous errand: he was supposed to help Judge Ira Rothgerber plan a testimonial dinner for U. S. Senator Charles Spalding Thomas. On arrival in Judge Rothgerber's courtroom, he found that oral bar examinations were in progress. Just as he lighted a cigarette to help kill the time, a crazed woman, with revolver in hand, entered the courtroom. "Where is this Gene Fowler! Someone at his newspaper told me he was here! I want him!" she cried.

With imperturbable self-assurance, Pop stood up, turned to face the woman, took a slow puff from his cigarette, and said: "Madam, no doubt you are referring to me. *I* am Gene Fowler. What seems to be your problem?"

Two volleys in Pop's direction deafened everyone in the courtroom.

Dropping his brave pose, Pop leaped over the rail and found temporary sanctuary behind Judge Rothgerber's high-backed leather chair. Now he was puffing rapidly on his cigarette.

Two more volleys ripped through the courtroom as the crazed woman shouted that "this Fowler" had caused her daughter to be in a family way.

Judge Rothgerber, the only one who seemed to be keeping his head now, turned around to Pop, who looked as if he was sending up distress smoke signals, and said (*sotto voce*): "What the hell did you do now, Gene?"

Pop dropped his cigarette and said: "It wasn't me, Judge. I swear! It was my by-line in the paper. She must have mixed up my name with the guy I wrote about . . . The one who knocked her . . . up . . . I guess . . . I'm innocent, I swear!"

The sergeant at arms arrived to subdue the irate mother. The judge soothingly explained that Pop had "merely written the story under orders by his newspaper editor." This placated the woman.

As she was escorted from the room, Pop began to howl: "Call the fire department! Get Chief Healy! I'm ablaze!"

While cowering, Pop had dropped the cigarette in his trouser cuff, and he truly *was* ablaze. From then on, the gossip about City Hall was that Gene Fowler was the "hottest reporter in town."

Old-timers who knew Pop's work as the third man in the boxing ring said he was sure-footed. In his August 19, 1946, column, "The Brighter Side," Damon Runyon wrote: "Fowler could drop a light, but thoroughly restraining hand on a dangerous right duke about to be discharged at the chin of a gladiator managed by a friend with as much delicacy and precision as any referee that ever lived."

Rereading this precise bit of innuendo from an age-yellowed clip, Pop chuckled and said, "Little did the 'Demon' [as Pop called Runyon] know the trouble I had the night I refereed for my own fighter, Battling John Johnson, against the greatest defensive fighter of all time, 'The Chocolate Tar Baby,' Sam Langford."

The afternoon before the Langford-Battling John Johnson fight, Pop visited Langford's manager, Joe Woodman. "Do you think Tham would mind my refereeing for my own fighter tonight?" Pop asked Woodman. (Close friends were allowed to call Sam "Tham"; Langford had a lisp.)

"Why don't you ask Tham hisself," asked Woodman. "He's an old sparring partner of yours."

Later Langford walked into the hotel room.

"Gene, you ol' buck," he said, "I'm glad I'm in this town just to see you. How's ol' Kid McCoy? I hear he's sellin' some sort of belts in a show-go-'round he's got."

Pop asked Langford if he objected to his refereeing the match that night: "I'm sort of managing Battling Johnson," he added.

Langford smiled wide. "Gene, I wouldn't care if Jesse James refereed. I can beat him."

Then Pop became solicitous: "Do you have to knock him out in the first round?"

"Well, we'll see how he behaves," said the Tar Baby.

Pop's heavyweight was already in the Baker Street Theatre ring. The Negro behemoth was dancing about and snorting as the audience sat in quiet awe.

Langford shuffled down the aisle, dressed in a worn maroon robe, smoking an expensive cigar. He took a puff from the cigar, then laid it on the edge of the ring apron, hopped into the ring, stepped out of his frayed robe, and listened while Pop gave the instructions. As Pop later recalled:

"My boy Johnson does well. He's ferocious. He plants a right cross on Sam's forehead. I see Sam is off balance when he falls right on his backside. I count two, and Sam gets up, chuckling. As I rub the resin off his gloves, I say: 'Well, what do you think of my boy now?' Sam laughs: 'I'll outpoint him.' 'A knockdown will count against you,' I say. Sam chuckles again.

"In the second round, Sam begins to pick up the pace after

Battling Johnson makes another play for glory. Sam begins to cut Johnson to ribbons. Johnson's face swells up from the beating. Sam starts to catch every blow Johnson throws.

"Suddenly, Battling Johnson, my fighter, spits directly in Sam's face. Sam gives him a left hook that sounds like the first shot at Fort Sumter. Johnson is on the mat. I could have counted fifty."

Pop went to his defeated fighter's dressing room to ask: "Don't you think that was a pretty terrible thing, spitting in Tham's face?"

As Johnson sat having his nose stitched up by the club physician, he explained: "I *had* to do it. He was gettin' mad at me. If I turned just a quarter inch to the right—*boom!*—I'd get a right cross. If I turned a bit to the left—*whack!*—I'd get a strong hook from that side. I didn't dare look away. So, there was only one place to . . . pardon me, Mr. Fowler . . . to spit . . . and I spit there . . . Straight ahead. . . ."

Recalling Langford's fights in Denver, Pop said, "Tham would get $1500 a fight and two tickets. An hour after the bout, he'd start drinking gin and playing dice. Then Joe Woodman would have to carry him until the next contest."

One night Pop refereed for the leading flyweight Kid Louisiana at the Stock Yards. "The Kid was notorious for fouling his adversary," Pop told me, "and I warned him that he would lose a round if he started getting fancy with me in the ring." But the Kid was a rude little fellow, and told Pop to go to hell. The result was that the Kid fouled himself right out of a decision that night as Pop awarded the fight to his opponent who was doubled up on the canvas, clutching his groin. When Pop stepped out of the ring to talk to a newspaper friend regarding his decision, Kid Louisiana hauled off and caught Pop on the back of his right ear. Though grabbing the top rope a little tighter, Pop composed himself, hid the pain he was suffering, turned to the boxer and said: "Is that all the harder you can hit?"

Another night at the Baker Street Theatre, Pop refereed a fight between aging Jack Bratton and an up-coming Mexican boy named Young Joe Rivers. Bratton stunned the eighteen-year-old Rivers in the second round. Before the third, Pop examined the boy's eyes. "If you don't look good to me," said Pop, "I'm going to call the fight." Young Rivers' manager assured Pop that there was nothing to worry about. In the third round, Bratton hit home with a three-count delivery: a startling left jab, followed by a left hook and right uppercut. The Mexican boy's eyes rolled back and Pop stopped the fight before there was a knockout. Pop was booed out of the ring.

As the main event came on, Pop went down to Young Joe Rivers' dressing room to see how he was feeling. The boy was sitting on the rubbing table. His gloves were off, but his hands were still bandaged. Pop put his arm about the boy's shoulder and said, "How are you feeling, kid?" The boy slumped over into Pop's arms. He was dead.

When word got around during the dreary main event that Young Joe Rivers was dead, members of the crowd made an effort to see Pop, to tell him that he had made a wise decision in stopping the fight. Pop took two of them to task before he left the Baker Street Theatre. He went to the nearest saloon, sucking his knuckles, and swore that he would never referee another fight.

There was a coroner's jury to be satisfied. Opponents of legalized boxing were crying "manslaughter" in the streets of Denver. The papers were having a difficult time playing it down. Fortunately, Coroner Horan was a mortuary owner. Pop winked at promoter Jack Kanner: "I think this boy should get the finest, most expensive funeral right here in Denver before his body is shipped back to Mexico. Let's get the finest casket we can . . . from Coroner Horan's stock, of course. . . ."

This episode was not only a narrow squeak for Pop, but it soured him, and from that time on he took offense at fat-bellied ringside know-it-alls who called out that fighters were "bums." No one, Pop felt, who was doing his best should be called a bum. "The real bums," he would snort, "are the booers, most of whom could not walk once around a ring by themselves."

Chapter Six

LOVE THAT BEGINS WITH LOVE,
AND REMAINS LOVE,
AND ENDS WITH LOVE
THIS KIND OF LOVE HAS NO END.

GENE FOWLER

The razor-sharp Colorado winter winds were yielding to a tenacious sun that blazed through a clear, blue sky. From afar, the foothills of Mount Evans, Mount Grizzly, and Pikes Peak took on the aspect of three unkempt miners with straggling black-and-white beards as the heat began to melt away streaks of snow. The columbine began to thrust through the surface of the pale earth. A herdsman was joyfully reunited with a flock of sheep he thought he had lost months ago to the cruel winter. Mountain grass was growing from the wool on their shaggy backs. Outbuildings soon would fall victim to Nature's swift seasonal change and be carried down the angry Platte River past Mullen's Mill Ditch estuary. The spring thaw of 1916 was at hand.

Spring seemed to be in my father's heart as he continued to make up the sporting page for Otto Floto on the *Denver Post*. Floto was in Kansas City at the time arranging a stage appearance for the long-deposed heavyweight champion Bob Fitzsimmons.

Pop's desk became a gathering place for the local sports world. This day, a bulbous-nosed fellow had come to ask Pop if he would manage him as a fighter. In a moment of whimsy, Pop said, "Let me take you over to the Press Club and introduce you around."

At the Press Club, Battling Brant, the heavyweight he had in tow, devoured three thick steaks, then informed the group which had gathered around the table that he was not only a boxer and philosopher, but also a musician of sorts. To prove it, he sat down at the Chickering and began to pick out a tune with his right index finger and pound the bass keys with a gnarled left mitt that looked like the butt end of a Virginia baked ham. Before he had reached what was supposed to be the end of the first chorus, the grand piano had suffered eight fractured teeth. Pop was informed by the club steward, Jim Wong, that he and his boxer would be barred from the premises until eight dollars were spent to repair the piano.

Within a few days, Pop's finances had been practically ruptured It was necessary that he put Battling Brant to work immediately, or there would be no money to bring home to Granny.

Fortunately, Norman Selby, better known as Charles "Kid" McCoy, who had won the welterweight championship of the world from Tommy Ryan in 1896, was in town.

"He was selling health belts at the time," Pop told me, "and he had also sold Tammen a bill of goods regarding the rejuvenative qualities of these belts. I called him 'Norman Sell Belt.' The Kid and I were old pals. We had a mutual girl friend. When he found out about my acquaintance with his girl, McCoy used to ask me to spar with him in the ring at the Denver Athletic Club. The Kid was forty-three, and I was very young. So he used to punch hell out of me during the first round for having taken up with his girl friend. But by the middle of the second round, if there was one, I could outdance him, and then was fortunate enough to get the better of the gladiator."

Tammen had hired the Tabor Grand Theatre at Sixteenth Street off Curtiss so McCoy could give lectures on breathing exercises and sell his health belts. The program's climax came when McCoy displayed his prowess by disarming five men, carrying among them a gun, a knife, a chair, a rope, and a blackjack. Pop worked on the Kid's generous nature to hire Battling Brant at $1.50 a performance to wield a blackjack.

The Tabor Grand was packed on opening night. It was a cinch that McCoy would sell a carload of his health belts. The audience was breathless during the finale as McCoy, after making a few perfunctory feints, threw two men threatening with gun and knife over his shoulders with consummate ease as two more, with chair and rope, advanced toward him.

Battling Brant, blackjack in hand, merely stood by while McCoy swung another adversary in such a violent arc that the fellow ended up in the violin section of the orchestra pit.

McCoy then turned to dispatch the man with the blackjack. Battling Brant, who was not overly intelligent, forgot that this had been a prearranged stunt. He saw his opening and took advantage of it, knocking Kid McCoy out cold. The curtain was swiftly lowered and no health belts were sold that night.

The following day, Jack Kanner suggested that Pop forget about managing pugs and look to greener fields. "You're twenty-six," said Kanner. "It's time a wild man like you settled down. Get married. Have babies."

"I wouldn't know where to start looking," rejoined Pop.

Kanner reminded him of the girl he had introduced my father to some three years before in the Health Department. "Remember? When you were a police reporter on the *News?*"

"You mean that cute little one with the auburn hair?" asked Pop. "Is she still working there?"

"Why don't you go over and see?" asked Kanner.

"But I don't even know her," Pop replied.

"You will," Kanner said confidently.

"What makes you think so?"

"I have a matchmaker's eye. It's my business to know a good match when I see one."

Late the next morning, before reporting to work at the *Post,* Pop walked briskly up Larimer Street toward the old City Hall to introduce himself to the blue-eyed Health Department complaint clerk, whose name was Agnes Hubbard. Although a trace of winter crispness was still in the air, his heart was blooming with the thoughts which come to young, healthy males in springtime.

Agnes Hubbard had been appointed complaint clerk in the Health Department in 1912 by Evelyn Arnold (now Mrs. D. Sturges), daughter of Denver's Mayor Henry J. Arnold. Agnes made $75 a month, which was more money than many Denver men brought home at the time. Her job was to take complaints over the telephone and at the office counter regarding matters that fell under the jurisdiction of that department.

Agnes, a second child, was born March 10, 1890, in the small town of Renick, a few miles from Mexico, Missouri. Her parents were Edgar L. and Catherine "Kittie" Hubbard. She had a slightly older brother named Herschel, who died an invalid as the result of a boyhood accident when a livery stable door fell on him, crushing his back. After three years at North Denver High, she and a beautiful tall blonde named Carol Summer decided to quit school and "pink tea it." Eventually tiring of the gay social-go-'round of sipping tea, rowboating in City Park Lake, and playing the early version of bridge called five hundred, Agnes had taken her present job.

Young Fowler scaled the City Hall stairs by threes, then halted at the top to consider what approach he might use on Miss Hubbard. He waited in line at the counter behind an aged woman whose face was half-eaten away by cancer. Agnes took the stopper from a gallon apothecary jar and poured out a few dozen pills to hand the old lady.

What a lovely package of beauty, Pop thought as he watched the blue-eyed girl smile at the sick woman. He introduced himself: "My name is Gene Fowler. I want you to be my wife and the mother of my children. Pick your church."

For Pop, the meeting was a dismal failure. Although Agnes Hubbard was gay and pleasant, he felt he had made no headway. But he knew he must pursue the matter.

Two days later, after discovering when Agnes would receive her pay envelope, he figured she would repair to the nearest dress shop. He posted himself in a doorway on Sixteenth Street near Champa during the lunch hour and waited. He had picked the right street, for here came Agnes Hubbard, all alone, dressed in white middy blouse and ankle-length dark blue skirt. He leaped out from ambush, grabbed the girl by the shoulders and said: "I told you that we were going to get married!"

"*I* am," said the composed Agnes. "In six weeks. To a doctor."

"Do you want to drive me to drink?" Pop pleaded.

"I don't think you have to be driven very far, from what I hear," she said.

"So you cared enough to look into my spotless past, eh?"

"It's not so spotless," she countered, and moved on.

What independence, Pop thought to himself as he watched her step into the Denver Dry Goods Tea Room.

Undaunted, the following morning Pop made another trek to the Health Department offices. He brushed past several desks on the run. Agnes, observing the look in his eye, took to her heels and headed toward Mayor Arnold's "getaway door," her crinoline petticoats swishing as she ran.

Pursued and pursuer rushed past the mayor's secretary, Miss Benson, and burst in upon the mayor's meeting with members of the Burlington railroad in the executive sanctuary. Mayor Arnold attempted to reassure the startled railroad executives with a chuckle that never got past his pursed lips, as Pop shouted: "Whether you like it or not, you are going to be the mother of my children!"

Soon Pop was hopping from a streetcar each night at the corner near Agnes's house. It was usually ten P.M. by the time he settled down with the girl on a Victorian love seat in the front parlor to talk about his day's work and the future plans he had for them.

"I had been kissed before by a high school boy friend, and by the young doctor to whom I was engaged at the time," my mother later told me. "But I guess I was really kissed for the first time by this crazy newspaper reporter on our front parlor love seat. I suppose millions of people have experienced the first kiss without saying much about it, but for me it was the first kiss anyone in the whole world ever received. I was twenty-six years old myself, and had wondered why and how I had waited so long for the right man. Now this tall, skinny guy with wavy brown hair had finally given me the answer. He awakened something in me that I never dreamed had been hiding inside my body. He opened the gates of love, a love which I wouldn't be ashamed of. I had been taught to hold down my emotions, as was every girl I grew up with. I knew this was right, but I hadn't had time to figure out what was happening to me."

Kittie Hubbard, her mother, was forever at the top of the stairs shouting down: "You go home, young man! My little girl has to go to work in the morning!"

"I won't go home until she says she'll marry me," Pop would reply.

One day Agnes suffered an acute case of tonsillitis. Just before she was given the anesthetic in St. Luke's Hospital, the Health Department head, and knife wielder this time in surgery, Dr. J. M. Perkins, said, "Agnes, you've had a lot of trouble with your appendix. Shall we do both at the same time?"

"It's all right with me," said Agnes. The last thing she remembered was Dr. Perkins' gold watch growing six feet in diameter as the anesthetic began to take effect.

When she awakened after the operation, Agnes was in a private room. Young Fowler stood over her with a potted sweetheart rose plant under one arm. He said, "Now will you marry me?"

Agnes, not yet having recovered her full senses from the anesthetic, said, "Yes."

When she began to regain her strength, Agnes looked at the card attached to the sweetheart rose plant. It read:

To the only Mother and sweetheart I ever knew.

The day before Agnes was to come home from the hospital, Pop sat in on an exclusive poker session with his three colonel friends: Colonel McFall, Colonel Jamieson, and Colonel "Buffalo Bill" Cody. He was allowed to win $63. The following afternoon, Pop purchased $50 worth of long-stemmed American Beauty roses. He tucked a $10 bill in his watch pocket and, with the remaining $3, hired a horse-drawn cab. While he was piling the roses in the back seat, Colonel Cody happened by and asked, "Who's dead? Someone I know?"

"The lady is very much alive, *Pahaska*," Pop replied, using his Sioux-given name, and the horse galloped off.

Pop asked for and was given a day off on July 19, 1916. Jack Kanner promoted an *automobile* from a Denver gambler known as Cincinnati. The open-top sedan looked like an English tallyho as they headed south of the city toward a spot in the Red Rocks. In the car were Pop, Agnes, her mother, best man Jack Kanner, former mule skinner and ex-wrestler, the Reverend James Thomas, and the gambler Cincinnati, acting as chauffeur. This was Pop's wedding party.

Crawling down the Red Rocks, Agnes began to hum Mendelssohn's wedding recessional, better known as "Here Comes the Bride." Reverend Thomas, perhaps forgetting his own youth, frowned at the young lady. A few minutes later he was reading the marriage lines.

When Kittie Hubbard was assured that everything was legal, she and the rest were driven back to Denver.

For the first time, Agnes noticed the greatcoat Pop had been wearing. It was orange, with mother-of-pearl buttons that seemed as big as demitasse saucers. "Where did you get it?" she asked.

"My friend Jack Dempsey, who is going East next month to become champion of the world, loaned it to me," said Pop.

"We must take good care of it," she said, "although I don't think anyone would want to steal such a monstrosity."

"I have ten dollars," said Pop, "and I think we should go alone to Rocky Mountain Lake and have a moonlight dinner. But I can't dance."

"Who wants to dance?" Agnes laughed.

The only place to go following their moonlight dinner was Agnes's home. The two crept in shortly after midnight.

That was the extent of their honeymoon. Early the next morning Agnes was up making coffee. The reporter had to go to work. He kissed Agnes at the front door and said, "I'd better spend tonight at Granny's house. I don't know how she'll take this. I'm her only source of support."

"I'll keep working," said Agnes. "That will help."

Knowing he would not be back with Agnes to share her bed that night, Pop wrote her a three-page letter, thanking her for her womanhood, and her gentleness, and the great gift of understanding. The third page contained a poem, an ode to his bride. Written in haste, its sentimentality was unabashed. A copy boy delivered it to Agnes. The poem read:

The whole night thru I held you in these arms of mine
And wondered at the Heav'n born thing
That men call Fate—the Destiny of Hearts, divine,
That turns the peasant into king.

And all night long the silver moonlight fell, and I
Could do naught but whisper, soft
And lo, the love that even now does make me sigh
A message to the skies aloft.

Oh! All night thru your hair lay like a mist of light
Upon the pillow white. It seemed
That angels gathered there with love bedight
To kiss the lips of her that dreamed.

And all night long I loved you, held you close to me,
Forgetful that another world there lay
Beyond the jeweled stars and moonlit, midnight sea—
Forgotten all I'd heard the wise men say.

And once again the whole night thru I'd hold you, love,
And once again I'd kiss you, sweet.
And if the life of mine were called by Him Above,
I'd kiss you, whisper: "God, 'tis meet!"

As soon as possible, Pop decreed that Agnes would not be a working wife. At his suggestion, now that he was making $70 a week, Agnes quit her job at the Health Department. Edgar Hubbard had been building a small brick house on Carona off Speer Boulevard. Financially, everything was looking up. Put Pop had no days off now. He began to take Agnes with him on assignments and other missions in Denver's sporting world so they could be together.

Pop was to have refereed the world's lightweight championship bout between title-holder Freddie Welsh and former champ Ad Wolgast at the Denver Stock Yards, but a problem of ethics arose.

"The champion was not in too good physical condition," Pop told me. "He was looking for an easy fight, but the high climate of Denver, a mile above sea level, worried his manager, Harry Pollock. Many a tiger had become short of breath in Denver."

Otto Floto told Pop that "the Champ has to be protected." Pop said if the bout appeared to be a draw he *would* protect the champ's title, but added that if Wolgast had a slight edge, he would have to transfer the world title.

Worried about Fowler's honesty, Floto decided to referee the bout himself. "No reflection on your"—Floto searched for the right words—"I mean, you've refereed world championship title bouts, Gene, but I just gotta do this one myself—know what I mean?"

Pop was overjoyed because he would be able to bring his bride to see her first boxing match, and the seats were Otto's, at ringside. He proudly ushered Agnes to their seats. Word had gotten around that Welsh might not have to fight too hard. Shortly after the newlyweds sat down, eight loaded revolvers were laid on the ring, two at each side of the squared apron. Upon seeing this demonstration of distrust, Pop stood up and shouted, "These guns belong to gambling men! If one shot is fired tonight, there will never be another bet placed on a fight in Denver!"

The fight was all Wolgast's through the tenth round. In the eleventh, Wolgast raked Welsh with a left hook. The champion was floored! "Immediately, Jack Rose, one of Welsh's seconds, jumped into the ring to claim 'foul,'" Pop told me. "Floto was about to count the champion out when a doctor appeared from nowhere to ascertain if Welsh had really been fouled. Rose had spirited Welsh off to his corner. He had a diamond ring which he turned around, then reached into Welsh's trunks and raked the Champion's skin under his trunks. When the medic saw blood (there were no protective 'cups' in those days), he stated that a foul had been committed. But he added he would allow the fight to continue after a ten-minute rest."

Pop's bride was aghast. "Does this happen all the time?" she demanded.

"Never saw it before," said Pop as he stared at the little savage that was Ad Wolgast. He knew Wolgast, a bit ring weary, was apt to throw fouls, even at the referee. Following the ten-minute respite, Wolgast held true to form. He wound up and hit Welsh three successive times in the groin. Referee Floto stopped the fight and awarded it to the "still champion, Freddie Welsh!"

Floto later became irate with Pop, who had been sending the

blow-by-blow fight description over the telegraph. Pop had Wolgast way ahead until he started fouling. "Up until the last round," Pop said to Floto, "you would have seen it that way, too."

Odd as it may seem to the passionate boxing fan, Mrs. Welsh and Mrs. Wolgast, wives of the respective gladiators, had spent the evening together at a Denver motion picture house. They were not really interested in how their husbands made a living.

Once again Pop tried to prove to Agnes that prize fighting was respectable and that the battles were restricted to the squared ring. This time, two months later, he escorted his skeptical bride to Colorado Springs where a clever boy named Charlie White claimed he could lift Welsh's lightweight crown.

To start with, a grandstand collapsed during the semi-final bout, and three spectators were killed.

"It was late afternoon," Pop said, "and Welsh chose a corner that kept White's eyes in the sun during the one-minute rest period. It went twenty rounds. The champ had really won the fight, but I knew when Otto Floto raised Welsh's hand in victory that trouble was coming."

The crowd roared its disapproval. Bottles were thrown into the ring as Floto ducked under the ropes to seek sanctuary. Three had already been killed that afternoon. He did not wish to be the fourth.

Pop was still writing the blow-by-blow description as Frank Newhouse grabbed Agnes, who was sitting next to him, and hauled her to safety beneath the ring. Convinced now that all prize fight contests were excuses for general brawls and disasters, Agnes refused in future to visit the arenas with her husband.

Almost as hazardous was Pop's assignment to cover the 1916 Calgary Rodeo Roundup in Cheyenne, Wyoming. T. Joe Cahill, who would become sheriff of that city until arthritis forced his retirement, had sent Pop a pure white, broad-brim $100 Stetson for the occasion.

Pop called his friend and manager of the Plains Hotel, Harry Hynds, who reserved his best suite for the Fowlers. Pop introduced Agnes to Mrs. Cahill, gave her a handful of money and said, "Go shopping, darling. I'm going to enter the Indian dancing contest where the Hunk Papa Sioux are camping out of town."

"But you said you didn't know how to dance," said Agnes.

"Not American dance," said Pop, "but I can *Indian* dance."

He joined the Hunk Papa Sioux braves, shared a bottle of fire water with them, removed his shoes, pulled the brim of his $100 Stetson tight on his head, and entered the contest. He was wearing through the soles of his stockings when a bullet creased his expensive hat. Instead of frightening him, the shot encouraged Pop to stomp his heels deeper into the dust and start whooping like a war chief possessed of the spirits, including those he had drunk.

When it was announced that Pop came in second to a young full-blooded Indian brave, he defied the Sioux judges, claiming "racial prejudice." Considering he was the first white man ever to enter the Sioux war dances, the council explained (between peacemaking draughts of fire water the young newspaperman had brought to share with the rest), "To come in second was a great honor."

A chief, next in command to Sitting Bull III, offered Pop his tepee "for rest before the big day." Fowler tried to sleep, but several papooses cried bitterly throughout the early morning hours.

What sleep he had left was interrupted when a squaw insisted that Pop hold her damp child. One never refuses an Indian's request, even though the tepee is poorly ventilated. "How the Sioux could track down game by their sense of smell was beyond me," Pop said. "This bit of Indian lore must have been a myth. They couldn't have been able to smell anything. That night in the tepee proved it to me . . . But then, I love children, so I got my ailing papoose to sleep."

Later that night, Pop loosened a peg holding down a section of the tent and rolled outside. Breathing in fresh air was nearly worth the risk of a scalping as Pop galloped off into the star-filled night.

Exhausted, he found refuge beneath a canvas-skirted stand, the judges' rostrum where the Calgary Rodeo Roundup would be inaugurated some hours after the sun rose that day. He fell into a deep sleep.

Pop was awakened by what he thought was screaming. What he actually heard was cheers from grandstand spectators as they watched the wild horse race, an event since outlawed in rodeos because of its dangerous aspects.

Pop crawled from under the judges' stand and ambled out onto the track just as a score of wild horses with riders began to descend upon him. First he saw his bride sitting with T. Joe and Mrs. Cahill. He waved to them. Then he was caught up in the stampede. Riders began to tumble. Soon all were unhorsed.

A telegraphic query arrived at the Plains Hotel the next day from Mr. Tammen. He congratulated Pop on his graphic descriptions of THE OLD WEST BEING RELIVED ONCE AGAIN, then asked why he had not included the exciting incident when the wild horse race had been disrupted by a lunatic straying in front of the onrushing blasts, of which rival papers had made much. MANY BONES WERE BROKEN, MR. FOWLER, the telegram read. YOU MUST HAVE HAD REASON FOR NOT INCLUDING THIS ASPECT IN YOUR STORY.

Pop's return wire read:

INCIDENT MOST EMBARRASSING.
FOWLER WAS MAN WHO BROKE UP WILD HORSE RACE.
COMING HOME TOMORROW, BUFFETED, BUT UNBOWED.

FOWLER

When Agnes and Gene returned to Edgar Hubbard's rented house, the bride of several months now said, "I can't understand how you live so long, Gene. Do you mind if I don't go on *any* assignments with you for a while?" She told her mother she was not feeling well, and that she wished to go to bed.

Mr. Hubbard announced that the whole family would soon be able to move into the new home he was building.

"I hope it's soon, Daddy," said Agnes, "because we're going to have a baby in the family come May or June."

On March 16, 1917, the Hubbards and the Fowlers moved into the new brick house on Corona Street. The younger couple had just celebrated their twenty-seventh birthday, Gene on March 8, Agnes two days later, and doubtless they were more than a little dismayed by the fact that family finances made it necessary for them still to share her parents' home.

At least the Fowlers had the upstairs to themselves, thanks to the consideration of her father.

It was just in time, that bit of privacy, for they were about to welcome the first addition to their own family.

One May night when Pop arrived at the Corona Street house, he was greeted with the news that his wife had started her labor pains.

"I had my mind set on getting the greatest obstetrician in town, Dr. T. Mitchell Burns," Pop told me. "He charged $50 a delivery, and he owed me a few favors, so he was going to do it for nothing, or next to nothing. But no. My mother-in-law had her own physician. Somehow I believed then that if a person was solemn and rigid in ideas, that person knew what he, or she, was doing."

Awaiting the doctor's arrival, Pop went upstairs to be with his wife. The long pains came. "My boyhood friend Jack Dempsey saw Mother in pain many times," said Pop, "and he told me he wished he possessed her courage."

The doctor had not arrived yet, and Pop wished that Buffalo Bill, whom he had buried five months earlier on Lookout Mountain, could have been by his side with a competent squaw.

When the doctor came, he apologized for being late. "He looked like a desiccated prune," Pop said. "He was affable, but he had nothing. He was a lightweight physically, and, as I ascertained later, mentally and professionally. So we went into labor (I use the editorial 'we').

"This pipsqueak attended the case for some hours, and I ventured to ask him how things were going. He said: 'It looks like a difficult case.' I did not know much about medicine or surgery or obstetrics, but I was worried."

Agnes continued through a second day of labor. She did not complain.

"I saw that she was not doing well at all," Pop said. "I had observed these things as a reporter, both in ambulances and in the emergency hospitals. I told the doctor he was tired, and that he should call in another physician as a consultant."

The doctor, although growing weaker during the second day, refused assistance. Mrs. Hubbard also vetoed calling in another doctor.

"Do you think this birth will be normal?" Pop ventured to ask the doctor.

"I think so."

"Are you sure?" Pop rejoined.

"Nobody can be sure," said the doctor as Agnes lapsed into unconsciousness.

"Don't you think someone like Dr. T. Mitchell Burns could come in now?"

"No!" Mrs. Hubbard insisted. "No one but our family doctor may come in this house to see my baby in this condition!"

Pop told me, "I know now that I had a great weakness of character there. I succumbed to all this sort of thing, and by the forty-second hour we all had had it. Agnes was game as usual, not complaining of the obvious pain she was enduring. It was already the twenty-sixth of May when the exhausted doctor suggested that high forceps would be needed to get the baby born alive."

Pop took over the forceps himself when the doctor suddenly folded up—there was nothing else to do in the emergency. "I had never held instruments before," Pop said. "I'd seen it done, but I never had the responsibility before. And it was my baby's head that I was pulling on.

"I kept a constant pressure there with that awful impersonal thing made of steel. I dared not let go, and I was afraid not to keep pulling. *It was the most positive emergency of my life*, and I was helpless to do what I was ordered to do.

"The doctor revived and took over the forceps just as one shoulder got through. When it all happened, I could only see my son's face. It was as black as a politician's heart. He had one eye closed. I thought I had killed him."

Pop said that Agnes was in and out of consciousness so often that she was not aware of what was happening. "We finally got him into this world, whether that was any favor or not," Pop concluded.

After nearly three days of labor for Agnes, Pop watched the umbilicus tied off. He went to the cupboard in the kitchen, took down a bottle of cooking sherry and drank it all. Kittie Hubbard came into the kitchen and said, "I can't understand a man getting drunk when he is having a child born to him."

During a brief tour with the Denver Grizzlies baseball team, Pop wrote Agnes a short letter. For the first time in his life he understood the meaning of loneliness. He wrote in part:

Essentially, I am a creature of impulse. I am moved by varying motives. I never know myself, and I do not expect anyone else to know me as I am. But you, dear girl, seem to grasp my wandering fancies much better than anyone else ever did or ever will. So that, perhaps, is the chief reason why I find myself perpetually in love with you.

A time for decision came Pop's way soon after. My father thought that Damon Runyon, who was climbing the ladder of newspaper fame in New York two rungs at a time, had forgotten him. Pop was happily settled in his job at the *Denver Post*. But his various wire stories had made Eastern cosmopolitan newspapers take notice of his talent.

Runyon wired him on August 11, 1918:

JOB HERE FOR YOU. WIRE ME IMMEDIATELY IF YOU CAN COME ON AND SEE MR. WILLICOMBE, SECRETARY TO MR. HEARST. SUGGEST YOU ARRANGE INDEFINITE LEAVE OF ABSENCE OUT THERE. I AM GOING ABROAD MIDDLE OF MONTH AND IF YOU CANNOT GET THERE BY THAT TIME, LET ME KNOW SO I CAN WRITE YOU LETTER. PLANNING MORE FULLY, BUT MY ADVICE IS TO HUSTLE TO NEW YORK SOON AS YOU GET THIS. LOOKS LIKE YOUR OPPORTUNITY.

DAMON RUNYON

Pop's answer regarding the prospective position on Hearst's *New York American,* the largest paper in the country at the time, has been lost, but Runyon was excited enough to wire back on August 15:

YOUR NIGHT LETTER RECEIVED OK.
I AM WRITING YOU.

DAMON

This was the professional turning point in Fowler's life.

Some forty years later, Pop made a penetrating observation to me about Runyon. "Well-intentioned appraisals of this man leave much to be desired," he said. "He was not a plaster saint. Writers and newspapermen who knew him mostly in his last days complained that they could not get close to him. To the few remaining friends who knew him for nearly a half-century, such as Arthur Robinson and "Bugs" Baer, this seems a bit absurd.

"Damon was very shy and the way in which he cloaked it by assuming an aloof manner and making sardonic comments was a sham. Although he might at times have appeared selfish in the extreme, this was compensated by his never-ending search for promising young writers and his private advice to them and continuous interest in their development.

"Runyon worshippers of late seem to find it necessary to hush-hush anything to do with his early alcoholic history. Let's face it! He was a lush all his life, but from 1911 until the day he died, he was a non-practicing drunk. Instead of booze, he drank at least thirty cups of coffee each day. The solemn revelation that he constantly craved liquor is a tribute to his courage."

Complications of the usual sort—monetary ones—set in the moment the move to New York was decided upon. Agnes agreed he should go, but they couldn't scrape together enough money for his fare, even in the day coaches. How Pop finally made it to New York is one of the giddier legends of the newspaper world, particularly since it first brought him into contact with two other notoriously blithe spirits, Ben Hecht and Charles MacArthur, whose theatrical set-piece *The Front Page* was a decade in the offing.

In his dilemma, a mortician friend named Rex Yeager finally extended a helping hand. An old lady had just died in Denver and had to be sent to her relatives in upstate New York for burial. The law required that she have a chaperon on her journey back home. So Yeager offered Pop a ticket to New York if he would take on this mission.

All went well until Pop and his charge reached Chicago. Feeling the need of fresh air and exercise, Pop detrained to stroll around the streets near the station. A cop braced him and demanded to see his draft card, which Pop characteristically had misplaced. Off to police headquarters he went, while the corpse continued eastward unescorted. Hecht and MacArthur, reporters on Chicago newspapers then, heard that a brother journalist had fallen into the clutches of the law and went over to see whether he was worth rescuing. The first meeting between Fowler and two men who were to be his lifelong friends took place with jail bars supervening. Hecht and MacArthur persuaded the police to turn Pop loose, but now he discovered his corpse had gone astray. He wired her relatives:

NELLIE AND I DOING WELL. EXPECT TO SEE YOU ANY DAY. KEEP IN TOUCH.

The body, happily enough, but through no effort of Pop's, finally arrived at its destination two weeks later.

By then Pop had reported to Joseph Willicombe, William Randolph Hearst's factotum. He told Willicombe that since he was making $90 a week in Denver, he'd have to get $100 a week in New York. Mr. Willicombe demurred, and the question was left unresolved by the time Pop decided to return to Denver, on borrowed money, and think it over. The big city frightened him stiff. That was all he could talk about—his fear of not making good in the big time, under the competitive pressures of Park Row—when he arrived back home and Agnes met him at the station. They stayed up most of the night while he talked out his fear of failure.

As she told him over and over again, "We'll go to this city, and together we'll lick whatever you're afraid of."

Faltering though his spirit was at the moment, chilled though he was by the prospect of leaving Denver and its easygoing ways, Agnes convinced him that he could make the jump from home town to metropolis. Without her redheaded spirit, he might have been content to drift in the backwater and spend the rest of his days in the city rooms and saloons of his native city, gradually going to seed like so many newspapermen who never quite make it. To reach for fame, Pop needed the spur, gently but firmly applied, and Agnes applied it with wifely tact.

"All we need is train fare to New York, the first month's rent on an apartment and a little spending money," she told her parents. "After Gene has licked the big city, we'll send for you."

Chapter Seven

SUCCESS IS A GREASED PIG.

GENE FOWLER

Gene and Agnes Fowler arrived at the Pennsylvania Station in mid-Manhattan on a cloudy day which only deepened their melancholy. As they claimed their trunk and three suitcases, she looked about at the mass of hurrying strangers and asked Pop, "What are they all running to?"

"You'll have to get used to not hearing fire alarms when you see people rushing," Pop answered.

They registered at an old midtown hotel after paying sixty cents cab fare plus one dollar for the trunk and twenty-five cents each for the three suitcases. Agnes bought an evening newspaper and began to study the APARTMENTS FOR RENT columns of the ad section. Pop headed downtown to check in at the *New York American*. He gave his hotel address on 48th Street and was told to "go write some poetry, and we'll call for you when we need you." It was August 25, 1918.

A week passed as Pop scribbled verses in longhand and delivered these poems each day to the paper. The couple moved into an apartment on 112th Street between Broadway and Amsterdam Avenue. It was situated one block south of the apartment house where Ellen Runyon awaited Damon's return from France, where he was covering the final campaigns of the war.

At the close of the third week, the poems were getting shorter as no pay arrived. Had Pop demanded too much money? Runyon had instructed him to start at $60 a week. Pop continued to insist upon $100 when he resumed negotiations on his return to New York.

"I always took into consideration how Damon counseled me," Pop said, "then I did just the opposite. Strangely enough, it always turned out right."

Down to their last $5, Agnes said, "Why don't you go to the office and ask why you haven't been paid?"

When he appeared at the *New York American* caged window the following day, the paymaster pulled out three checks and handed them to Pop. They were for $100 each. "I guess you Westerners are all rich," said the paymaster. "Colonel Van Hamm left a note here for you to report to work when you showed up."

Always a pessimist in money matters, Pop hurried down to the Manhattan Bank and cashed the $300 worth of checks. Hearst's money, he found, was good.

Pop did not sleep all night. Instead, he stroked his sleeping wife's hair, lying in their double bed, then arose to look out the window at the sunrise presenting itself to this big city that had frightened him so. He kissed his sleeping wife and headed downtown toward the *American* for his first day's work since his return. He walked all the way, taking in the sights as he went. There were not many people on Broadway at this hour. This made him feel less hemmed in as he gawked at the skyscrapers, veiled gray from years of coal smoke settling on their outer walls, their thousands of windows looking down in judgment on this young man from Denver.

Pop could not recall to me what his first assignments were, but he said that within a few days he and Agnes had moved around the corner to a less expensive apartment at 1028 Amsterdam Avenue. It had four bedrooms. The rent was $80 a month. Pop sent a telegram to Denver, requesting that Grandma Maria West bring little Gene, Jr., to New York. Agnes began to buy used furniture, making her purchases near the new apartment so Pop would not have to carry the load too far. He soon became known in the neighborhood as "the moving man," walking down Amsterdam Avenue with the head section of a brass bed, a table top, or stuffed chair on his back.

Thursday, November 7, 1918, was what Pop called "The beginning of the '20s." It was the day of the false Armistice. The New York newspaper headlines read:

GERMANS SEEKING TRUCE REACH ALLIED LINES

SEDAN FIRED AS AMERICANS DRIVE FOE BACK

SMITH ELECTED GOVERNOR BY ABOUT 10,000

DEMPSEY LANDS KNOCKOUT BLOW ON LEVINSKY'S

CHIN IN THIRD ROUND

The New York Times headlines read the next morning:

CITY GOES WILD WITH JOY

Supposed Armistice Deliriously Celebrated Here
And In Other Cities. Crowds Parade Street.
Judges Close Courts.

The real Armistice took effect November 11, and soon thereafter, with the first contingents of the A.E.F. scheduled to return home, Pop was given his first important assignment.

William Randolph Hearst, owner of the *New York American,* had expressed the desire to meet personally the first of the returning heroes. But petitions were passed about New York to restrain Hearst from greeting them. When Mayor John F. Hylan appointed Hearst to his welcoming committee, it roused a storm of protest from his journalistic rivals.

During this time, Hearst kept calm and assigned my father to hire not a yacht, but something much larger, to greet the homecoming troops. With unlimited funds at his disposal, Pop paid $3000 for the use of a ship to steam on an "evening's cruise out beyond the breakwaters" to greet an ocean liner carrying returning troops.

Pop went to a Childs Restaurant and ordered 500 ham sandwiches, 500 chicken sandwiches, 200 gallons of coffee, and invited all his friend's friends to join him on this cruise.

Just as the ship he had hired was about to haul in its lines, Pop halted the action to climb ashore and call Hearst at his apartment

overlooking the Hudson. "I made a great mistake, Mr. Hearst," said
Pop. "I got all ham sandwiches. I ordered chicken sandwiches, too.
But the chicken sandwiches didn't arrive. Now I've got 500 ham
sandwiches, and a great part of my guests are Jewish."

Hearst was quiet for only a moment on the telephone, then said,
"If they get hungry, young man, I'm sure they will eat the ham
sandwiches."

Rain had threatened in the early evening, but now, as Pop's ship
got underway, the threatening storm became a reality. The troop
ship had to lay off some ten miles to await a calmer entrance to
New York Harbor. Pop's guests were too seasick to care about the
bill of fare.

The next day, Pop hired the same ship again. This time he had
chicken sandwiches. He also rounded up another shipload of greet-
ers from the Bowery. When small- and large-craft storm warnings
were run up by the Coast Guard, and his ship was not allowed to
cast off, a riot broke loose at the docks. The troop ship spent yet
another night beyond the haven of New York.

"All I remember," said Pop, "is that I ran up a Bowery street
and sought the refuge of McSorley's Ale House as many disen-
chanted potential travelers sought my scalp. I sent word back by a
brave young man, 'The ship is yours until 2 A.M., at which time the
food will be cut off.'" The rented ship's galley opened the stores,
which also included several barrels of beer. Further rioting was
averted, but Hearst gave up the entire venture.

Fundamental requirements of newspaper reporters then were
sound health, vitality, and ability to work long hours with little
sleep, the Newspaper Guild and the eight-hour day being far in the
future. A reporter needed stamina, both as a journalist and a
drinker to hold his own on Park Row. Pop had that kind of endur-
ance and liked to work with men who could match his best efforts
in both departments. This led him to take the unusual measure of
calling the New York *World* city desk and asking that his opposition assign either Donald Henderson Clarke, then a top-flight reporter and later the author of a string of best-selling novels, or
Joseph Jefferson O'Neill, a reporter and rewriteman of legendary
skill at the typewriter and heroic capacity at the bar, to cover cer-

tain stories with him. Clarke recalled that Jack Gavin, city editor of the *World*, would reply to his request, "If I do, will you promise to come back to your offices after the assignment is over?" And Pop would reply, a trifle haughtily, "We always produce, don't we?"

One assignment on which Pop wanted to see a friendly face was the Sing Sing execution of Gordon Fawcett Hamby. The handsome but homicidal Hamby had been captured in Portland, Oregon, and could have been tried for a holdup-murder in that state, which did not have the death sentence. Instead he confessed to a prior murder of two East Brooklyn Savings Bank employees and agreed to extradition to New York, where he could be electrocuted. At his trial he needled the assistant district attorney handling the case, saying, "This isn't a trial. It's a farce. I've pleaded guilty. I am guilty. Why this nonsense? I don't want to spend the rest of my life in prison."

Pop arranged with City Editor Gavin to have Clarke cover the execution—the first nighttime electrocution in Sing Sing's history—with him.

When Hamby entered the death house, he was nonchalantly puffing on a cigarette. He inhaled deeply, tossed the butt away, thanked Warden Lewis E. Lawes for his consideration, then turned and told the newspapermen about to witness his death, "All I wish to say is that no one ever died in front of Gordon Fawcett Hamby's gun without having a chance." He paused, glancing around the chamber thoughtfully.

Nodding at the door through which he had been escorted from his cell, he said, "Tell the boys back there [in the death cells] that the Little Green Door is brown."

Until the observant and composed Hamby offered his correction, newspaper accounts of executions had always referred to that dismal portal as the Little Green Door—and Hamby was a stickler for accuracy.

Father Cashin (appropriate name for a Death Row priest) offered Hamby the Crucifix to kiss, and then the guards strapped the condemned man into the electric chair. A few moments later Hamby was jolted by successive shocks as the lights of Sing Sing dimmed and notified the countryside that one more malefactor was being separated from his life. Father Cashin fainted and had to be carried off. The prison doctor stepped forward to supervise the removal of the body. Before that could be done, Pop strolled over to the executioner, who was examining his handiwork with professional interest, and kissed him on the forehead. "A very workmanlike job, my good man," he congratulated the executioner.

Chapter Eight

MONEY WAS MEANT TO BE THROWN
FROM THE BACKS OF TRAINS.

GENE FOWLER

To his generation of newspapermen, and to succeeding ones who have heard their barroom reminiscences, Gene Fowler was one of its raffish, hard-living heroes. His legend was built upon countless escapades, wild nights in the Park Row speaks, jousts with authority, uninhibited scrambles after news or excitement, during the last days when journalism was a three-ring circus. Many of the stories, of course, are true, as Pop was always ready to confirm and elaborate. But if he drank all the bootleg booze and greeted all the uproarious dawns he was supposed to have, he wouldn't have reached half of his seventy years. There was a lot more to him than hell-raising and legend-making.

The domestic side of his nature, though less romantic, was as much a part of the whole Fowler as the bravo of the city rooms and saloons. His great love of children, his own and everyone else's, was illustrated by two incidents which occurred on and just after New Year's Eve of 1920.

The day of New Year's Eve, Pop was off-duty and occupied part of his afternoon watching some children playing around the Cathedral of St. John the Divine across the street. He saw the caretaker slap two of the children for not dispersing quickly enough, and rushed down four flights of stairs from his apartment to box the caretaker's ears.

"No offense, my friend," he said, helping the man back on his feet, "but you shouldn't hit kids, especially in front of a church."

That night Gene, Jr., came down with a fever and was fretful all that New Year's Eve. Next morning Pop found a note in his mailbox which read, *"If you can't keep that Goddamned brat of yours from squalling all night, get the hell out of this building."* The note was, of course, unsigned.

Fuming with rage, Pop composed his answer and placed a copy in every tenant's mailbox. *"You coward!"* his note read. *"I know who you are. Anyone who writes an anonymous letter is either insane or about to become insane! I'll dash your brains out the next time I see you, you cheap son-of-a-bitch!"*

The scattershot technique of dealing with a poison-pen letter worked beautifully. Gene, Jr., resumed his vocalizing that night, but nobody complained.

Pop was now keeping a diary. His scribbled entries were made in a little date book Ellen Runyon had given him for Christmas. A few of the entries read:

March 1—Cool and sunny. Baby starts in kindergarten. Agnes goes with him. He has a fine time and tells about it all afternoon. Home at 3 a.m.

March 2—The old payday. Down on rewrites. Disciplined for taking time off for haircut. Baby's first love affair. He is wild about Gloria, 4 years old. He raves about her, says someday doorbell will ring and there will be Gloria.

April 24—Cool and clear. Agnes worse—looks like problem in addition. Work until 2 a.m. Take bus ride. Grandma ill. Baby has cold.

This last entry indicated that another child was on the way. Agnes and Pop hoped for a girl.

Pop, pregnant Agnes, and baby Gene were now spending their time on the seashore at Far Rockaway during the summer months. They rented a cottage on the beach where they slept during fair nights out on the front porch. Pop spent all the time he could bathing in the ocean. He had never learned to swim, so he stayed among the breakers where he could get a foothold in the sand. Meanwhile, he was assigned to cover Sir Thomas Lipton's last attempt to win back the America's Cup for Great Britain.

"Sir Thomas had lost his very fine yacht, *The Aaron,* when he loaned it to the British Navy," Pop told me. "We were sitting in Sir Thomas's scow during an off-sailing day of the big race," he continued. "Westbrook Pegler [the future choleric columnist] and I were chatting with Lipton and Lord Dewar, the man who made Scotch Whisky. His Lordship had one leg. He lost the other in a hunting accident, or in some damned war."

Pop was looked upon as an impudent fellow by the society people visiting Sir Thomas's yacht that day because he had said, "Would you like to go into partnership with me, Sir Thomas?"

"What are your qualifications?" asked the gentleman who had a corner on the tea market.

"With my brains and your money," said Pop, "we couldn't miss." Then he turned to Lord Dewar and said, "I am a big whiskey man myself, Your Lordship, only I'm on the consumer's end."

Sir Thomas tried to change the subject by telling one of his limited repertoire of jokes. He asked, "Gentlemen, did I ever tell you about the regatta when we were standing off Cowes, and the Queen of Spain . . ."

Pop interrupted, "Sir Thomas, you not only told it to us once, but you've told it to us three times!"

Sir Thomas mumbled in his whiskers as Lord Dewar glowered at Fowler and said, "A gentleman never has heard a story twice!"

Pop rejoined, "A gentleman never *tells* a story twice!"

Pop's September 16 diary entry read:

Warm and fair. Good dip in ocean. At office. Wall Street explosion. Cover with Otto Winkler. Army of reporters. Buy fiddle for baby. Agnes in town. Letter from Father.

This brief entry referred to the Wall Street bomb which killed thirty persons and injured one hundred others when a horse-drawn vehicle with a cargo of explosives blew up across the street from the banking house of J. P. Morgan & Co.

While covering this disaster, Pop noticed a Colorado postmark

on the envelope he was carrying, on which he was about to scrawl
some notes. Instead he opened the letter. It was the first communication of any kind he had ever received from his long-lost father.

Pop stood near the statue of George Washington on the steps
of the old United States Sub-Treasury building and read:

Dear Son:

I hesitate now, as I long, long have hesitated to write to you. I am
bringing the ashes of my father to Elizabethport, New Jersey, to bury
them as he wished me to at the feet of my mother. Would you mind if I
called to see you? If you don't want me to, I am sure I wouldn't blame
you in any way after all the years I never wrote or did anything for you.
But I always have been very proud of you.

> *Your father,*
>
> *Charles F. Devlan*

When he returned to the *American* with only fifteen minutes to
deadline, Pop stood in front of his city editor, Martin Dunn, and
said, "I just got a letter from Denver."

"You don't mean to say," said Martin Dunn. "From Lord Chester-
field, no doubt."

"From my own father," said Pop, still stunned.

A few weeks later, while covering Alfred E. Smith's guberna-
torial campaign, Pop opened the door of his Amsterdam Avenue
apartment. He looked down at a man who wore a graying Vandyke
beard. The man's eyes were fine and gray, and, as Mark Twain
once said of Robert Louis Stevenson, the eyes gave beauty to his
face. My thirty-year-old father was seeing his *own* father for the
first time.

The two were wordless for a few moments. Then, referring to the
beard, Pop said, "So *that's* where you've been hiding all these
years!"

The two shook hands. Pop's father stepped inside and was offered
the easy chair. Pop shut the window against the clatter of streetcar
wheels, then drew the blind to blot out the silhouette of the unfinished Cathedral of St. John the Divine. The two talked the night

through. Once renewed, the contact between them was never to be broken again.

Martin Dunn, city editor of the *American* during Pop's first years in New York, who now lives in retirement in Hartsdale, New York, recalls my father as a hard-working as well as high-spirited young man at this period. Dunn wrote me:

Gene Fowler was courteous and congenial, but not a smoothie. Neither was he a softie. Although he would use a jest to avoid a quarrel, he knew when to stand his ground . . . So evident was his personality that it dominated him and his work. No matter what he produced, however wonderful and fine, it would not equal his personality—that something which shines out of men and makes them superior individuals . . . When young Fowler was the spirit of youth, tall, straight, fine looking, he moved with grace and charm. Usually he was in a playful mood, which deceived many into believing he was a playboy. The outward banter concealed industry. He worked fast, hard and long, but spoke of it as nothing. He never complained of being tired or over-driven. He would not admit that work was a grind. He was doing what he liked best to do, being a reporter, and was satisfied. . . .

In this letter, Martin Dunn recalled an episode concerning a Mrs. Harris, "a very busty lady involved in an interesting divorce." Mr. Dunn went on to say, "When she won the case, she invited all the reporters to a party at the Hotel McAlpin. During the convivialities [there was a bit of drinking], Mrs. Harris's mammillary glands became an object of adoration."

It seems there was enough breastwork showing so that Pop, with soft pencil, printed on one of the gorgeous mounds, "Borden," and on the other, "Sheffield." Borden and Sheffield were the leading milk companies in New York.

By the time the sun started to rise and the reporters began to nod, Mrs. Harris had retired to her bedroom. Jack Carbery, who had recently come from Denver, began to spray the recently divorced lady's cloying Hour of Joy perfume around the room until all were well scented. In each of the sleeping reporter's pockets, Carbery slipped a rose with the attached note: *"Meet me at the McAlpin."*

Arising that morning, Agnes saw the condition of her husband's suit and decided to send it to the cleaners. As is the custom of a dutiful wife, she emptied his pockets and found the mangled rosebud and the *"Meet me at the McAlpin"* note. Pop explained the circumstances.

Reporter Lowell Limpus' wife was going to file suit for divorce until Agnes explained that other reporters were also dupes of Mr. Carbery's joke.

During this period, Pop was suffering through another prenatal siege. "They tell me that in every person there are mixtures of male and female tendencies," he told me, "and I don't think that I'm a *nance*. But I do have and I recognize it, a fierce maternal instinct, and that goes for adults, too. It certainly applies to your little daughter Claudia. I just beam on her. I love to hug her. I love to hold her close. I think that's sort of a maternal thing . . . I even comfort old men, anybody who needs mothering, anyone who's down-and-out, and it's nothing to my credit. It's my nature . . . I've given much of what I have had away. But the money you give away is not important. It helps people, but you must give some of yourself, too. I think that is your duty. It isn't anything to be given credit for at all. You can't save the world. But a man must try to help the person next to him. That, I don't think, is noble, nor is it to your credit. It isn't exactly your duty. It's something that wells up from within. If a person needs help and you're there, no matter how tired you are, you must give of yourself. Unless you give of yourself, you have given nothing. . . ."

His fierce joy over coming parenthood was not, however, shared by his mother-in-law.

"Our children were always unwelcome to her," Pop told me. "But we must not condemn her for this. She might have had something in her life that caused her to become this way. We must remember that her son, Herschel, was a cripple. Agnes had been injured during the first birth," he continued, "So this second birth was also a difficult one. Knowing that, and knowing my great love for children —not an affected love, but an entire and—well, hell—that was the reason I got married. I wanted children."

A nine-pound daughter was born on December 13, 1920. She was named Jane. Pop was so jubilant over having been presented with a daughter that he cried out, "Persons ask, 'What are miracles?' They doubt miracles. The greatest miracle of all is Birth. The occurrence of life before your very eyes. Birth is the Fourth of July of Sex!"

Early in 1921 Pop was assigned to cover a breach-of-promise suit which promised plentiful sensation. Shortly before court convened, one of the many attorneys for the defense of the Wall Street tycoon who was being sued for a half-million because he allegedly failed to tell his girl friend that he had already been married for twenty years, came into the press room. The lawyer asked each of the reporters to step into the nearby men's room with him for a private conference. Finally it was Pop's turn. The lawyer cautiously checked the compartments to be sure there were no possible eavesdroppers, then turned to Pop and offered him a letter, the contents of which refuted the young lady plaintiff's suit. "It's worth $20 to you if you print this letter in your newspaper," he said.

Pop glanced at the document. "You know, sir, I always thought I was worth at least $40."

Not realizing that my father was joshing, the legal wizard said, "For God's sake! I'll make it fifty!" He reached into his breast-coat wallet and extracted a fifty-dollar bill. He thrust it at Pop. "Here."

Pop smiled. "I can see now, sir," he said, "that we came in here for two completely separate reasons." Then he turned his back on the money and entered one of the stalls.

It seems that one of the reporters had not been true to the unwritten laws of the Fourth Estate, for the letter was printed that evening on the front page of a New York newspaper. Rather than explain to his editor the facts in case, Pop allowed the word to be passed around the city room that he had been scooped. As punishment, he was put on rewrite for the rest of the day and that night.

"I showed up for work the following morning with a black crepe armband on my coat sleeve," he told me, "so I could go into official mourning for having been scooped." This bit of humor was not appreciated by Hearst executives until yet another day when the letter in question was rejected as evidence at the trial because the plaintiff's attorney proved it to be counterfeit.

As a reward for his "good judgment," Pop was allowed to go home early. He sat in the Amsterdam Avenue apartment and played with little Gene while Agnes nursed Jane at the breast. When the baby finished, Agnes put her on Pop's lap. He was distracted by the glimpse of a lady across the court beginning to undress. Her shade was not only up in the fully lighted room, but her window was open. Walking about in the nude, the lady took some currency from her purse, folded it neatly, looked about suspiciously, then secreted the money in one of her slippers and put it beside the other beneath her bed.

Spontaneously, Pop shouted from across the way, "That's the first place they'll look!"

A report emanated from the northernmost regions of Ontario, Canada, in January of 1921 that three U. S. Navy aeronauts had been found alive after an unexpected wind carried their balloon far into that country nearly a month before. Pop was assigned to travel to a settlement in Ontario named Moose Factory to interview these miraculously fortunate explorers who had escaped freezing to death in the sub-zero weather. The balloonists were expected to arrive at Moose Factory within the week.

Pop registered the following day at the King Edward Hotel in Toronto with a host of reporters representing the opposition. In his pocket, he carried a map of Canada he had torn from a book at home just in case he himself became lost in the northern wilds. He obtained a wad of Canadian currency and went on a shopping tour. Among other things, Pop purchased a typewriter and leased a private railroad car which he stocked with all the forethought of an Egyptian pharaoh preparing his tomb for a happy time in the next world. There was an abundance of fancy food and vintage wine so the trek into the north might be reasonably comfortable.

It took about a week longer than was anticipated until the brave balloonists finally arrived at Moose Factory. The interviews were gripping enough to make the front page for several days. All this time, however, Pop had been doing some high living, and was also a loser in several high-stake poker games. When he arrived back at the *American,* the first man ever to simultaneously suffer frostbite and the gout, Pop was braced by the editorial auditor to explain in detail exactly how he had managed to get rid of $3000 in expenses during his Canadian caper. It was now my father's task to call upon his latent talent for composing swindle sheets, a talent unrivaled, I have been told, in modern journalism. If the auditor could not disprove his accounting, chances were that he would not be fired.

Beyond more or less legitimate expenditures, such as the renting of a private car, Pop invented the purchase of a mythical fully equipped dog team and sled, but this did not yet cover the last $500 sent him. He then soared into complete fantasy as he jotted down the illness of his lead dog, who required expensive medical care. Next to this, he entered the amount: "$215." He recited the fact that the lead dog's "wife" had given birth to pups shortly before his eventual death. And next to an explanation of the mythical funeral given his brave lead dog, he entered another amount. He had a copy boy deliver the expense account to the company auditor. Within five minutes, the expense account was bounced back at Pop with a terse note from the head bookkeeper that "You have yet to account for $60, Mr. Fowler."

Pop stared out the window, searching for inspiration. He smiled, then scribbled: *Flowers for bereft bitch, $60.*

Pop was now covering the fast breaking stories in the daytime, and was filling in as drama critic at night. There was little time for pranks as his diary showed:

February 15—Clear and windy. Payday. Cover Frank Tinney divorce. Paderewski interview postponed. Home early. Fight over gas bill. Play with my dear children.

February 16—Gas bill adjusted. Bank and call on King Features. To write detective yarns, playlet biography on Mother Goose. Cover bad Shakespeare play. Bad night's rest.

February 17—Like a Spring day. On Caruso story at Vanderbilt. At night with Whitaker to see Lionel Barrymore's Macbeth. Peg O' My Heart. Dine at Jack's.

March 27—Warm and clear. See St. John crowds and go to office to make out expense account. Another expense account wrangle. I blow out of office. Dinner with Martin Dunn. Calms me down.

March 31—Warm and drizzly. On Black and Tans in afternoon. To Carmel on Stillman case. Shooting in our apartment. Find gang at Carmel, nothing doing until Monday. Back to town on slow train. Interview May Cochrane. Home at 11 p.m.

The last day's entries were the most interesting because Pop told me many personal angles associated with "Black and Tans" and "Stillman."

Black and Tans: "While they were shouting 'Up the Rebels' in Ireland," Pop told me, "I happened to meet a young boy in a Bowery speakeasy. He was being dragged, bodily, by two men. Not wishing to see a boy mistreated this way, I beat the hell out of the two bullies, and shoved a guy who tried to intervene over the bar. When I took this handsome lad with his mint copy of an Irish smile to a more peaceful speakeasy, I ordered two Jameson's straight and asked him what it was all about.

"He said that he was a Rebel, and he had a date with a firing squad back in Ireland. The two men who were tugging at him had been sent all the way to America to bring him back for that appointment with death."

On succeeding days, Pop took the young man with him on various stories. "You must give him a call," Pop reminded me many years later. "I'm surprised you don't know him. His name is George Brent. You know, the actor."

Stillman: "James A. Stillman was president of the National City Bank in New York," Pop filled me in. "It was rare then, but he filed suit for divorce from his wife, Anne. He named a Canadian half-breed Indian guide named Fred Beauvais as co-respondent. I was lucky enough to get Beauvais' exclusive story after he saw me leave a Montreal hotel where he was hiding from reporters. I was walking down an icy path, lost my footing and fell right on my backside. It seems Beauvais was watching through a window and saw me laugh out loud. Beauvais got hold of me on the telephone and said that he thought he might want to give his story to a man who laughed at himself."

Some time later the Indian guide visited Pop. "I took a walk with him into Forest Park in Queens, Long Island. It was a tiny postage stamp sort of a park. We both got lost, and I ended up having to show this master of the wilds how to retrack our path only a quarter of a mile back to civilization. I had a secret, though. I just listened to the passing trolley cars on Myrtle Avenue and walked in that direction."

Pop's diary continued:

August 25—To Bronx and interview Douglas Fairbanks and Mary Pickford. Doug offers me job to write movies for him. Home late.

(Pop didn't accept the job.)

September 24—Warm and clear. Move from beach. Write in office all afternoon. First night in new home. A real house at 8401 115th Street, Richmond Hill, Long Island. Start life anew.

December 6—Cold. Home early. Call on F—— to rescue him from suicide.

December 13—Jane's first birthday. To office late. Give Martin Dunn some birthday cake. Rewrite all day.

December 24—Home early to trim tree. Play with my darling children.

December 25—Sunday. Great Christmas. Gene's sword crowning achievement. Great tree. Down to work at 4:30 p.m.

December 27—*Payday in more ways than one. Agnes not well. Seems there is another Fowler on the way.*

"A father loves his children," Pop once told me, "but he must not be possessive. Each child has his own life, and must pursue it. The child belongs to the future and the parent to the past. No matter what one's pull, intention or inclination is toward his child, he may lie there in the dark of night and think back to the only time when one has his child really. That is when the child is very young, knows no other heroes, and thinks his father or his mother are the gods and goddesses of this world. The father glories in that temporary reign. When the child grows up and gets wise to his father, of course, and sees that other men are not only larger and stronger, but indeed wiser, then the old man is sort of sunk and has to fumble around until the child finally gets big enough to lick his father."

One day early in 1922 when it was definite that a third child was to be born into the family, Pop got up from his desk at the *American* and asked City Editor Dunn if he could go home.

"You sick?" asked Dunn.

"No," said Pop. "Just have an uneasy feeling . . . like something's wrong."

When he arrived at the Richmond Hill house, Pop asked the colored housekeeper Ethel where Agnes was. Ethel told him that Mumsie, his mother-in-law Kittie Hubbard, had taken her to a certain doctor's office. With a rising temper, Pop ran out of the house and headed toward the medic's establishment. It was common knowledge in the neighborhood that this doctor was able to bring on miscarriages by administering an overdose of X ray to an expectant mother during the first months of pregnancy.

By the time Pop arrived at the office, he noticed his wife leaving by the front door. She was crying. When she saw Pop, she fell into his arms. "When I looked at the X-ray burns on his hands," she cried, "I decided I just couldn't go through with it."

In later years, Pop said to me, "Had your mother not changed her mind, you would never have made it into this world. And looking at the mess it's in today, she might not have done you any favor."

As the pregnancy progressed normally, Dr. Howard Moss told Pop that Agnes was not getting enough exercise. This seemed always to be her problem. "She must do a lot of walking to tone her muscles," the doctor prescribed. Pop took her for her first walk, over her objections. Walking along crowded Jamaica Avenue, Pop stopped in front of Lipschitz' Stationers and shouted so all passersby could not help but overhear, "Look, madame! How do you know you're that way? . . . I am not responsible for your condition, and you cannot blame this on *me!*" A jeer from a nearby onlooker caused a group to assemble. Pop declared, "I will not marry you!"

To the gathering crowd, it appeared that Agnes was pleading for her honor. What she really was saying was, "I want to go home, Gene. I'm tired."

"I will not accept this kind of talk," Pop went on, fortissimo. "I did not do it! Someone else did it! I will not marry you, and that's that!"

A brave man stepped from the crowd and said, "You got good teeth, pally. Would you like to try for an upper plate?"

Realizing he had gone far enough, Pop lowered his voice and said, "Well, if you insist. Come on. I'll marry you."

By this time, Agnes was a bit miffed and began to berate Pop for his practical joke. Pop walked ahead at a fast clip. Agnes exerted herself to keep up with him as he took a circuitous route back home. Agnes had been duped into taking the kind of walk Dr. Moss had prescribed. The following morning she felt exceptionally well for the first time, and from then on, was the first to suggest an evening's stroll.

Late in August, Pop was assigned to interview a judge in Salt Lake City, Utah, who was accused of having strangled his wife. The trip by train took four days and Pop was reluctant to take the assignment since his third child was not yet born.

Arriving in the city of the Mormons, Pop prepared to interview the judge who, it was reported, was about to be freed of the murder charge because of insufficient evidence.

"Utah was the only state where a man could be shot in expiation of his crime," Pop told me. "He had his choice, and there are not many choices in this world, but in Utah one could choose between being shot or being hanged. If you chose to be shot," he continued, "a group of six high-minded citizens were picked anonymously. When the sharpshooters entered the prison on the morning of the execution, they were all masked. There was one blank bullet in the one rifle, which I always thought was a big piece of chicanery, so each might think that perhaps he did not shoot the condemned man. Here's an open confession that capital punishment is wrong. It's an indictment of society itself when it makes these concessions. You must not kill living human beings under any circumstance. You must take care of these vicious people in a medical way; put

them away so they will not hurt anyone. God is our judge. Most
people take the Old Testament saying, 'An eye for an eye, and a
tooth for a tooth' to mean, a tooth for a set of false teeth. You must
not take the life of another human unless it is in self-defense, a horrible moment of desperation when somebody is stealing your child
or raping your wife or going to kill you."

When Pop was ushered through the adobe prison's bakery to
interview the accused judge, he noticed a Mexican prisoner playing
a guitar. "As I came in, the Mexican tried to hide the guitar behind
him. It seemed an instinctive sneaking quality of this dear fellow,
thinking he had done something wrong . . . Men usually hide their
greatest pleasures."

Pop was naturally disappointed when the judge haughtily refused
him an interview. He was, in fact, incensed. His anger so impressed
the warden that this official decided to permit him to confront the
judge, who knew he was about to win his freedom. All the judge
would say was, "No interview. Nothing to say." And when Pop
tried to argue the point, the judge snarled, "You can go jump in
the lake!"

"Just for your inhospitable reception," Pop replied, "I am going
to do something you won't like. I came here with no preconceived
ideas. But just because you have rebuffed me in a rude manner, I
am going out and find some kind of evidence to not only keep you
in jail but eventually to prove you guilty beyond any doubt." And
he added, before stalking away, "I live on the other side of this con-
tinent, and on the other side is my wife who is expecting to have a
baby at any moment. And because of you, I am not at her side.
Think that over, my friend."

Infuriated mainly because he would not be home with his wife
in time for the birth of their child, Pop tracked down every clue he
could, although he was at a disadvantage because he was a stranger
in town, and was trying to pin a murder on a man well liked in
the community. He began digging for the real motive for the crime.
This led him to the home of the judge's stepdaughter, an Oriental.

On August 29, Pop found and talked to the judge's stepdaughter
at length. She admitted that her stepfather had seduced her. This
evidence Pop presented to the local district attorney. When he
faced the judge with his stepdaughter's story, Pop told me, "he

1. Pop's mother, "Dodie" Wheeler Devlan. It was 1889 and this teen-ager was carrying my father at this time.

Bellsmith, Denver, Colorado

2. Gene Fowler, age one, 1891. He had big ears from the start.

Beebe, Denver, Colorado

3. Agnes Fowler at Sweet Sixteen, 1906.

4. The first formal portrait of Gene Fowler. Here we see the steel, staring eyes of the young reporter of twenty-two, when he joined the staff of the *Rocky Mountain News* in Denver.

5. Here is the youngest managing editor of any New York City newspaper. Pop was thirty-four; the year, 1924; the paper, the *New York American*. Dressed as neatly as Mayor James J. Walker, with cuff-links and matching vest, he sported a pencil in his coat pocket.

6. Hair disheveled, necktie twisted, and pocket handkerchief awry, we see the same Fowler a few days after his formal *New York American* portrait. *Pictorial Press Photo*

7. When William Randolph Hearst suggested in 1925 that "that young man from Denver" take a trip because he was such a wild, impetuous fellow, Pop grabbed Mother and the two sailed for Europe. In mid-Atlantic Pop sent the following radiogram to Hearst: "On my way to Egypt. Is that far enough?" Reading from top to bottom: Pop, Mother, Gene, Jr., Jane, and me. *International Newsreel*

8. The Seaview, Fire Island, New York, summer home completed in 1933. It was the biggest house on the island at the time. It was not meant to turn out that way, but Pop had designed it on the back of a shingle. It ended up with ten bedrooms, slept twenty-two comfortably. *Photo by J. A. R. Duntz*

9. Two beaux from Broadway are **Walter Winchell and** Fowler in 1933 as they pose for a Hollywood photographer. During this time, there were only two radio programs for which the motion picture houses stopped the reels: Amos and Andy, and Walter Winchell. Here the two fashion plates pose in overcoats and Itailan crush fedoras. This was Pop's maroon era. He had a maroon suit, shirt, and maroon speckled tie. He was *the* Hollywood writer at the time.

10. Who was the movie star and who was the writer? Pop (on right) poses with the rage of that era's cinema, Maurice Chevalier, at Paramount Studios. Pop was writing Chevalier's scripts at the time but he could have easily become a star with his handsome looks.

11. Honolulu, June 1941. First day in the private home we had rented on Waikiki Beach. It was six months before World War II and one year before Pop would begin writing his most publicized book *Good Night Sweet Prince*. Pop is fifty-one, just two days older than Mother (at left). I am nineteen, full of muscles and hair on the head. *Photo by Allan Campbell, Honolulu*

12. A few members of the Bundy Drive group in John Decker's living room. Left to right: Film editor Al McNeill, myself, John Decker posing as John Barrymore, Sadakichi Hartmann, the poet Whistler's former secretary (and a bitter sage Pop made famous in his book *Minutes of the Last Meeting*) and lastly, Pop. It was 1941, just before World War II.

13. Another meeting of the Bundy Drive group. Six philosophers, 1942. Left to right: W. C. Fields, Pop, John Barrymore, one month before his death, Barrymore's emulator John Carradine, actor Jack La Rue, and artist John Decker.

14. Gene Fowler at the top of his career. In spite of paper shortages, his latest book *Good Night Sweet Prince,* the biography of John Barrymore, outsold everything in sight. He was fifty-three at the time and happy that he could make a living writing books. Note the pin on his collar where a button is missing. In spite of his dashing dress, one could always find a flaw. "But," as he said, "there is a flaw in every man."   *Photo by Will Fowler*

was non-plussed. I said, 'Judge, I am sorry I had to uncover this thing. If you had been decent enough, even in your extremity, to see a reporter who has come so many thousands of miles, it might not have happened.'"

The evidence Pop dug up caused local authorities to re-evaluate the possibility of the judge's guilt. During intensive grilling by the police, the judge eventually confessed that he had murdered his wife to be able to marry his stepdaughter.

After he had filed his story of the new evidence and confession to the *American,* Pop returned to his hotel. There was a telegram awaiting him. It read:

FINE TEN POUND BABY BOY BORN. BRING PAPA A POUND OF TINSLEY'S MIXTURE CHEWING TOBACCO. LOVE.

AGNES

When Pop walked into the nursery at Jamaica Hospital four days later, he spied one which was obviously the largest, for ten-pound babies were then uncommon, and said to a nurse who was attempting to shoo him from the room, which had been germ-free until he arrived, "If this one isn't mine, I don't want any other!" He was taking a chance, for that baby was *me*.

There were times when our Jamaican housekeeper, Ethel, would ceremoniously place her little daughter, Mavis, and myself in Pop's bed just before we were carried away for our night's sleep. Then there were days when Pop would roll Mavis and me down Park Lane toward Jackson's Pond in a perambulator to watch the toy sailboat races. One day the champion racing car driver Barney Oldfield and the wrestling promoter Jack Curley visited Pop in Richmond Hill. They sighted him coming out the front door with Mavis and me in his arms. Oldfield was dumb-struck as he saw one child (blue-black) and myself (cream-white) in either arm. "Gene!" cried Oldfield. "What the hell! What happened?"

With his usual aplomb on such occasions, Pop said to Oldfield, "Well, you know, Barney. They tell me this happens every so often. I don't know much about genetics—but aren't they wonderful, these kids? You'd never suspect they were twins, would you, now?"

Putting it bluntly, Pop told me in later years, reflecting upon Barney Oldfield's consternation on seeing a black and a white baby in his arms, "I never needed any of that integration stuff. I love people as people. None of that big bazoo lip service. If a good person is a good person, he's a good person. If he's a bad person, he's a louse. I don't care if he's colored green. I reserve the right to like or dislike any one."

Fortunately, he seldom disliked any one for longer than five minutes. As for his kids: We were brought up in New York where there were then no problems with integration. We went to school at P.S. 99 in Kew Gardens with Negroes, Jews, and Catholics.

Pop stocked his first writing room with books. He called it the "study." It was an enclosure just off the bedroom. The study seemed large to me in childhood, but upon returning many years later I found it to be only about six-by-ten feet. When I returned, most of the bookshelves had been taken down. Only two large Egyptian water colors, one of Rameses II, the other of the God of the Upper Nile, remained. These had been painted by my father.

Now that Pop had the money, he started to collect vintage editions of the classics. This was a period when he would sometimes work sixteen hours a day, then go home either to do some of his creative writing or go to bed with a good book. And then there was always Agnes and his children. He had little time with us then. His bed was placed beside an outer wall of the house. And on this wall, he daubed India ink to silhouette the likeness of his three children's heads.

"I never slept well," Pop used to say, "and when I awakened at night, I would look over at Agnes, then up at the silhouettes of you kids. It brought me comfort."

On my first birthday, Agnes, whom I shall now respectfully refer to as "Mother," left home to visit relatives and friends in Southern California. She arrived at Cambridge Street in Los Angeles where she shared the second floor of a private residence with two girl friends and stayed there for two months.

Back in Richmond Hill, Pop was still at work on the *American*. He now wore *pince-nez* glasses with black ribbon attached to his coat lapel. His detachable white collar was high and starched. A tightly knotted black tie hid the gold collar button. But with his flair for never being completely dressed, he wore no stick pin in his tie, nor did he have a pocket watch or chain attached to his vest. He never did carry a timepiece as long as he lived, yet could tell the hour, usually within five minutes.

During Mother's absence, it was not exactly peaceful on the home front.

Actor Wilton Lackaye gave a speech at the Lambs Club. During the convivialities afterward, the manager of the New York Giant's baseball club, John J. McGraw, for some reason hit Lackaye in the jaw. Lackaye suffered not a broken jaw, but a Pott's fracture of the leg caused by falling on the marble floor. Then four Irishmen in the bar took offense at what the actor said about their "forefathers" in his speech. To this, Lackaye snapped back: "If you have *four* fathers, you're all bastards!"

Up the Rebels!

Pop stood in front of the actor to save him further injury, and received a broken nose from one of the four Irishmen. Pop demanded a brandy as a restorative just before someone asked him if he would "like to go outside and settle this thing as a gutty Irisher himself." Outside, Pop was set upon and received another drubbing.

The next day Gene Fowler showed up for work with smoked glasses and a tin cup filled with used pencils. He asked City Editor Martin Dunn if he might cover Central Park that day.

Shortly following the recovery from his honorable injuries, Pop covered an insignificant story as far as the reading public was concerned, but it held a fascination for him even though the story was buried back among the financial pages. It happened that a wealthy Park Avenue lady's cook was placed in a private room at Bellevue Hospital with a malady never discovered before. Instead of sweating like most other overworked ladies of the pantry, this female emitted *sand* from her pores. Observing this phenomenon among a group of learned but puzzled diagnosticians, Pop broke the silence with: "Very simple, gentlemen. She swallowed an hourglass," adding, "Too bad, though. It broke up a marriage with a cement man."

"What that man could do with minor stories," Martin Dunn told me. "He would pick out some special angle and dress up a drab event so that it shone as resplendent as a window display at Tiffany's."

One afternoon, still during Mother's absence, Pop told Martin Dunn that he wished to get off an hour early to meet Don Clarke uptown. Dunn said that he was counting on Pop to write the obituary of Thomas Fortune Ryan, the wealthy financier who had died that day.

"All right," Pop replied. "I can do that."

"But I want three columns," said Dunn.

"I can write three columns in an hour," said Pop.

He did it. And he met Clarke uptown at the prescribed time.

Shortly before Mother's return, Pop was assigned the duty of interviewing the French statesman Georges Clemenceau, "who," Pop told me, "was over here to hit the good old U.S. for some money. But," he added, "it had been diplomatically stressed that we of America were to consider this as a privilege, and should be cautiously polite to this dignitary."

Feuds often are over matters that seem trivial to the observer. In Pop's journalistic world there were three kinds of feuds: between the editorial department and the business office (mainly over expense accounts), between the reporters and the copy desk, and between the reporters and their photographers. Reporters liked photographers individually, but collectively they were a menace on many occasions to good reporting. Pop said, "It was necessary for the photographers to get their pictures first so that their negatives might be developed and the prints passed upon for publication and sent to the art layout room and then to the engraving department." He added that in those days engraving took some time and to complete a plate within an hour was considered fast work. "The photographers also were a daring and impudent group of gentlemen who ordered celebrities about on land or sea as if the visitors were common ignoramuses," Pop said, adding, "and on occasion they were right."

When Clemenceau, the Tiger of France, arrived on our shores this day, a large group of journalists and photographers went down the Bay aboard Mayor Hylan's committee vessel, the S.S. *Macom.*

"Many other persons crowded the venerable tub to the gunwales," Pop related. "Whistles were tootling in the harbor and streams of water flourishing from the fire tugs, a kind of hydraulic gesture that I never did quite understand the meaning of."

The Tiger of France seemed a bit annoyed by the general bedlam, but for the time managed to keep his temper, perhaps bearing in his great mind the dominating purpose that brought him to the United States.

As soon as Grover Aloysius Whalen, silk-hatted and with a white carnation in his lapel (not a gardenia as was popularly supposed), had run interference for the Tiger and got him aboard the *Macom* without wetting his gloved claws, the photographers went into action. To the plain dismay of the eminent statesman, these picture snappers converged upon him and began to give an exhibition of what coyotes can do to a tiger.

"They called him 'Clem,'" said Pop, "bellowed at him, criticized his stance. He began to wave his gray-silk gloved hands and his shrugs became violent contortions. He either couldn't or wouldn't speak English, although it was afterward established that he could pronounce the word 'dollars' as clearly as a bell."

When Clemenceau appealed to members of the Alliance Française for advice and protection, the photographers began to lay hands upon him and force him into postures suitable for their daguerreotypes. This went on for perhaps twenty minutes with all the aspects of a rough-and-tumble, punctuated by Gallic screams and the East Side-West Side accents of the lensmen.

Finally, when the perspiring Tiger was brought below decks for the interview, he was so mad that Pop and his fellow journalists had difficulty in getting so much as a *oui, oui* from the cantankerous Saviour of France.

On dry land the following day, Pop and other reporters continued to follow the movements of Clemenceau for the simple reason that they wanted to know how much money he might be taking away. And by this time, too, no matter what sort of feuds reporters had with photographers, they meant to be recognized by this man as Americans on American soil; to be paid respect, even though it might have to be offered by a translator.

"We reporters were spurned again and again by the Tiger," Pop iterated, "as for example when he visited Otto Kahn's Cold Springs château with its lane of juniper trees and its thirteen Rolls-Royces. When Mr. Kahn, a most amiable and approachable man, discovered us hiding to get a story, he smuggled sandwiches to us in his garage."

Clemenceau met in secrecy with great editors and publishers of the time at the estate of Thomas Lamont. When Pop and other reporters entered this mansion, a dignified but horror-stricken English head-servant treated them as if each and every one was carrying the original germs of the Great Plague into the place.

"The foyer looked something like the interior of Notre Dame Cathedral," Pop went on, "although there were no cardinals' hats hanging from the ceiling and no candles burning before shrines.

"The photographers were not even allowed to stand near the entrance and enjoy our discomfiture when we were <u>bounced</u> from the premises.

"I believe that we were a rather resourceful group in those days. We did not much give a damn what the Tiger said in the privacy of Mr. Lamont's mansion, but our pride was hurt."

It occurred to Pop that one of the guests at the session was an old and valued friend, the lawyer and orator Chauncey M. Depew. It had been Pop's privilege to call on him many times over the years, sit in his Egyptian library, and talk about the man Depew knew and loved, Abraham Lincoln.

"Now Mr. Depew was not exactly a great emancipator," Pop said, "but he had one thing in common with his hero and mine: a monumental sense of humor and a great gift for mischief." He went on to say, "The 'Senator,' as we called him, was then in his nineties. At any rate, he was older than God."

Pop consulted some of his confreres, among them that great reporter Alva Johnston, and expressed a belief that Mr. Depew would not be sworn to secrecy, and that if the reporters waited until the meeting adjourned and then called upon the good Senator and boldly conveyed their problem he would be delighted to snitch.

Meantime, Pop had another good suggestion, which was for the reporters to retire to the nearest speakeasy and drink to their own health.

"At about eight o'clock in the evening," Pop went on, "we visited

Senator Depew's house which my memory seems to suggest was somewhere off Fifth Avenue, mid-town." What he did remember clearly and warmly was that the Senator had an elderly butler who restored one's affection for England.

The butler welcomed the reporters with great sincerity and courtesy but conveyed the disappointing news that the Senator had retired to his bedroom. They really liked the old boy for himself and of course said that they would not disturb Mr. Depew under any circumstances. To this the butler replied, "Oh, no, gentlemen. Senator Depew would be greatly offended if I did not at least look in upon him to see if he is awake." In a few minutes, the butler returned to say the Senator insisted upon dressing and coming down to see the boys.

"We went into his library, which contained a real collection of books to be read and not displayed," Pop recalled.

In perhaps fifteen or twenty minutes, the tall, twinkling old gentleman with his muttonchop whiskers and his high florid brow came into the room. "His first remark as I remember it was, 'Gentlemen, this is indeed a pleasure. I am getting lonely in my old years. I made a horrible mistake when I was a young man in forming friendships with men older than myself and now all my playmates are gone.'"

Senator Depew shook hands all around, telling his guests, "You know, I don't get many visitors from the Press any more, but your grandfathers used to visit me and they always were nice. Of course," and he smiled, "there were a few editorials in the papers that were not complimentary, but they never bothered me much. Be seated, gentlemen. What, if anything, can I do for you?"

The Senator knew my father fairly well so Pop took it upon himself to say, "Senator, we are in a jam. We are reporting the actions of Mr. Clemenceau and we are not getting very far with the assignment. Today we were barred from the home of Mr. Lamont."

"Mr. Lamont," said the Senator, "is really a very nice young man." Mr. Lamont was then about fifty and seemed quite old to the young reporters, but they did not dispute the Senator.

"Senator," Pop said, "will you help us out by revealing what went on at the meeting? That is, of course . . ."

The Senator broke in with another twinkle: "Of course, I shall."

He looked benevolently at the reporters and added: "Naturally I shall expect you to treat my confidence as your grandfathers always did, and, shall we say, refer to me as an 'authoritative source.'"

Pop and his fellow reporters agreed to this gladly and the Senator then proceeded to tell them how Clemenceau had appealed for American dollars to save France and Europe. Not only did he give them this information, but he added information regarding just how this money might probably be spent in France, once the loan had been made.

The chief editors of the papers usually went home before the morning editons were "put to bed," as the saying is, and usually received their early editions at their various clubs or homes. You may well imagine the consternation of one and all, when the headlines appeared to the effect that the Tiger of France had his eye upon U.S. gold. Indeed the horrible impression that had been created in Clemenceau's mind on his first meeting with the press was now confirmed.

The editors themselves were flabbergasted, but they could do nothing about it because they were so flattered to have been introduced to Clemenceau that they had neglected to instruct their various subordinates concerning their solemn vow. They had not foreseen such a development as a *leak*. And this leak was fostered by a young reporter who often looked as though he took his job lightly. When Hearst called Pop in to compliment him on his excellence as a reporter on this particular story, my father left the newspaper mogul with these words: "You know, Chief, I never did find out if Mr. Clemenceau also slept with that damned skull cap he always wore about in public."

Pop was so versatile that his editors switched him from sports to the theater, from police stories to international politics at will. Another important assignment during this period was to help cover the heavyweight championship fight at the Polo Grounds in New York on September 14, 1923, between Jack Dempsey, his boyhood friend, and Luis Firpo of Argentina.

Pop was the only newspaperman allowed in Dempsey's dressing room before the fight. Dempsey, as Pop recalled later, seemed a nervous wreck. "If I didn't know Jack well, I'd have thought he was truly frightened. He walked about nervously and seemed to shake a bit . . . but when the bell rang, you would have thought an animal had been loosed. Jack was a killer."

In the first round Dempsey was knocked flying out of the ring by the massive Bull of the Pampas. Afterward a throng of reporters claimed they had been the ones who pushed Jack back in the ring after that wallop. Films of the fight, however, show only one man trying to help him back up on the apron of the ring. In looking over that film, I spotted Pop sitting calmly three rows away, under a salt-and-pepper cap, as his old friend was clambering back into action.

Pop had good reason to stay calm. In the next round Dempsey stalked Firpo and clobbered him all over the ring, knocking him out in two minutes.

Dempsey was so dazed, however, that the day after the fight he still thought he'd lost it.

He went up to a newsboy near his hotel and asked, "What round was I knocked out in?"

The newsboy gave him the news that he was still champion of the world.

Mother wrote that she was finally coming home, after stopping off in Denver to visit families and friends, adding, "We dug up some spruce trees and shipped them by express tonight. You will no doubt get them by the time you get this letter. Put them out right away. I do hope they will live as they are so pretty."

A load of spruce trees was all Pop needed at the moment, his life at home already being complicated by the necessity of digging up baby-sitters. As a result, I had two of the oddest temporary nursemaids any child could boast—one a Congressional Medal of Honor winner, the other a kidnaper-turned-evangelist. The first was Sergeant Mike Donaldson of the "Fighting 69th." Pop had waged a letter-writing campaign to get the nation's highest military award for Big Mike, who finally got his medal five years after the war ended in a ceremony at Governors Island.

The other baby-sitter was Pat Crowe, who had kidnaped Edward Cudahy, Jr., the fifteen-year-old heir to a meatpacking fortune, in 1900 and collected a $25,000 ransom. Somehow, after being arrested and tried in 1905, he had beat the rap. Now he was touring the country as an evangelist. Pop and he were friends, in token of which he allowed the ex-kidnaper to watch over me while he was downtown at work.

If my mother would have been alarmed to know Pat Crowe was watching over her youngest child, Pop got a worse shock when he reported for work the day of Mother's arrival.

Assistant Editor George Tuttle, whom Pop dubbed "Typhoid Mary," had recommended him for the Albany correspondent's job. This meant that Pop might become a "beat man," a stodgy fate for a man with Pop's restless temperament.

"If Tuttle's recommendation went through," said Pop, "it meant that I would be stuck in Albany for the rest of my life. So I used reverse psychology. I let it be known that I had been striving for two years to get this post as the State's correspondent. When it got back to Tuttle, the man was so mystified by my allegation that I was refused the position."

When Pop greeted Mother at Penn Station, her first words were: "Is everything all right, Gene?"

Pop blandly replied, "Nothing has been so placid, my darling."

Chapter Nine

MY MIND IS FULL OF LARCENY,
BUT MY TONGUE REMAINS HONEST.

GENE FOWLER

January 5, 1924—Cool and clear. Beginning of a cold wave. At office, rewrite. Home early and see all three babies in bathtub at once. Visit with Daddy and retire to room to read and write, having told Agnes that for a woman to deck herself with a multiplicity of costly furs is a frank admission of such a woman that other animals are more handsome than she—else, why borrow the skins of the fox, or beaver, or squirrel? Read the Ibsen *A Doll's House* and then picked up Darwin's autobiography wherein he reveals himself as a dumbbell at school. Retire at 4 a.m.

Our family was complete now. There would be no more children. Pop's life, as indicated by the diary entry above, was bounded by his home, office, and intensive reading that ranged from Darwin to Tolstoi to Aristotle.

The night Lenin died, January 21, Pop consumed Karl Marx's *Das Kapital* and went off to work without sleep. His book purchasing kept Mr. Mendoza feeling prosperous in his store on Ann Street. What was left of his time at home, Pop spent in conversation with Daddy, his father-in-law, who was beginning to grow weak from his asthmatic condition. On the night Woodrow Wilson died, February 3, Pop wrote three columns for the *American* on the passing of this great man, "The first Democrat I really understood."

Later on, Mumsie spilled ice water on Daddy while giving him a bath. "The air was blue," Pop remarked in his diary.

Came March and Pop had lunch with Christy Walsh, late sports promoter and manager of George Herman "Babe" Ruth. The two talked about the possibility of Pop's quitting the newspaper profession. This was a gloomy time in my father's life because he had heard that Hearst had in mind to make him an executive on the *American*.

"I never wanted to be anything more than a reporter," Pop said, "and the thought of becoming an editor frightened me. I could never handle men in the executive manner. I did not want to give up calling my friends by their first names."

Now he began to dwell on death—a morbid trait little suspected by his friends—and this would never again leave him. He began telling me, and this persisted through the years, that he would never live to be fifty, then sixty, then seventy.

On April 1, Pop stayed home to do his Sunday feature story. Jane and I broke out with the measles imported by Gene. There was a heavy snow with lightning and thunder, a phenomenon and a true April Fool spring. The next day he visited McFadden Publications where he was offered the editorship of their two best-selling magazines. Then he went to work to interview theatrical producer Morris Gest and opera diva Mary Garden at the Ritz-Carlton. That same day his Newspaper Club Reporter edition was received as a great success. He was nominated for re-election as president.

The editorship of McFadden Publications could have been the beginning to a successful, wealthy life, but Pop remained true to Hearst. "Random impulses, contradictory ideas, conflicts of desires bounced and whirled about like roulette balls inside my skull. Out of this hit-or-miss scramble one thought kept reappearing to the mind's eye. The thought became my first desire, and later on, almost an obsession; to keep the spirit unbroken, win or lose, till kingdom come. Often I was wrongheaded in my defense of this manifesto, and Damon Runyon once said that I specialized in kicking success."

Pop tried to keep his spirits up, but on May 23, he saw that Daddy was sinking rapidly. His duties at the paper would have put any man of weaker character into a delirium. At night, he sat at the bedside and talked with his father-in-law. He bathed him and he read to him. He sat through the nights with Daddy as the older man slipped in and out of a coma. During Daddy's sleeping times, Pop would go outdoors and smoke under the stars "to do some of my usually aimless dreaming."

It was nearing Gene, Jr.'s seventh birthday, so Pop took his son and his son's friend shopping. He bought both of them baseball mitts. The following day, he completed constructing a rock path that Daddy had started in the garden shortly before taking to his bed for the last time.

May 28—Cool. Daddy is like a withered leaf that threatens to fall from the tree at the least whisper of a kindly wind. The end is not far off and he is prepared. He has done all his suffering. He rallies slightly in the evening and his extremities take on a faint, renewed glow, the forerunner of the Great Visitation.

May 29—Daddy goes home at 5:15 a.m. on a bright spring morn and without a semblance of a struggle. Rain in the afternoon. A long siege ended and a good man has earned his rest. Three weeks without food and with only a few drops of water. He went out like a Gentleman he always was; silent, placidly, unafraid—not conscious for three days except at rare intervals. He was a friend. God, be good to him, I pray; and to us who err.

May 30—Cool, sunny. Mumsie leaves with Daddy to bury him in Denver.

May 31—Cool and clear. Build on Daddy's rock path and finish it. Outline shrubs with pebbles.

On June 1, after motoring to Great Neck with Mother, Jane, and myself, Pop went on a drinking spree which lasted two days. Before he started, he sat down at his typewriter in the office and rolled in a piece of blue linen stationery with the *American* masthead.

One of the poem's stanzas read:

> They will sing you hymns, good heart,
> Kind heart,
> And the hymns are beautiful.

On the way to his first drink that day, Pop entered a speakeasy on 48th Street operated by Wilson Mizner. The prime game of chance there was *chemin de fer*. Pop found Runyon and reporter Alva Johnston seated at a far table. After tipping his hat to a phony stage prop of sixteenth century armor halfway down the stairs of the basement night club, Pop joined Runyon and Johnston.

Pop ordered a large gin. Alva Johnston asked for the same. Runyon called for another pot of coffee. The Demon was out of sorts again with Pop because he had stolen into Editor Arthur Brisbane's Cadillac limousine, which was equipped with a dictaphone on which Brisbane was accustomed to inscribe his latest large thoughts.

It seems that, seeing the limousine unattended outside the Ritz Tower, Pop had climbed in and recorded an editorial warning against universal disaster in an era of airplanes driven by intelligent apes. A secretary had transcribed the parody and it was reportedly set into type at the *American* office shortly before the hoax was discovered.

This was not the night to try Pop's temper. When Runyon continued to point out his shortcomings, Pop stood up and said, "Al, you're just like Powder River. A mile wide and an inch deep!"

Runyon stalked out mad.

Alva Johnston took offense at Runyon's sudden departure. Rendered a trifle giddy by the raw prohibition booze, Johnston weaved in Pop's direction as my father ordered a fresh bottle at the bar.

"I don't think you are so tough as the boys say you are," Johnston told Pop as he squared off menacingly. "I've got a mind to hit you on the chin."

"Go ahead," Pop obliged.

Johnston did hit Pop on the chin, but his punch was as light as a daydream. Pop took it and pretended that it staggered him. Johnston was so overjoyed and eager to tell all of his friends he had knocked Fowler down that he staggered up the turn of the speakeasy stairs and ran right into the phony suit of armor. His head was cut badly, and he was taken away and given first aid by one of the club's bouncers.

Mizner had come in from behind the locked gambling-room door to sit with Pop. He reassured my father that Johnston had not cracked his head too badly after colliding with the suit of armor.

The eloquent con man put on an act to disperse the rich gamblers who had congregated at the table. "I remember when I was in State Prison," he said. "We cons were on a hunger strike, I recall. I was the leader, and it was up to me to decide whether the warden should live or die . . ." He was never in a state prison, but that line of conversation was good for startling a group of snobs.

As Mizner poured a stiff one for Pop, a poor loser dashed from out the gambling room to complain he'd been cheated.

A trained bouncer immediately broke a wine bottle on the guest's skull, inflicting a small but bloody wound.

"Send for a croaker!" roared Mizner, as his hearties dragged the stupefied customer to the private office.

Dr. Smith, we shall call him, a lodger at Mizner's nearby Rand Hotel, responded. Like several other guests of that caravansary, Dr. Smith was an opium addict. Mizner had lured him with difficulty from his Shanghai flute. When the poppyfied Dr. Smith examined the wounded playboy, blood, mixed with red wine, had seeped into the crevices separating the victim's three pendulous chins.

"Holy smokes!" diagnosed the still somewhat opiated doctor, *"his throat is cut!"* He proceeded to sew the three chins together from ear to ear.

A week passed with Mizner trembling every time he saw a policeman before the corpulent loser reappeared. He had changed. His head was bent over—literally sewn to his chest—and he couldn't for the life of him raise his eyes higher than a storm sewer. He shook the trembling Mizner's hand and said:

"Sir, I want to thank you for saving my life."

During his second day of drinking, Pop decided to repair to the Hotel Pennsylvania, then the largest hotel in the world. Pop had made an appointment with Dr. J. Darwin Nagel, medical director of the hotel, for a coffee enema and steam bath which would get him in shape to get to work that day.

So much has been written about Pop's spectacular drinking that I wrote Dr. Nagel at his Winter Haven, Florida, home to ask his opinion regarding Pop's drinking habits. Dr. Nagel died a few months ago at ninety-four. He had observed many topers come and go. This is what he put down:

In reply to your question as to whether your father was an alcoholic, I can definitely state *no*. Your father was a periodic drinker but he never drank too much, when his spell came on, not to know what he was doing. In my 26 years experience as Medical Director of the Hotel Pennsylvania and the Hotel Vanderbilt, I have had more experience than the average doctor in treating alcoholics, both periodic and confirmed, and I learned the truth of the old Latin saying: *in vino veritas*. That is: "There is truth in wine." This means that the use of alcohol shows the real character of the drinker. Some get gay, some get bellicose, some get lachrymose, but when your father drank, he was always full of fun and strongly inclined to be satirical.

As Pop pulled himself together to go to work from Dr. Nagel's cure-all station on the tenth floor of the hotel, he reached into his coat pocket to find a typewritten poem which Mizner had placed there two nights before. Pop told me in later years that this verse had been scribbled by a now deceased buddy whom Mizner had comforted during his last binge. Mizner told Pop this man, named DeLange, paused at the Rand Hotel to write his poem, then proceeded to Mock's Hotel where he killed himself. Whoever wrote it, it read as follows:

> New York—vulgar of manner, over fed,
> Over dressed and under bred.
> Heartless, Godless, hell's delight,
> Rude by day and lewd by night.
> Bedwarfed the man, enlarged the brute,
> Ruled by thief and prostitute.
> Purple-robed, pauper clad,
> Raving, rotten, money-mad;
> A squirming heart in Mammon's mesh,
> A wilderness of human flesh;
> Crazed by avarice, lust and rum—
> New York, thy name's Delirium.

That night after work Pop took his reporter friend Joe Gordon home with him for company. They chatted until two A.M. A message arrived in the middle of the night that Pop had been selected by Jack Hastings and Walter Howey of the Hearst brass to become sports editor of a proposed tabloid newspaper.

Mulling it over the following day, Pop conceived the idea that radio, which was beginning to become popular, should have a time table sort of reference place in newspaper columns. Just a few publicity pamphlets were being mailed to newspapers regarding particular programs going out over the air. Burying his indecision, Pop collected all the radio publicity sheets he could find and took them to the composing room to make up the world's first radio log.

"At first," Pop told me, "I thought this thing should be called a Radio Time Table."

As a sample, it was rolled off in a two-column spread with boxed twenty-four point bold face type reading: *RADIO TIME TABLE*. Below this in parenthesis was the explanation in italics, bold face and asterisk directives: At 11:25 A.M., a radio listener could hear *Ted Lewis's Symphonic Clowns* on WHN, Wave Length 360; *Harry Richman's Entertainers* at 11:45 on the same station; *Joe Cook* of *"Vanities"* interviewed, on the same station; *Weather and Market Reports* on WEAF, Wave Length of 492; *Waldorf-Astoria Tea Orchestra* on WJZ at 4 P.M.; and so on to *Phillip Spitalny's Orchestra Programme* on WHAZ (Troy) at 2 A.M. Pop had already created the "double truck" on the sports page, a headline which was spread across two open pages. He had also created a box index on the front page from which a reader could thumb to his favorite subject posthaste.

On June 17, Pop was notified by the assistant publisher of the *American*, Victor Watson, that he was officially appointed as Sports Editor of this tabloid which would be named the New York *Daily Mirror*.

There followed an enormous effort by Pop and the men he called in from throughout the country to become members of his sports department. He had only eight days to organize his staff and plan the layout of his section.

Pop learned that Walter Howey, a famous editor and organizer, had been made managing editor of the sheet. Hearst informed Howey: "We do not expect this newspaper to be a great success, but I wish it to cut seriously into the *Graphic's* circulation."

Howey's retort, Pop told me, was, "Mr. Hearst, I have never been associated with a failure."

The blithest gesture I ever knew a newspaperman to make (and

I was a Hearst reporter for about ten years myself), was made by my father: he took a day off to play with his children with only five days more to put this New York newspaper in shape to publish.

The following day, Pop gathered his staff to brief them on his policy. The next day they had a dress rehearsal. His diary read:

The dress rehearsal—hard day. We get to press at 12:35. See the new paper go over the presses. Here in the great presses there is an expression of civilization greater than government, for the press is the government of the mass mind. States govern only property and body.

June 23—The paper is born at 9 p.m. A sweltering night over hot metal.

The first edition was dated June 24, 1924, and contained thirty-two pages. The top headline read: *FLIES IN DAY FROM SEA TO SEA*. This had to do with Army Lieutenant Russell L. Maughan who flew a 375-horsepower Curtiss pursuit plane from New York's Mitchell Field at dawn and landed (following four stops) in Los Angeles within 24 hours flying time.

The four back pages of this five-column tabloid were dedicated to sports. Above a multi-spaced cartoon was the line: *Milk Fund Advance Passes $100,000*. This was on the second page to Joe Gordon's recounting of how the Yankees dropped the American League baseball lead to Detroit.

On the same page was Pop's signed column under the title *Hammer and Tongs*. It cut two columns for a pica, then rested down to a one-column side, starred and lined to finish off with half-column cut photos of Luis Firpo and Georges Carpentier.

In his first column Pop sounded a bit like his friend Westbrook Pegler.

An unnamed boxer was about to travel across the ocean from France to fight Pop's boyhood friend, Jack Dempsey. Nobody could lick Dempsey, in Pop's opinion. The *Hammer and Tongs* column led off:

A French woodcutter, possibly stronger in the arms than he is in the forehead, is the latest candidate for American boxing dollars. His sponsors are preparing to tout him into the ring with certain of the army of set-ups that clutter the Heavyweight Highway. He will not be permitted to carry his broadaxe into the arena. This will be a handicap. For he will be called on to face more or less dead wood.

This French tree-surgeon is only one of many foreigners who are planning to invade this country where crutch-kicking is a profitable profession. A brief survey of pugilism's array of low and narrow foreheads discloses odd goings-on. Bunk is still in its infancy.

In the column, Pop went on to say that Dempsey would fight for a million dollars. And so he did, when he finally met Carpentier.

There were four entries in the last of Pop's diary:

June 24—Very hot. Quarter million is our first day's circulation. My staff beginning to simmer down. Dan Parker looks like a good boy under fire.

June 25—Rain. Very tired. Adjust income tax. Am unusually short and cross. Grind out much work and come home to read and write. These are long hard days, but satisfactory ones.

July 19—Eighth Wedding Anniversary.

September 2—Six years in Hearst Service. Twelve years in newspaper work.

Pop put himself in jeopardy with Arthur Brisbane when the editor sent him a note suggesting that he write his sports column in imitation of his (Brisbane's) *Today* editorial column on the front page of the *American,* and Pop's return note to Brisbane was: "I shall imitate only one man. His name is Fowler."

The scuttlebutt now was that Fowler was marked for "bigger things in the Hearst Service." Pop told me, "Here I was still a reporter, and enjoying it in covering sports."

Celebrating the *Mirror's* first edition, Pop and Walter Howey went on the town early. During the evening, Howey remembered that he had promised his wife to escort her to the opening of a most expensive speakeasy. The two rushed to Howey's apartment where they dressed for the formal opening.

"This speakeasy was a splendid place," Pop told me. "It was

rather large, and there were flowers everywhere. The host was a phony Count. Shall we call him Count Smith? Smith seems to be the safest name to use in these matters. He had a nose like comedian Danny Thomas. But he lacked the sense of humor of Thomas. As we sat down, I told Count Smith that I could not tell the difference between cider and wine. This put into action a private vendetta on the Count's part."

Count Smith eventually asked Mrs. Howey to dance. On the third pass, during a Strauss waltz rendered by a five-piece string orchestra, Count Smith made a remark too loud and offensive to be ignored. Howey stood up and punched in the direction of the host's outsize nose. He landed on target, and blood spouted.

"The battle started," Pop continued. "Howey and I stood back-to-back. I got a chair and jabbed at everyone who came at me. I kicked several field goals under this chair. I'm sure some of the ones I kicked never became fathers."

The Count's son came up brandishing a revolver. Mrs. Howey knocked the gun from the young man's hand. Someone called for outside help. The police arrived to save Pop and Howey from being killed. The place was closed down and Count Smith's backers suffered a $40,000 investment loss, not to mention the fine crystal and napery destroyed.

When they got into a taxi, Mrs. Howey slammed the door on two of Pop's fingers on his right hand. Apologizing, Howey sent his wife home. The newspapermen repaired to Chinatown where Howey joined in a dice game with proprietor Johnny Keyes and won the restaurant from him. Pop, during this time, had been tending bar in the front and had given away all the money in the cash register, along with free drinks to any stumblebum who happened by.

Pop and Howey were on the job the following morning to put out the second edition of the *Daily Mirror*. As a whim, Pop sent his assistant, Ray Helgeson, to Johnny Keyes' place to claim the restaurant for Howey. Keyes put up a row, but compromised with the pledge that he would give one free shot of straight whiskey to each of the first ten moochers who entered his establishment for twelve months running providing the deed of ownership was returned to him. . . .

Mirror circulation soared. Pop often worked with Howey to keep in touch with big news events, but most of his time was dedicated to putting out the sports page. Pop was becoming more and more impressed with the talents of a tall, rangy young copy boy, Dan Parker, who eventually became the *Mirror's* sports editor and is still on the job after thirty-eight years.

In one of his recent anniversary columns, Parker wrote:

There was plenty of money in circulation, the stock market was booming, and radio hadn't yet developed to the point where it offered competition to newspapers. In this wonderful newspaper era, Gene had a picnic. I can still see him sitting on the other side of a double row of desks from me in the dingy sports department of an old brick building down on Frankfort Street under the shadow of the Brooklyn Bridge—a section known as "the Leather Swamp." I have never seen anyone equal Gene for facility in pounding out copy. And no one had a better time doing it. As witty lines, either in polished prose or hilarious verse, flowed from his swiftly moving fingertips onto a sheet of copy paper in his typewriter, he would chuckle, laugh out loud, occasionally twitch his neck as if his collar was too tight and pay no attention to those seated around him, as if oblivious of their presence—which he probably was, so great were his powers of concentration.

Promptly at four o'clock every afternoon, Pop would call a tea interval and join the staff in a dish of oolong, dedicated to cricket players everywhere. Sometimes this would develop into a musicale as Pop, on the accordion, joined in some red hot harmony with Charlie MacArthur, who would drop in tootling on a saxophone.

As often happens when a man is sipping a good brew of tea and laughing his heartiest, bad news arrives like the apple salesman in Eden. Just as Pop was enjoying the happiest days of his newspaper life, a message arrived from Hearst announcing that, as of the following day, Pop had been appointed managing editor of the *New York American*. Hearst never gave his editors time to burn bridges or heal professional wounds. "While I had qualities of leadership," Pop told me, "I knew I was not a managing editor. I was too young, to start with, only thirty-four. I fought it from the start, unknown to several office Babbitts who could not then realize that there exist a few men in the world who do not care for money, fame, power, or professional advancement. I demanded $500 a week and a three-year contract. To my surprise, I was granted these terms."

Pop went up to Hearst's apartment on Riverside Drive in the middle of the night. To his surprise, the Chief answered the door. He was fully dressed, except for being in his bare feet. He showed Pop into the kitchen where, spread over the floors, were the latest editions of all the New York papers. It seems that Hearst would stand up, sipping a glass of milk and chewing a piece of whole wheat bread, and turn the pages on the floor with his toes. "I get a better perspective of the makeup this way," he told Pop. "Now what do you want, my young man from Denver?"

"I protest my appointment as managing editor of the *American*," Pop insisted. *"I don't like editors!"*

"Neither do I," said Hearst. "But they are a necessary evil. Won't you have a glass of milk with me?"

Chapter Ten

Most morning newspaper managing editors arrive at work shortly after the lunch hour. His first day in office with this new title, Pop appeared shortly after sunrise to talk with the night men who were about to leave the plant. He wandered into the composing room and through the banks of linotype machines. He would not sit in the chair behind the dark mahogany desk in the front office. Doing so seemed to him to be a final act of submission to the job. Rather, he stood at the layout table and composed a directive to his staff. He put down two major points. One was that the use of articles such as *a* and *the* be no longer used in headlines, banks, or captions. "This sort of practice is poor journalism." He insisted that any use of the verb *to be* should be discontinued in heads. He explained: "Where *is* and *are* appear in twenty or thirty heads in a given edition the effect not only is sloppy, but the punch—which choice of better verbs insures—is killed."

Other points reminded his staff that they should scrupulously avoid repetition of the same words in heads and sub-heads. He further stated that no head would begin with a verb unless a "freak head is being built." Finally, he urged that his copy men get better acquainted with jazz heads and human interest heads and captions. He cautioned, "This must not be interpreted to mean that facetiousness or levity in heads should mar a good story which is obviously serious. But where a light, humorous, or human interest angle develops, please jazz up heads and captions with a few exclamation points or question marks that lift the yarn out of the ordinary groove." The Hearst bible was being rewritten; a new Daniel had come to judgment.

Pop's directives were not meant to cramp his editors or copy readers. His aim was for improvement in the "show windows" without curbing his staff's imagination through rigid rules.

Next, Pop sent for a rundown of the *American's* expenditures. The weekly budget broke down to a grand total of $25,795.04. Including Pop's salary, city side, exclusive of copy readers, etc., totaled $4138.24. This also represented the salaries of only nineteen general assignment reporters.

After a few weeks, when everything began to run smoothly, Pop visited a Cadillac agency and asked if they had a sedan of gunmetal gray. It just so happened that there had been one on the show-room floor for the past month. "Immediate delivery?" Pop asked.

"Greased and oiled to be at your front door tomorrow morning," said the salesman.

As Pop started off toward Manhattan in his new four-door Cadillac, the following morning, we three children had practically bid goodbye to our kissing stone.

The sidewalk on the periphery of our block along St. Ann's Avenue separated Richmond Hill from Kew Gardens to the north. Slate squares which maple tree roots had upended looked like forgotten tombstones. Gazing east to 116th Street, halfway down that block, there was a granite rock to the side of the turning asphalt roadway. The rock was covered on the sides with green moss a child could rub and pretend it was a cat. This was our kissing stone.

When Mother received a telephone call that Pop would be coming home early, we would wait on the corner where Park Lane ended and peer up the two blocks until Pop came into view. When we spied his first great strides, we would race to the kissing stone and wait for him to pick us up in his arms. I was usually the last to arrive. Pop would wait patiently. Then all at once, he would kiss us. He would kiss us on the cheeks and mouths each time as if he had been away for a long time. What strength he had left was dedicated to carrying us in his arms and wrapped about his legs for the last half block until we released him at the front door where Mother would be waiting. This was perhaps the most precious time of our young lives.

Not familiar with the mechanics of his new automobile, Pop traveled nine miles over the Queensboro Bridge into Manhattan *in low gear*. The car broke down on 54th Street just west of Fifth Avenue in front of John D. Rockefeller's town house (which today is part of the site occupied by The Museum of Modern Art).

Three caretakers appeared. Their spokesman said, "You cannot park here. This is the residence of John D. Rockefeller."

"The hell I can't," said Fowler. "I have a flat tire."

Fortunately, Rockefeller's mansion was situated across the street from the University Club. Two of Pop's friends, Cameron Rogers and Stanley Walker, the latter city editor-to-be of the New York *Herald Tribune,* came to his rescue to help change the rim-bolted tire. As they labored, Rogers and Walker berated the Rockefeller factotum for not having recognized the *American's* new managing editor.

Pop's relaxed Western ways caused newspaperman Ring Lardner to dub him "the Last of the Bison," adding that "Fowler never left the plains or the prairies or the mountains."

Arriving at the paper a bit late this day, Pop discovered an old prize fighter awaiting him. "Gene," the man said, "I ain't got much talent with the dukes any more, but I can remember any amount of numbers you can put in front of me all day."

This gave Pop an idea. Now that the automobile had become a standard piece of modern-day equipment, many were beginning to be stolen in the City of New York. "Here's $10," Pop told the ex-fighter. "If you can do what you say you can, I'll give you five more if you come back tomorrow and check all the license plate numbers I put before you."

"How come you give me ten now and only five if I come back, Gene?" asked the scarred boxer.

"Because I think you need the ten now," said Pop. "You know if you come up good," he spoke in the boxer's vernacular, "you'll get better than what you might sparring with boys at Stillman's gym."

The ex-pug stood at the Manhattan entrance to the Queensboro Bridge an entire day, then reported back to my father. By this time, Pop had secured a "hot sheet" which listed stolen cars. The retired fighter was able to report that eleven of the automobiles stolen from Manhattan during that day had coursed over the bridge. His talent was so respected by the police following publication of this information in the *American* that two cars were assigned by the department wherever Pop placed his memory man. This was the first fully organized action taken to recover stolen cars in Manhattan.

One of Pop's weaknesses, from the viewpoint of his superiors, that of compassion for his fellow man, began to affect his prestige with the brass hats. His revolutionary ideas did not set well with the higherups in the Hearst domain. As an example, Pop was the first to hire copy girls. "Girls were good at this work," Pop told me, "and if one of my reporters called in that he was sick, I would tell him that Joan, or Jill, or Mary pined for him. It was remarkable how these reporters who needed only a bit of nudging came to work, even with high fevers, or high hangovers, just to get a smile from a good-looking girl who would deliver a piece of copy from the bull pen to the city editor's desk. If I possessed any record at all," Pop continued, "I had the lowest editorial-side absentee record. The Hearst Service has yet to match it." His head rewrite man, Eddie Doherty, and sob sister Elizabeth Beecher dubbed the copy girls "Fowler's Follies."

Martin Dunn told me that there were so many women reporters on the *American* that it was necessary for a particular editor to be assigned to find jobs for the girls. "This onerous chore fell to the lot of Gene Campbell. Campbell ordered the girls to phone in their stories—which were rarely printed—then come into the office only to pick up their weekly pay."

When Eddie Doherty was stuck for a lead, Pop would offer him inspiration by emerging from his office to play Brahms' *Lullaby* on his accordion.

When Pop's rather unorthodox operation was reported to Hearst at his San Simeon Ranch in Santa Barbara, California, the Chief called my father on the phone to ask if it was true that he had been serenading his men in the bull pen. Receiving the Chief's call on top of a deadline, Pop answered, "Yes. It is true that I have been putting music into yours and my newspaper with an assist from my accordion. Hold on," he said. "I'll get the instrument, and you will judge for yourself if my playing is not up to what you have been hearing."

Hearst, with a rare and patient indulgence, listened while Pop took out his squeezebox to play a full thirty-two bars of *Asleep in the Deep,* then a chorus of *Goodbye,* and *The Last Rose of Summer.* At the end of his impromptu concert, Pop spoke into the telephone to ask Hearst, "Don't you like my playing?"

"I can assure you that it is high class, young man," said Hearst, "but circulation is dragging. Don't you think you should do something about *that?*"

A directive followed this phone conversation. Pop was ordered to visit Hearst in Santa Barbara for a "meeting of minds." Pop got as far as Los Angeles, where he decided to visit a friend who had been the first to interview Calvin Coolidge when he became President of the United States. This friend was Harry Brand, publicity director for Joseph M. Schenck shortly after creation of United Artists Studios.

It happened that upon his arrival in California, Pop was the worse for wear. While waiting for Brand, Pop felt the need for a bit of exercise. He began jogging around an open stage—it was still the day of the silents and movies could be made without soundproofing—just below the open window of the office where Schenck, Brand, and other executives were conferring on an important deal. Schenck caught sight of Pop doggedly running around the stage but didn't remark on it until Pop shouted:

"Lap three! I'm breaking Paavo Nurmi's record!"

"Who's that man?" Schenck asked Brand.

"Don't pay any attention, Mr. Schenck," Brand said. "He's my friend from New York."

"Nurmi! Lap four!" Pop sang out.

"He's just nervous and letting off a bit of steam," Brand explained to his chief.

By Lap fifteen Schenck was suggesting that the window be

closed. Pop, however, folded on the next lap. Brand poured him on the next train for Santa Barbara.

Arriving in the great reception hall at San Simeon, Pop took a seat and waited, hungover and dejected, while other Hearst executives from around the country exchanged knowing looks. The word had gone out that "Gene Fowler was insolent to Mr. Hearst on the telephone," and his fellow hetmen expected he would be fired. And when Hearst came out to announce, "I now wish to speak with that young man from Denver," Pop followed the Chief like a condemned man. His fellow executives sensed that the ax would be falling within minutes and silently congratulated themselves on a greater sense of discretion.

Hearst rarely spent more than five minutes in conference with any one subordinate. If condign punishment was to be meted out, no more than a minute would elapse. So when Hearst emerged from his office after spending nearly an hour with Pop, his arm about my father, he announced, "There will be no more interviews today, gentlemen."

During his "free reign" as managing editor on the *American*, Pop wrote many stories himself. His boyhood friend, Jack Dempsey, married motion picture actress Estelle Taylor. Gerald Chapman, the mail bandit-murderer, was caught and convicted to hang. Floyd Collins, a Kentucky coal miner trapped by a cave-in, was found dead after seventeen days of excavation. E. G. Barrow, secretary of the New York Yankees, stated that Babe Ruth was not "broke" and had at least five more years of professional ball to play (and in two years more, he would hit 60 home runs in one season). The old Madison Square Garden went to the hands of wreckers, and a man to help build the new stadium, carrying bricks, would eventually emerge as the great novelist John Steinbeck. A biology teacher in Dayton, Tennessee, named John T. Scopes, went on trial because he had the effrontery to tell his high school students that man descended from the ape, rather than from the rib of Adam. Sing Sing celebrated its one hundredth birthday, but no original lifers were at hand. Pancho Villa, the liberator of Mexico, was assassinated. John D. Rockefeller, Jr., paid the top income tax in the country: $6,-277,699 and some cents. Sandow, the Strong Man, died.

Also—of even more importance to all Hearstlings—there was an earthquake that shook Santa Barbara. At the epicenter was Hearst's castle at San Simeon.

"What can I tell you, son?" Pop asked me. "I had an allegiance to Mr. Hearst, but I also had to tell the truth to my subscribers. The first wire story told that a severe earthquake had wrecked Santa Barbara. Eleven persons had been killed and property losses were in the millions. The Santa Barbara City Manager said $3,000,-000. A figure put out by the City Engineer was $30,000,000." Pop began assembling an "extra."

Duplicates of the following two wires were forwarded to him as guidance on how to handle the story:

R. E. Boyd
International Newsreel Corp.,
226 William St., New York

Filed six good Santa Barbara quake pictures with American Telephone Company. Should reach Chicago by 11:15 and New York by midnight. They were the first to be filed as the opposition plane cracked up. Los Angeles bureau is sending complete bureau Hearst papers and fastmail service. Managing Editor of *Examiner* wants me to send telephoto one air view of Santa Barbara to *Chicago American* also *New York Journal*. Advise. We should have complete beat.

Jack Gum. *International Newsreel Corp.*

Publishers all morning Hearst papers: While there has been heavy property damage and apparently a few lives lost at Santa Barbara, the early reports are manifestly exaggerated. *Examiner* sent its own men to the scene, which is over 100 miles away, and we will have really authentic reports for you this afternoon. As Chief has many millions invested throughout the State I am sure you will not want to use wild stories from non-Hearst sources.

Young

Concerned as to how his "flagship" of the chain, the *New York American,* was treating this story, Hearst put in a phone call to my father. He asked, "How are you treating this earthquake out here, young man? I hope you have not made too much of it."

"I have alerted the circulation department to awaken all news-boys. As of now, I am in the throes of replating for the second time. We have sold a half-million extras to date, and I expect a record sale for one day, but am only putting out a third extra of a quarter million, feeling that there will soon be a slackoff. In a few words, I am merely mentioning the matter all over the front page!"

"You are doing a fine job, young man," Hearst chuckled. "Just keep selling your papers." He hung up with what Pop told me must have been a smile. "I felt it." Breaking a circulation record most likely appealed more to the Chief, on second thought, than playing down the catastrophe.

Shortly thereafter Hearst purchased a twelfth-century castle in Wales. He had the structure taken apart stone by stone, ordered it boxed, then mailed it Parcel Post to the United States. "During his lifetime," Pop told me, "I believe that it was never unpacked. But, anyway, I wish I might have had the thrill of saying to an inquisitive postmaster: 'It's a castle . . . Mail it! . . .'"

Looking back on his reporting days, and the times when he was a thirty-four-year-old managing editor of the biggest paper going, I asked Pop: "Do you mind if I refer to the time you were stopped by a mounted policeman on Broadway while driving the new Cadillac with Joe Gordon at your side?"

"You mean the time I asked Gordon to take my place at the wheel as a diversionary tactic?"

"The same," I said.

"The story was simple and true," said Pop. "I harassed the cop so that he dismounted from his clopper and Gordon slipped over into the driver's seat. While Joe placated the cop, I merely rose into the stirrups and heeled the horse in the flanks, and we two galloped down Broadway as I shouted 'Yipee!' The cry of '*Hy Yo Silver*' might have been more appropriate, but then, The Lone Ranger had not yet been created."

Thomas H. Ince, a veteran film producer reported to be trying to organize the entire motion picture industry under his dictatorship, was a guest on Hearst's yacht late in 1925. On December 10, it was reported that he had died under mysterious circumstances. Because he was a guest on the Hearst yacht, there was a flood of rumors about the way he died. Gossip claimed that Ince had been stabbed, then died from loss of blood. Other accounts had it that he was shot and died aboard ship.

Apprised of the tragedy by wire, Pop contacted two reliable acquaintances in Los Angeles. The two shall remain unnamed here. They were directed to visit the morgue where Ince's body lay, and "find traces of anything that might indicate murder, then report back to me immediately."

It was later found that Thomas Ince had died of a heart attack. "As the result of acute indigestion," San Diego District Attorney Chester C. Kempley reported.

"It was reported to me," Pop went on, "that Ince had drunk too much booze. He had a heart history prior to this incident. So take it from there. One Los Angeles newspaper hinted at murder. This rumor was probably instigated by other factions trying to fight Ince for the generalship of the movie industry. Anyway," he concluded, "this settles the mysterious Ince death once-and-for-all."

Later that month, annoyed at Pop's lighthearted editorship, Hearst, according to word that reached Pop, expressed the wish that "that young man from Denver might take a long trip."

Receiving this news as a personal affront, Pop stormed home and asked Mother, "How long will it take you to pack so I can show you the sights of Europe and other places?"

Mother said, "Well, if you sit down quietly and have the pot roast dinner Mumsie cooked, I should be able to be packed by the time you're finished."

It took forty-eight hours until a special passport was issued from Washington, D.C., then Pop and Mother were off on the ocean liner *Paris*.

After two days at sea, Pop sent Hearst a wireless. It read:

ON MY WAY TO EGYPT. IS THIS FAR ENOUGH?

An assuaging answer came back from Hearst, suggesting that Pop take a good vacation and rest, adding that all expenses were on the house. It also mentioned that when Pop returned, there were other executive plans for him.

When they arrived in Rome, Pop and Mother took the first taxi they could find. It brought them to the Hassler Hotel at the foot of the Spanish Stairs. There was a group of fine-looking girls living at the Hassler. They seemed to be quite unattached, ready for fun and games. Pop eventually dubbed the hotel "The Hustler."

While Pop was out shopping for a Christmas tree, a Hearst correspondent took it upon himself to spirit Mother to another hotel he believed more suitable. As the moving process went on, a number of the local gentry gathered to salute "a lady climbing up to another bracket in life." Although she had had a short stay at the Hassler, Mother was regarded by the natives as being an exceptionally good-looking woman of the streets.

Moved to a suite in the Grand Hotel, Mother awaited her husband's discovery of the new address. Her errant husband arrived with an entourage of guides seeking traveler's checks as payment for gifts. After settling with his guides, all sang a round from Puccini's *La Bohème*.

Alone in their suite, Mother and Pop trimmed the Christmas tree with shreds of napkins and silver utensils from the kitchen. They drank toasts to their children, then Mother opened her gift. It was a white Spanish shawl with intricate hand-sewn designs. "It's difficult to get Spanish shawls in Rome," Pop told Mother.

What was Pop coming home to now? He had a house to pay for in Richmond Hill. He had a family to support. What had Hearst in mind for him? The surprise appointment was that of director of the Koenigsberg Syndicate (known popularly as "King Features"). This meant he would head all syndicated magazine stories and cartoons for Hearst interests throughout the nation.

It was a job which lasted sixteen months; then on June 18, 1927, Pop was put back to work out his contract as a reporter on the *American*—still at $500 a week.

One of Pop's more memorable assignments was coming up, the Ruth Snyder-Judd Gray murder case.

"Damon Runyon called it 'the dumbbell murder,'" as former Hearst editor Ward Greene recorded in his book *Star Reporters*.

"Never did two conspirators slay their victim with less cunning than Ruth Snyder and Judd Gray on the night they fell upon Albert Snyder in his sleep and hammered him to death with a window-weight."

Ruth was a Queens, Long Island, housewife grown tired of her middle-aged husband whose only recreation was bowling once a week. Judd, a corset salesman, had a wife and child in East Orange, New Jersey. After the two met in a speakeasy in 1925, their subsequent relations led to the murder of Ruth's husband. Shortly before the murder Ruth had tricked her husband into buying more insurance than he thought was necessary. Ruth and Judd purchased a sash weight, rubber gloves, and a can of chloroform. Sucking on a quart of bootleg booze to get up his courage, Judd concealed himself in the Snyder home. The Snyders returned home, with their own child, at 2 A.M. from a neighborhood party. The little girl fell asleep, then Ruth went to Judd.

She led him to the bedroom. Seeing only a shapeless form under the bedclothes, Judd Gray raised the sash weight with both hands and began to pound where he thought Ruth's husband's head was. He bungled the job; the sash weight dropped from his shaking hands. Albert Snyder was fully awake now because Judd's blow had been diverted when the weight hit the bed's headboard. Snyder grabbed Judd's necktie and nearly won the fight. Then his wife, Ruth, picked up the sash weight and battered her husband as he shouted: "Mommie! Mommie! For God's sake, help me!"

Clumsy in their greed, Ruth and Judd were apprehended when they attempted to cash in the life insurance policy. Ruth's story about a sudden intruder did not stand up. Fingerprints were everywhere about her home. The story was a tabloid sensation. Of all the murders of that decade, it seemed to typify the 1920s the most acutely.

The lovers went to trial in 1927, and on January 12, 1928, they were executed in Sing Sing's electric chair. Two facets remain in the mind of the older reader. One was that Warden Lewis E. Lawes allowed newspapermen witnesses to the execution not to be frisked by his guards. A man with an ankle camera shot a blurred photo of Ruth dying in the chair. It was printed the following day on the front page of the New York *Daily News*. The second was Gene

Fowler's account of the double electrocution, which stands today not only as a fine piece of reporting but as a lasting argument against capital punishment.

"What did you do that night, Gene?" Ward Greene asked many years later. "I hear that you drank steadily before and after the knockoff."

"I behaved in a most prosaic manner, contrary to legend and my own character," Pop told Greene.

"Do you remember anything else about it, any sidelights?"

"Only the flowers blooming outside the deathhouse. They were planted, you know, by Charlie Chapin, the *World's* city editor who killed his wife. I'm sorry, but I can't recall anything else. But I'm like most reporters," Pop added. "I never relished seeing people hanged or electrocuted—since none of the victims ever seemed to be moving picture producers."

On the night of the execution, Pop was, as usual, without pencil. He had the gift of seeing, then reporting. While other reporters sat down at their typewriters to compose their accounts of the executions in a little store a few miles from the prison, my father dictated his story cold over the telephone to a rewrite man on the *American*. There was no editing of his copy. It was set up in print as the man on the other end typed his story in short takes. Doing it this way he beat the opposition to the street by one edition. It read:

SING SING PRISON, Jan. 12—They led Ruth Brown Snyder from her steel cage tonight. Then the powerful guards thrust her irrevocably into the obscene, sprawling oaken arms of the ugly electric chair.

That was about 30 minutes ago. The memory of the crazed woman in her last agony as she struggled against the unholy embrace of the chair is yet too harrowing to permit of calm portrayal of the law's ghastly ritual. Ruth was the first to die.

The formal destruction of the killers of poor, stolid, unemotional Albert Snyder in his rumpled sleep the night of March 20, 1927, was hardly less revolting than the crime itself. Both victims of the chair met their death trembling but bravely.

Each was killed by a sustained, long-drawn current that rose and fell at the discretion of the hawk-eyed State executioner, Robert Elliott. In Ruth's case, he administered three distinct increases of current. For Judd, Elliott had two climactic electric increases.

Ruth entered the death chamber at 11:01 o'clock. She was declared dead at 11:07. Less than three minutes after her limp body was freed from the chair, Gray entered—not wearing his glasses and rolling his not unhandsome eyes rapidly from right to left and then upward. The current was applied to Gray at 11:10 o'clock. He was pronounced dead by Dr. C. C. Sweet, chief prison physician, at 11:14.

Brief as was the time for the State to slay Ruth and Judd, it seems in retrospect to have been a long, haunting blur of bulging horror—glazed eyes, saffron faces, fear-blanched, that became twisted masks; purpling underlips and hands as pale as chalk, clenching convulsively in the last paroxysms.

And as these woeful wrecks passed from life the shadows of attendants, greatly magnified, seemed to move in fantastic array along the walls, the silhouettes nodding and prancing in a sepulchral minuet.

The football helmet, containing the upper electrode, was pressed to the skulls of Ruth and Judd, one after the other, in a manner suggesting a sordid coronation of the King and Queen of Horror. A passing noise emanating from the bodies of the current-paralyzed victims rose like a hideous hymn by a serpent choir. No regal incense for these wretched beings, but from the skull of each in turn there curled upward thin, spiral wisps of pale smoke where their scalps were seared by the killing flame.

As Ruth entered the room she responded to the prayer for the dying given her by the Rev. Father John T. McCaffrey.

Ruth's voice, bereft of the maddening, hysterical scream that sometimes has risen from her throat in the condemned cell, now was high pitched, but soft in texture. It sometimes was the voice of a little girl—such a one as might be seen and heard during the Times Square rush hour, lost from her parents and among big, strange men.

In response to the prayer of the priest, who wore his black cassock and stood sadly over her, Ruth muttered parts of the responses, the last one being:

"Father, forgive them, for they know not what they do."

The leather helmet was pressed to her blonde hair, a patch of which had been clipped to make place for the electrode. Two matrons who had walked, one on either side of the woman, departed from the room before Elliott shot the hot blast into her once white, lovely body.

The matrons and Principal Keeper John J. Sheahy, had stood before the pitiful woman to shield as much as possible her helpless form from the gaze of the witnesses. Ruth wore a brown smock of the sort stenographers and women clerks use in their office work. It had white imitation pearl buttons. She had on a short, washable black cotton skirt.

Ruth had black cotton stockings, the right one of which was rolled down to her ankle. On her feet were brown felt slippers. She wore blue bloomers.

"Jesus have mercy!" came the pitiful cry. Ruth's blue eyes were red with much weeping. Her face was strangely old. The blonde bobbed hair, hanging in stringy bunches over her furrowed brow, seemed almost white with years of toil and suffering as the six dazzling, high-powered lights illuminated every bit of her agonized lineaments.

Ruth's form seemed more slender than usual as she dragged her feet and groped with her hands.

"Father, forgive—."

The failing voice was interrupted. The holy litany was snapped short. No priestly ministrations could save her body now. Ruth's felt-slippered feet were at the great abyss, her blanched face, only the lower part of which one could see, was chalky.

She who had pleaded earlier in the day for life—just twenty-four hours more of it—seemed to have lived a thousand years and a thousand torments in the hellish prelude. Tightly corseted by the black leather bands, Ruth was flabby and futile as the blast struck her. It swept into her veins with an insidious buzz. Her body went forward as far as the restraining things would permit.

The tired form was taut. The body that once throbbed with the joy of her sordid bacchanals turned brick red as the current struck. Slowly, after half a minute of the death dealing current, the exposed arms, right leg, throat and jaws bleached out again.

Executioner Elliott, in his alcove, gazed as dourly as a gargoyle at the iron widow, who now had turned to putty. Then he shut off the current. Dr. Sweet stepped forward. He adjusted the stethoscope, exploring for any chance heart beat. Ruth's right hand had been clenched. The back of that hand rested flush against the chair. The forefinger and thumb were placed together, in the position of one who is holding a pinch of snuff. As the current was opened, the hand slowly turned over in the wrist strap; the forefinger and thumb, which had been pointed upward, now were turned down.

All this time there had been a fizzing, whirring monotone. That was the only sound in the white-walled death chamber except the light rattle in the silvered steampipes.

Two attendants hastily donned white interns' coats. A porcelain topped wheel stretcher, virtually a movable operating table—which hitherto had been behind the chair, was brought to Ruth's feet. And now the small audience was nauseated by the repellent work the chair had done.

One attendant screened Ruth's legs with a towel. Water from the moist electrode was dripping down her right leg. As a guard removed the electrode it proved to have been a ghastly garter, one that scalded, branded and bit deeply.

A greenish purple blister the size of an egg plant had been raised on her well-formed calf. No mawkish sentiment should be expended on lady murderers, we are told, but somehow one did not think of what this woman had done, but of what was being done to her. It was a fiendish spectacle as they lifted her to the white-topped table.

Two men hoisted her. Her arms hung limply. Her head had been burned. Her mouth, the purplish lips now as white as limestone, was agape in an idiotic grin. What a sorry gift the State made to Eternity.

No longer was Ruth trussed in those oily black straps. One of those binders had seemed to press her ample bosom cruelly where once a baby daughter had nestled and found life. Another belt had imprisoned her waist. The humble folds of her cheap girlish smock had retreated vainly and formed puffy plaits under the rude familiarity of the chair's embrace.

Ruth was a broken butterfly in a spider's web.

In looking back—back to the death of Ruth—the adjusting of the helmet, imagine a football helmet of regulation brand on a woman's head as an instrument of death; I say, the adjustment of that dripping helmet was such a striking symbol of Ruth's futile search for worldly joys through sin.

It spelled all that she had dared, suffered and paid in leaving her doll's house in staid, home-loving Queens Village. That helmet was death's sordid millinery. No fluffy ribbons or bows or gaily-hued feathers so dear to the fun-loving Ruth.

Just a snaky wire at the top of this hateful hat, a wire that coiled beside her and was ready to dart into the brain with searing fangs. They wheeled her out to the autopsy room. There were three minutes of mopping up, retesting of the machinery. Warden Lawes stood sadly aside. Father McCaffrey, his head bowed, departed.

The chair *Moloch* of civilization in this year of enlightenment was yawning for another human sacrifice. Principal Keeper Sheahy left the room to summon the little corset salesman to his doom.

Everyone had expected Judd to die first. But at the final hour Warden Lawes moved Ruth to the last-minute cell only 20 paces from the chair chamber. Judd was shunted to the east wing and had to walk 160 feet.

Judd Gray met his death like a man. It is true he seemed horribly shaken. It is a fact that he was so moved by the enormity of the price he must pay that his voice could not be heard above a guttural, jumbled monotone. His lips framed the words, but the words died in his throat. It was the voice of a man being turned into mummy-like catalepsy.

Judd, his roving eyes apparently seeing naught before him, looked shabby in the full, white light against the background of severely tailored medical men and uniformed guards. Yet there was in his bearing a sense of dignity incompatible with criminality and disgraceful death. Judd came of good people and his breeding now told.

Yes, his dignity as he tried to repeat after Protestant chaplain, the Rev. Anthony Peterson, the phrases from the Sermon on the Mount, was impressive. One forgot his cheap, frowsy gray trousers and the grotesque, flapping right pants leg that had been split at the inner seam to receive the electrode.

He had figured woolen socks of a mauve shade. The right one was rolled down over a brown felt slipper. His knitted long underwear of light buff color had the right leg rolled high above the knee. Gray's leg was well developed and evidenced his athletic days of tennis and quarterback on his school football eleven. Now he too wore a football helmet just the sort he used to sport when directing the attack of his team.

"Blessed are the pure in heart," intoned the chaplain.

Gray's white lips moved. A deaf person would have understood the words by the lip-reading system. But only a cackling scramble of sound got past Gray's rather boyish mouth. It seemed that Gray came into the death house supported by a religious ecstasy. His chaplain was wearing his gown as a doctor of divinity. He is a large, finely set-up man with gray hair and a large kindly face.

Gray sought the eyes of his spiritual advisor, both when he walked into the chamber and before his eyes were masked. In walking Gray moved with leaden feet. At times he seemed to be treading on thorns and the two lines between his eyes and at the top of his nose were black streaks in his ashen face. That face seemed to be fed by lukewarm water instead of blood.

Brisk and facile fingers of veteran guards, whose powerful hands displayed an astounding cunning, worked at Gray's straps. The big hands manipulated the buckles and the spidery accoutrements of death with the ease of a Paderewski ensnaring the notes of a rhapsody.

Gray had entered the death room at 11:08 o'clock. At first he walked stiffly as though his knees were locked together. His steps sometimes were like those of a person trying to climb a steep hill. His chin, which has a deep cleft in it, was thrust forward and his nostrils were slightly distended.

There was evidence of a terrible inner strain, but there was not one whit of cowardice manifest in the march of the little corset salesman. His jaws were as yellowish white as saffron and his lately-shaved beard still showed enough to lend shadows to his sunken jowls. But there was no saffron and no yellow in his backbone, no matter what his crime was or how brutal he may have been when he held a sash weight over stodgy, middle-aged Albert Snyder.

The doctors, Sweet and John Kearney, watched in a detached way as the well-trained prison attendants proceeded to kill Judd in the name of the State. Elliott sent the short copper lever home. Judd, who had been sort of crumpled beneath his leather manacles, now shot forward and remained erect.

A blue spark flashed at the leg electrode. Soon his sock, not quite clear from the current as the water from the electrode dripped down his calf, was singed. Smoke came from the leg. Next the powerful pressure of the death stream singed his rather wavy dark brown hair. Smoke rose on either side of his head. For a moment he seemed a grotesque Buddha with votive incense pouring from his ears.

At the first electric torrent, Judd's throat and jaws were swollen. The cords stood out. The skin was gorged with blood and was the color of a turkey gobbler's wattles. Slowly this crimson tide subsided and left his face paler, but still showing splotches of red, which were mosaics of pain. The electricity was put on just as the chaplain got this far with his comforting words:

"For God so loved the world—."

Judd was not conscious, presumably, to hear the rest of the minister's "that he gave his only begotten Son . . ."

Gray's white shirt was open. When Elliott withdrew the lever of the switch, Dr. Sweet walked forward to search the chest of the night's second victim for heart action. He found none. He said:

"I pronounce this man dead."

The chair with its now lifeless burden still held the eyes of many with a bewildering fascination. There were not a few, however, who covered their eyes. The men in white coats made their second trip with the wheeled stretcher. Judd did not know that he had been preceded in death by Ruth. They had not seen each other or exchanged notes since they first entered the death house eight months ago. Nor did the former lovers meet tonight in life.

Still these victims, who were known as No. 79892 (Ruth Snyder) and No. 79891 (Judd Gray) on the prison rolls, are again together in death. For their bodies, shrouded in white sheets, are in the prison morgue, a small room not fifty feet from the chair. This, then, was the end of the road, the close of their two years of stolen love. Their bodies are cut open as the first hour of the new day comes hazily over town, prison and broad, half frozen river. Their skulls are opened by medical men, as in the stern letter of the law, and their brains are plucked therefrom by rubber gloved hands and are deftly turned this way and that for inspection beneath the bright prison lights.

It was an unhallowed spectacle, this reduction of a full-blooded woman of thirty-three years to a limp and blubbery cadaver. It was fearful to see a man cooked in the chair. The twenty-four invited witnesses file out of the death house. Warden Lawes' secretary, Clement J. Ferly, signs the death certificates.

A last minute move on the part of Ruth's mother, Josephine Brown, and her brother, Andrew, failed to prevent the autopsy that is being performed as this is written. An order was served on Warden Lawes forbidding the prison physician to make a surgical incision in Ruth's body. On advice of Attorney-General Ottinger, Warden Lawes did not obey the order.

No opiates and no sedatives were administered to either of the pair tonight, Warden Lawes said. They ate somewhat heartily of a last dinner of roast chicken, soup, coffee, celery and mashed potatoes. Gray, in ordering his meal, had underlined his written request for "good coffee." As he handed it to the guard, Gray said: "And I mean *good* coffee."

No typewriters and no telegraph wires were permitted in the penitentiary. Immediately after the reporters left the now empty, grasping, greedy chair—which seemed to clamor for still other human sacrifice—they dashed to waiting automobiles and through the tall iron gates. About a thousand persons were massed as close to the prison as the guards would permit. Through a long gauntlet of watchers, who stood anxiously to hear if Ruth and Judd had gone, roared the press cars.

The stories are now being finished in a cramped and crowded back room of a soft drink establishment, which has an old-time bar running the length of the front room, and where the air is thick with tobacco. Then, as the morning comes on, leaving the night with thinning shadows like ghosts departing, the fading click of typewriters comes with less rattle and the buzz of telegraph instruments, too, is subsiding.

Then the calm realization that the law had been obeyed and society avenged, and that the chair remains to jerk and rip and tear and burn those who slay. Then to bed for nightmares to distort your scrambled dreams.

The bodies of Gray and Mrs. Snyder will be released to relatives at 9 o'clock in the morning. Ruth's body will be claimed by her mother, Mrs. Josephine Brown. Judd's mother, Mrs. Margaret Gray, will claim his.

The children of our neighborhood used to cross to the other side of Myrtle Avenue as we passed executioner Elliott's house on the way to school. Elliott received $150 for each person he put to death. For the Snyder-Gray doubleheader, he was paid $300. Few in the neighborhood spoke to him. On the mornings following an electrocution, his house usually showed some evidence of mud thrown at his front door, or a garbage pail tipped over at the back. This particular morning, on the way to P.S. 99, we noticed that his plate-glass bay window had been smashed.

Chapter Eleven

MEN ARE NOT AGAINST YOU;
THEY ARE MERELY FOR THEMSELVES.

GENE FOWLER

Pop was offered a contract renewal with the Hearst organization, but he declined. He wanted to devote himself to writing books when his present contract ran out in 1928. His prime ambition then was to have a book published before he was forty.

His last assignment as a newspaper reporter was to cover the funeral of Lewis Rodman Wanamaker, late president of the John Wanamaker stores. It was a heavy gray March day that began with rain. A carillon had been imported from Switzerland to chime funereally. A circus tent, its interior banked with orchids, protected the mourners from the elements. Pop noted scores of dignitaries holding their top hats over their hearts. As the minister voiced the usual words, "ashes to ashes, dust to dust," the sun punched a hole through a thin cloud, and the superstitious sighed.

Pop had covered too many funerals in the rain to be moved by this possible omen. Instead, he looked across a gully to notice a strong, stout woman carrying a load of wash to hang on her back-yard clothesline. She broke out in song as she began to pin up sets of underwear. "I thought," Pop told me, "how much the lately departed Mr. Wanamaker would have surrendered his millions to trade places with a happy middle class woman doing her wash this day."

Pop finally purchased a bungalow at Ocean Beach, Fire Island, where he had been renting during the summer months for the past six years. There were no numbers on the houses of this small community. Instead, each bungalow had such quaint names as *EEEE* (For Ease), *The Billows, Fish-Inn,* and *The Dunes*. Pop's was *Anchorage*. He owed $2500 on it. He had $25 in the bank. There was a hint in Mother's voice that literary endeavors did not pay as well as chasing ambulances for Hearst. Pop declared he would remedy the situation.

Pop looked up his friend Jack Curley to suggest they join forces in a fight promotion. After a search, they brought a chap named Johnny Squires from South Africa to America to fight anyone for money. They took this unproved heavyweight to Detroit.

Messrs. Fowler and Curley obtained a match for their fighter with Johnny Risko, then the tough baker boy of Cleveland. Pop's boyhood friend, Jack Dempsey, traveled all the way from California to referee the fight for free. There was a gate in excess of $60,000 and Pop came home with a good share to pay off what was due on his beach cottage. "I should have been with the House of Morgan," he told me. "Anyone can make money." Pop added that he created another first in boxing history by giving his battered fighter, who had been knocked out in the second round by Risko, the lion's share of the purse, "plus the bonus of a paid ticket back home to South Africa."

Tex Rickard, most famous fight promoter of all time, and then head of Madison Square Garden, intercepted Pop before he caught the ferry from Bay Shore, Long Island, for his Fire Island cottage. "Gene," said Rickard, "be my publicity director at the Garden." Pop was hooked. And he knew taking this job would prevent his publishing a book before he was forty. He was halfway through writing it. It was about a whorehouse madame—celebrated years before in Denver—and was titled *Madame Silks*.

Late that summer Rickard sent out a news release that Gene Fowler was named Publicity Director for the Garden.

Many newspapermen were critical of Pop for having taken this job, which they considered beneath his talents. But he insisted on his right of free enterprise. He told me he had quit the newspaper business because it was no longer play for him. "I hate work," he said, "and when newspapering became work, I knew it was time for me to get into something else. Much as I liked it, sixteen years is enough time to devote to one's education, and I consider newspaper work an education, though not a thorough one. It teaches you how to run a lot of 100-yard dashes, but doesn't give you wind enough to run a long race." He went on: "Newspapermen were the brightest and best men alive then, and the work was never dull nor tiresome. Sure, there must be bank clerks and grocerymen and people like that. It's too bad for them. Everybody wasn't made bright enough to be a good newspaperman."

During his tenure as publicity director for Rickard, Pop helped his friend, Jack Curley, to bring professional wrestling over from the Seventh Regiment Armory on Park Avenue to Madison Square Garden. It was the heyday of Farmer Burns (who had a twenty-six-inch neck) and Jim Londos. "Jim's neck was twenty-one inches," Pop told me. "And if he had a few more inches added to the length of his legs, he would have been the greatest wrestler of all time. Jim could pull a starch collar down over his head without having to undo the button."

Pop and Dempsey were later pallbearers at Curley's funeral.

"Curley at one time wanted to manage Dempsey," Pop told me. "Well, at any rate, Jack and I were at the funeral in Bayside, Long Island. There was a bunch of sportsmen there, everybody of prominence. And among these sportsmen was a group of Curley's Boston wrestling promoter rivals who were pretty keen guys, and not very ethical. While the pastor was preaching, the rivals were on the long veranda, cutting up the wrestling empire. Dempsey and I thought that was a kind of a sad, lousy thing . . . a commentary on sports in our times. From then on, wrestling became phony."

The Garden was Pop's proving ground for theories on drawing crowds. Remembering his friend, T. Joe Cahill, Pop booked the Third Annual World Series Rodeo in the Garden. Forty thousand dollars in purses was posted, and T. Joe sponsored the affair. There was a parade down Broadway in which I rode my first horse, accompanied by Sister Jane and Brother Gene. I fell in love with T. Joe's daughter, Mary, when I saw her draw on a pair of sheepskin chaps. But Mary's eyes were only for Brother Gene. She had red hair, and an apple-cheeked smile.

From then on, the Rodeo became an annual event at the Garden.

Pop walked to Billy La Hiff's Tavern near the Garden following a long night's work arranging a boxing card. He had a few drinks, then ordered a thick steak. He met with his sports-writing pal Westbrook Pegler. The two were about to attack their steaks when Bill Gibson, manager of Benny Leonard and Gene Tunney, sidled up to protest that Pop had not included one of his lesser boxers on next week's card.

"I don't suppose any other place has ever housed as many homicidal grudges with so few blows struck as La Hiff's Tavern," Pegler later told me. "Some of them dated back so far that the parties thereto had forgotten what they were sore at, but they went on hating just the same, in some cases until the sod grew green above them.

"Fowler was an exception. I doubt that Fowler ever hated anyone. Yet Gene had a wild fight with Bill Gibson. Gibson slashed your dad's face very badly with a diamond ring. Not that Gibson was a dirty fighter. It just happened that the ring was home from the cleaners when the trouble broke out. That crazy Fowler, tall and strong and hilarious, stood up there *laughing*. And Gibson was a wise fighter. Fowler was actually laughing, and belting Gibson back until the waiters, four of them, went between the two."

Subsequently Pop was asked to become Managing Editor of the New York *Morning Telegraph*. This was a sporting and theatrical sheet, then as now. It was said that a whore's breakfast consisted of a cup of coffee, a cigarette, and a copy of the *Morning Telegraph*.

Pop took the job, knowing the book he was working on, the saga of Madame Silks, would have to wait again.

The *Telegraph* stood on the southeast corner of 50th Street and Eighth Avenue and was formerly a horsecar barn. Pop would often draw in a lungful of what the old bricks still smelled of and say, "Horse shit! Isn't it wonderful? Can you smell it, men? What an atmosphere for a horse paper!"

While on the *Telegraph*, Pop assisted Tex Rickard in promoting a prospectively dull ten-round welterweight fight which had little promise of attracting even a small crowd to the Garden. Nevertheless, Pop began the ballyhoo build up. He let fight fans know that he had hired ten of the finest available sports writers who would cover one round each for the *Telegraph*. He also made public that for their chores, each writer would be paid $500, and titled the bout "The Battle of the Aeon."

Among those occupying seats at ringside for the *Telegraph* that night were Lois Long, Ben Hecht, Charlie MacArthur, Westbrook Pegler, Walter Winchell, silent motion picture star and fight fan Lew Cody, and Ring Lardner.

Winchell wrote the first round. Hecht covered the second. Halfway through the fifth, catastrophe struck as one of the fighters was belted colder than the inside of an icebox. Pegler described the knockout. There was no sixth round, but Lardner considered that he should earn his $500. So he described in minute detail exactly *what would have happened* had The Battle of the Aeon gone six rounds.

The day following The Battle of the Aeon, Pop's publisher, who was rather miffed about laying out $5000 for ten sports writers to cover a single event, made a discovery just above the city room. He strode into the empty city room and asked, "Mr. Fowler, do you know there is a whiskey still on the fourth floor?"

Pop exploded. "I know that, but where the hell is my staff? We go to press in thirty minutes, and you are here complaining about some piece of plumbing! Where is my staff? Go out and find them!" Actually, the staff was out working hard, and Pop was aware of the progress of each assignment. His outburst was merely a diversionary tactic to direct the publisher's attention away from the whiskey still which continued to supply his staff and himself with booze.

Pop had no city editor on the *Telegraph*. All copy came through him, and he handed out all assignments to his reporters. He was not strict about their working hours. The only thing he asked of them was that they deliver.

Pop had hired Walter Winchell to write a column, *Beau Broadway,* anonymously, as Winchell sat out a contract with the *Graphic* just before he was to go to work for Hearst for a lot more money. When Winchell began his column for Hearst, many accused him of "imitating" the *Telegraph Beau Broadway* column, unaware that Winchell himself had been grinding it out for Pop.

Pop also hired Ring Lardner. Ben Hecht and Charlie MacArthur came along for the ride and provided their impressions of life and sports in the columns of the *Telegraph* for free.

During this time, Tex Rickard was suddenly stricken with peritonitis in Florida. Pop rushed to his side and held his hand. Rickard smiled and said, "You're a good boy, Gene," then died. Arriving back in New York, Pop wrote a poem dedicated to Tex Rickard in the form of an obituary. In a letter some years later, Pop explained it this way:

The Rickard poem was written in haste, as are most newspaper pieces. Pegler and I had gone across the street from the *Morning Telegraph* (of which I was then the editor) to the Garden, where Rickard's body lay in state. Neither of us liked to look at dead friends; so we sat in the gallery as the people moved below us. I was for a short time in 1928 the publicity chief for the Garden (having succeeded Ike Dorgan), and my regard for Tex, always high, was increased. The poem was an impromptu memorial, nothing more.

Requiem to Rickard

Not before the altar and the choir of the Cathedral,
With surpliced boys intoning,
And dirges of holy bells beating down on the congregation;
Nor with cross bearers and robed clergymen marching;
Candles burning and sunlight groping feebly through stained glass
    while swaying censers are uplifted—
But beneath the high and bare girders of the hippodrome hall—
With twice ten thousand seats strangely empty,
And the chill of a January day stalking through the bleak corridors—
There, in a bronze coffin, lies the tall and silent Texan.

In the high hall he built, he lies in state.
Along the torn-up avenue, the laborers peer at the silk-hatted men
    leaving their motor cars and at the throngs passing into the black-
    draped foyer—
And near the ring-space is a floral platform and a bronze box.
And here is his Peace, where only yesterday—and again tomorrow—
    the bodies of boxers were wet with straining and their flanks were
    cramped and tired from the blows,
While Gutturals of the gallery men, sadistic, growled like the surf of
    the Rockaways.

Not the Gothic sanctity of the Cathedral with its somber ecclesiastics
and the rituals—

But the stolid policemen in the hippodrome hall

The crepe-festooned lobby, where the mourners pass the picture gallery of the champions—

Portraits of muscular celebrities: Muldoon, his arms folded and his
loins draped bravely in a lion's hide and posing in a studio setting
simulating the arena of the Caesars;

Hairy-chested Jeffries in his ponderous crouch, poised for a left-hand
rip to the liver.

Huge, phlegmatic Willard, his unwieldy biceps flexed and his steam-
shovel fists framing a vacant face;

Dempsey, when his tapering legs were yet alert with youth and when
his body was a symbol of power;

Jack Johnson, the incorrigible black genius of defense;

Corbett in white tights, his pompadour suggesting a cockatoo's crest
and his darting left extended.

Skinny-legged Bob Fitzsimmons with his grotesque bald pate and his
abnormal shoulders—

The Maulers' Hall of Fame—and beyond it, in the high hall, the
sleeping Texan.

Upstairs, in the locked drawer of the bronze desk, are the dry and
shriveled gloves Battling Nelson wore when bludgeoning the con-
sumptive Gans;

And a trophy head of an African buck given by the younger Roosevelt, and a rhinocerous hide cane presented by T.R.

And an empty chair made from the horns of steers;

And a brass cuspidor the Texan seldom hit with his tobacco thrusts.

And drawn blinds on the wide windows fronting Forty-ninth Street,
where he often listened to the voices of playing children.

His friends—the millionaire and the beggar, too, come in to see the
Texan.

The gate is shut forever between him and them and there is only
Memory.

Lament and January Day—tomorrow the Spring, and flowers newly-
blooming on a grave.

Not beneath the vaulted roof of the Cathedral,

But under the high and bare girders of the hippodrome hall,

There, in a bronze coffin, lies the tall and silent Texan.

One day Pop telephoned from the *Telegraph* for Mother to come get him.

"Where will I pick you up?" Mother asked.

"Broadway and 42nd Street," Pop answered in a weak voice.

When Mother found him standing on the corner, she noticed that he looked pale. He was unsteady on his feet. For the past two months he had been getting no more than three or four hours sleep a night.

As he stood correcting the last page proofs for the next edition on one of the busiest corners in New York, Pop slowly sank to his knees. But he continued to work over the page as the copy boy who had been sent along with him helped Mother drag Pop bodily onto the floor in the back of the sedan. Pop finished his work while lying on the floor there. He was shaking so hard that the pencil dropped from his grasp, suffering his first nervous breakdown. "This is a hell of a place," he said. "I knew it would happen here, right on the corner of 42nd and Broadway."

The boy ran back to the *Telegraph* with the last piece of copy Gene Fowler would ever work over as a newspaper editor.

Mother brought him home to Fire Island where he would take his first vacation in sixteen years.

The wind is most always from the west on Fire Island. It is the habit of the sea to pile in beneath the whiplash of this west wind. In those days, the sand bar seemed lonesome.

If you had a musical ear, you could distinguish the wind-tune from the sea-tune. To you it might be just a noise. But to us who have lived on Fire Island for a time, it is a duet. This day the leaves of the huckleberry bushes were a warm russet, like the hair of my first girl. And the cranberries were plentiful in the hollows. There were many wonderful sights here. A Westerner has never really seen the Milky Way until he views it from Fire Island.

Here the mature Gene Fowler began his post-journalistic career. He felt slightly disabused, but was never cynical. He was still high-spirited and healthy, with not one gland given out and with not one vital organ limping excepting a confounded liver, which he said "might look like Plymouth Rock, and which prevented me from a workmanlike handling of modern toddies."

He was raw-boned and swarthy and his hair was beginning to show a touch of gray. He began to be concerned about what he called "malarial spots" that had lately appeared on the back of his tough hands and on his weathered face. One of his closest friends, Ben Hecht, upon seeing these white patches, dubbed him "Pinto." A later friend, W. C. Fields, called him "Spotted Bull." Cartoonist-writer Will Gould, who originated the sobriquet "Schnozzola" for Jimmy Durante, referred to Pop as "The Indian." Pegler addressed him in letters as "Booker T. Fowler." At first, he thought he was coming down with leprosy. "But when I found it was merely a sort of death of skin pigments from overexposure to the sun, I was relieved."

Once, while traveling on an airplane, during the pioneer days of commercial air transportation, a lady sitting next to Pop commented on his spotted condition. Instead of shrinking from the subject, Pop took special pains to point out that he had secret maps tattooed thereon so he might deliver the information to the enemy. "This is confidential, madam, and I hold you to uttermost secrecy."

The woman was enthralled. She asked, "And what are those eight little plateaus on the outer side of the back of your left hand?"

"Those, madam," Pop went on, "are the Hawaiian Islands. And toward the back of the thumb there, is the coast of the U.S."

"Ah, yes. I can see it all," she said. Now the lady wanted to show him how smart she was. "The big spot on the other side of your right hand looks a bit like the Rock of Gibraltar. Am I right?"

"Hah!" Pop cried, drawing the attention of all the other passengers, "Such an astute observation!" He stood up and began to loosen his belt now as all looked on. "And now, my dear," he said, "I am going to let you in on the *big* secret!"

The lady beat a hasty retreat to the powder room.

Pop was pulsing with life. He was ebullient, defiant, eager, careless, confused, naïve, timid in soul but bold in address, big-hearted, sensitive, given to nightmares and crying out in his sleep, jealous of solitude after a life of gadding about, incapable of sustained drudgeries, fond of good whiskey and forgiving of the bad, in love with children, an adorer of women, tactless, a blundering *moujik*—in short, it had not bored him to have lived with himself. Sometimes he laughed to keep from whimpering. Now Fire Island began to bring out his latent talent, provided him with the solitude he needed for something more ambitious than newspaper prose.

Pop completed his first manuscript, the one about Madame Silks. He took Captain Robinson's ferry from Ocean Beach, rode the Long Island Rail Road from Bay Shore to Manhattan, and deposited his work with publisher Horace Liveright. A week later, he received a check for $500 in advance of royalties. He spent the money on everyone he met in Manhattan, ending up at Ocean Beach (which we called "The Beach") with only a small oval portrait of Ulysses S. Grant which he had bought for Mother.

Mother was nonplused until Pop removed the picture from the tiny walnut frame to show her that the former President's portrait had been printed by the Treasury Department. It was a $50 bill.

Filled with remorse the following day, Pop returned to Manhattan and the Liveright offices. He asked a clerk if he might enter the vault and scribble a few corrections on his manuscript. When he departed Pop had the entire manuscript hidden beneath his coat. Brother Gene, who was twelve at the time, saw Pop walk over to the fireplace and toss his document in the flames. "I'll never forget it," Gene told me. "He just burned the whole thing up."

The next day, Pop awakened to discover he had been threatened with a lawsuit. "Either you return the $500 that was advanced you, or go to jail," said an impersonal attorney for the publishing firm.

Pop asked for a moratorium of thirty days in order to "deliver a *good* novel." The lawyer allowed this reprieve. And after twenty-one days of intensive work in the kitchen at the rear of Billy La Hiff's restaurant, Pop delivered a 100,000 word novel to Liveright. He titled it *Trumpet in the Dust*. It is still being reprinted every few years. . . .

Pop isolated himself again on Fire Island. There were no telephones, but we did have a lamplighter named Mr. Claus. We used kerosene lamps and candles for light in the evenings when the ever-present mosquito seemed as fond of citronella as we were. This was an extra-special place to live in now that the stock market had

ripped its seams and marginal speculators were leaping from Manhattan buildings. The best thing for Pop to do now was to dig in
and begin writing another novel.

Although he blazed the path for many people of the arts to Ocean
Beach, such as Moss Hart, Herman Shumlin, Rose Keane, Billy
Rose, Fannie Brice, Arthur Kober, Joe Laurie, Jr., Ben Hecht,
Charlie MacArthur, Helen Hayes, and Leslie Howard, there were
characters already there whom Pop loved dearly. They were the
ones who, like the Indians meeting the *Mayflower,* greeted Pop
aboard Captain Robinson's ferry when he arrived at Fire Island
back in 1922. As a character in point, there was Buck Fitting, a
husky fellow across from the Beach in Bay Shore. He tended a cor-
rugated-iron garage where he put up and serviced vacationers' cars
during the summer months.

"Who would believe Buck Fitting's story?" Pop asked me. "It was
a long time ago, I guess," he said, "when Buck was standing beside
the railroad gate at Bay Shore. A Long Island train was passing.
Everything happened quite suddenly. The train whistled. A man
staggered along the right of way and stumbled across the tracks.
Buck dashed out to save him. He succeeded, but himself fell beneath the wheels of the train. Buck's legs were cut off well above
the ankles.

"Ten years subsequent to the accident which cost the heroic Mr.
Fitting his props," Pop went on, "Buck was standing in precisely
the same place and beside the same gates, and looking at approxi-
mately the same spot where the Long Island train had ground him
under. And while he was so standing, he saw a man walking un-
concernedly along the tracks as the train bore down upon him."
Again Fitting made the dash, and again he bumped the man—not
the same one he'd rescued years before, however—from the tracks
in time. And again (God give the reader strength to believe this)
the train ran over Buck.

This time, Buck told Pop, he had it on Fate. The wheels cut
off only his wooden legs.

Buck was a bachelor. He had always looked up to my father who
was six feet one inch tall. One summer day Buck met Pop at his own
height.

"What the hell happened?" Pop asked the elevated Fitting. "You've grown a half a foot!"

"Well, Gene," said Buck, "I got married while you were away last winter. My wife is tall. She said she wouldn't marry a guy shorter than herself."

"So?" Pop asked.

"So I had a set of wooden legs made six inches taller," said Buck. "Now I'm as tall as my wife." He walked around. "How do you like them?"

It was late spring and the wild flowers were good to see. Not many of the summer colony had arrived, partly because of the fact that school was late in closing, but mostly because the stock market crash kept men chained to the city and their desks.

Billy Rose had rented a big shingle house on the bay front with his wife, Fannie Brice. His coming to Ocean Beach was assured when Pop told him that no one could contact him unless he cared to open a telegram delivered by Charlie Beuhler. "There are no phones," Pop continued, "and the only questions you have to answer down here are those asked by yourself."

Celebrating the Fourth of July some thirty years ago, Billy and Fannie had as house guests Ben Hecht, Charlie MacArthur, and the great Jimmy Durante. I carried a box of seven-inch firecrackers. We were planning a tuna fishing trip on Captain Bink's boat the next day. Pop happened to mention that Durante was still asleep in one of the Rose's many bedrooms. The sun had been up for five hours, and Fannie was painting a bayscape in greens and blues on a canvas downstairs. Unable to comprehend why a person should be still asleep at this time of day, I ran upstairs with my firecrackers. Invading Durante's bedroom, I lighted and tossed one under his bed, then quietly closed the door. When it went off, there was no place for the explosion to expend itself. Shortly after the firecracker exploded, Durante staggered into the hall cupping his ears in pain. He shouted: "When I get my hearing back, I wanna know who the *hell* did this to me!" Now I was more shocked than Durante. It was the first time I had ever heard a stage performer of his stature use the word "hell." When Durante reads this, he will finally discover the culprit.

We all met at 5 A.M. of the Fourth at Billy Rose's house, an unprecedented hour for Durante to be getting up. As we headed toward the pier to meet Captain Bink, Durante took hold of each tree he discovered along the way and shook it violently. Pop asked, "Why are you shaking all these trees like that, Jimmy?"

"If Durante don't sleep, the boids don't sleep!" he testily explained.

We met Captain Bink who, Durante complained, was unreasonably awake. Hecht, MacArthur, my sister, Pop, Billy Rose, Durante, and I climbed aboard. Rose complained that he was no sailor and was going along under duress. Hecht, a good fisherman and a man with a fair knowledge of the sea, appointed himself Captain *pro tempore*. Pop offered to take on the job of baiting the hooks. Jane and I stood on the extension (like a diving board) of the bow from which Captain Bink said he harpooned sharks, and watched the phosphorus gleam like a myriad of underwater fireflies.

It was still dark and calm as we passed through the inlet and headed out to sea where the tuna were expected to strike. Hecht was at the wheel. He said he had been through this inlet before and knew every sand bar. At this moment, the boat lurched. Ben said, "That was one of them."

Now that the sun was up, Rose and Durante broke out a deck of cards and began a game of nickel casino. "I began to lose interest in the cards," as Rose later recalled. "I looked at Durante's famous nose. It was turning a delicate shade of chartreuse. Fannie would have liked to capture this color in one of her canvases." Then he asked Durante, "Can I get you anything?"

"Yeah," said Durante, dropping his cards and staggering off to lie spread-eagled on the forward deck. "An island."

We had arrived at the tuna grounds, and Pop was cutting up the bait. He asked Durante if there was something he could do to ease his seasickness, adding, "Don't worry, Jimmy. No one ever died of it."

"Don't say that," Durante groaned. "Only the hope of dyin' is keepin' me alive!"

"If the fish bite today," he added, "they're gonna be bitin' each other."

Two hours later, way out at sea, Captain Bink suggested that everyone haul in his line and take a lunch break. The engine was cut off and we rocked in the swell.

Since no one had been posted on lookout, we were all taken by surprise when the German Lloyd liner *Europa* steamed past in all its majesty. We gaped at the impressive sight until, suddenly, the liner's wake began hitting the cutter and causing it to bob like a cork. Captain Bink hastened to warm up his engine. At this moment my sister was doing her best to interest Durante in a two-decker sandwich of peanut butter, cream cheese, and jelly. That finished off Jimmy's seafaring career.

"We've seen enough of the sea," he cried out. "Now let's find out if we can get back to America."

Pop directed his attention to the red Fire Island lightship. "The men live there on that iron boat for two and three weeks at a time," he said. "They have nothing to do but clean the light and their fingernails. And they don't drink, either. When the big foghorn blows, a lot of them get nose bleeds from the sound of it. And they all hate each other."

"You should write for the Encyclopaedia Britannica," said Durante as he pushed away Jane's double-decker sandwich. "What would ever happen," Durante continued, "if we *did* catch a fish?"

"Simple," said Pop. "If you don't know what to do, you just climb up the rod and strangle the fish to death."

As we approached the calmer inlet waters off Saltaire to enter the Great South Bay, Durante began to recover. He joined Hecht and the silent MacArthur on the fantail to watch a beachcomber poking his bamboo walking stick into the white sands, perhaps hoping to discover treasure. Durante said, "See that man on solid ground there?"

MacArthur rallied to say, "Yes? What about it?"

Durante sighed, then said, "How fortunate!"

We arrived back at the Ocean Beach pier with what I thought was nothing. No fish. It was shameful. Jane told me sometime later: "You don't usually know when you're having fun until a lot of years have piled up and we all get together to rehash it."

That night Fannie Brice's son, Billy, shot me in the seat of my bathing trunks with a Roman candle. Jane was kind enough to find

a bar of cocoa butter and rub it on my wounded posterior. At
this writing, Billy Brice is a professor of art at the University of
California at Los Angeles and a respected modern artist.

Some years later, when he was shocked that Charlie MacArthur
had died at the age of sixty, Pop said to me, "Here was a wonderful man. He was a fellow who never should have grown old. He
always seemed to be twenty-two, buoyant, grand, brilliant. Charlie
told me once: 'Old age is when false teeth cease to be funny.'"

We returned to our Richmond Hill home in time to prepare for
school and the oncoming winter of 1931. One day the telephone
rang in the piano room. Pop said, "Let it jingle. I'm no longer on
the paper."

The ringing stopped, then it started up again. "It might be important," said Mother. She stood up and opened the narrow
glass-paned double doors to the cold little piano room. She picked
up the receiver and said, "Hello?" After a few moments, she
called out to Pop, "It's Hollywood calling. I think you'd better take
it, Gene."

After Pop took the receiver, there were a lot of "no's" and
"yes's," then Pop hung up the phone. He sat down at the table and
said, "Agnes, they offered me a lot of money."

"What for?" asked Mother.

"To write a movie for Jack Barrymore," Pop answered.

"Is this what you want?" she asked.

"I don't know," he answered. "I want to do that book on Bonfils
and Tammen."

"Then do the book," said Mother.

"Whatever you say," said Pop. He added, "I already said 'no'
unless they paid the family expenses to and from Hollywood with
first-class train accommodations."

The phone rang again as we were finishing dinner.

"What the hell," said Pop. "It might be a new adventure."

Chapter Twelve

EVERYONE NEEDS A WARM PERSONAL ENEMY
OR TWO TO KEEP HIM FREE OF RUST
IN THE MOVABLE PARTS OF HIS MIND.

GENE FOWLER

The most direct way to travel to Hollywood thirty years ago was to take the Pennsylvania Railroad to Chicago, then transfer to the Santa Fe *Chief*. It was one day to Chicago with a three-hour layover, then three more days to the West Coast on the *Chief*. The family occupied three of the four staterooms in the observation car. Pop and Mother were in the first; Jane, Mumsie, and our new housekeeper, Evelyn Miles, the second, and brother Gene and I shared the third. Grandma West had died five months earlier at the age of eighty-two, and we missed her. To the end, she had carried on a platonic courtship with our ninety-year-old neighbor, Daddy Ottens, who had been a rivet boy during the Civil War on the Confederate iron-clad ship *Monitor*.

My brother and sister and I kept busy eating apples and chocolate until the train came to a halt in Chicago. When we detrained, Pop was greeted by a tall, thin gent wearing a hard straw hat and striped necktie with a large diamond stickpin. He was Spike O'Donnell, Chicago's beer baron; the man Al Capone was unable to run out of town. Spike was there to show us around the city until we were to board the *Chief* a few hours later. All but brother Gene and I got into Spike's huge black air-cooled Franklin limousine. We followed the Franklin in a new Dodge coupe with window glass two inches thick.

As we passed by the museum on the lake front, there was a series of explosions emanating from a truck on the other side of the avenue. Our taciturn driver pulled the biggest pistol I ever saw from the inside of his suit coat as Gene and I dove to the floor of the car. Our chauffeur jumped out to look around. His blank expression never changed.

Spike O'Donnell ran toward us and hauled Gene and me into the kitchen of an Italian restaurant where we greeted the rest of the family. Pop said as long as we were there, we might as well have dinner. We ate spaghetti back in the kitchen while Spike disappeared temporarily to make a phone call. Five minutes after Spike returned, about eight unsmiling men arrived. When we finished dinner, Spike, laughing and joking with Pop (obviously to take off the pressure for Mother), had us escorted back to our cars. This time there were two more black limousines flanking our own cars.

As the *Chief* pulled out of the station heading west, Spike O'Donnell gave us a generous smile and waved his straw hat as his men stared in every direction but the train's. I'll always remember them standing there with their right hands inside their suit coat pockets . . . like so many Napoleons. . . .

Pasadena was the fashionable point of arrival for the latest Hollywood importations. The studios would let it "leak out" that so-and-so was "sneaking into town" and would be getting off at Pasadena. This added intrigue to the arrival. Only the middle-class movie man, such as a character actor or associate producer whose last picture had flopped would think of riding the train all the way into Los Angeles. Next to Mecca, Hollywood is perhaps the most class-conscious city in the world. As we alighted from the train at Pasadena, Pop was greeted by a studio publicity man waving his arms wildly.

Pop hailed three taxis as the publicity man protested, pointing out two black, chauffeured limousines. "The studio arranged your transportation," said the publicity man, who had now used every dry corner of his handkerchief wiping away a hangover perspiration.

Pop assembled his family and insisted on putting us in the taxis.

"But the limousines, Mr. Fowler!" cried the bewildered publicity man.

My father handed the perspiring fellow a bridge hand of baggage claim tickets. "My dear young man," said Pop, "I wish to enter Hollywood the way I expect to leave it: *By a fast taxi!* . . . Now get the luggage and have it placed in your limousines after you give my lead man our new address."

Our cabs pulled up to the front of a fine stone house with shake roof which in 1931 was at the end of Canyon Drive, north of Franklin Avenue in the Hollywood hills. Above the house, against a high hill was a collection of thirteen tin letters backed up by timbers, each about forty feet high. They spelled out the word: HOLLY-WOODLAND. The first letter, however, the H, had been toppled half over.

Our baggage-ladened limousines arrived fifteen minutes later along with the nervous publicity man shouting directions as he hung on for dear life to the running board of a Pierce-Arrow.

Two of Pop's old friends were on hand to greet him. One was a former newspaper pal, Brick Terrett, presently regaining his eyesight following a bout with a questionable bottle of bootleg. The charming little man who drove Brick Terrett was the famous comedian Bert Wheeler, in town to appear in his first movie with his partner, Robert Woolsey, and Dixie Lee, who later became Bing Crosby's wife. "I live nearby," said Bert. "If I hadn't driven Brick, I'd of come up on my bicycle."

The day before Pop was to report to the studio, Wheeler pedaled up to ask, "Is there anything I can do for you, Gene?"

Pop eyed the blue bicycle with painted silver spokes. "You can sell me your bike." He further explained to Wheeler that he did not wish to become accustomed to grandeur within a week, "so I would like to ride the bike to work in the morning." Wheeler gave him the bike.

On his airy way to the studio the following morning, Pop jammed on his coaster brakes in time to avoid being hit by a glittering Rolls-Royce at the corner of Gover Street and Sunset Boulevard. Pop engaged in an argument with a policeman, then turned his ire on the bald-headed man in the rear seat of the Rolls: "You rich bastards are all alike! Always pushing the poor working man around!" The policeman began to take Pop's side and told the chauffeur of the custom-made English automobile to get along. As a parting shot Pop yelled after the departing auto: "You and your big new Buick!"

The bald-headed man in the back seat stuck his head from out the rear window and screamed back, "This is *not* a Buick! It's a Rolls-Royce! And it cost me $20,000!"

When he arrived at the studio gate, Pop rolled down his right pant leg and hopped off his bicycle to identify himself to the gateman. "I am the latest cinema-writer import. Do not detain me. They are paying me a barrel full of money."

"On a bicycle?" The gateman scratched his head.

"Benjamin Franklin *walked* into Philadelphia," said Pop. "And I can see that I am receiving the same doubtful reception he did."

The gateman phoned the front office to report Pop's arrival. He was put through to a studio head who was in the midst of an important story conference, a conference Pop later discovered was about "how Fowler is to be handled." After many "yes sirs," and without Pop disclosing his name, the gateman turned to my father and said, "I'm sorry, but the boss said no one's to be allowed on the lot riding a bicycle."

Pop thanked the gateman, rolled up his pant leg, then pedaled back home to play with his children at the side of the Canyon Drive goldfish pond.

Later that afternoon Pop was called to the phone by a distraught executive who was making plans for John Barrymore's latest talking picture, *State's Attorney*. He asked if Pop had arrived all right, if he was sick, or if he was just suffering a seizure of temperament.

"I showed up at nine o'clock," said Pop. "But one of your higher-ups told the gateman I was to be refused entrance."

"I can't understand it," said the executive.

"Perhaps it was because I was riding a bicycle," said Pop.

Early the next day Mother bought the first new gun-metal gray Pierce-Arrow she could find. Gun-metal gray seemed to be the Standard automobile color for the Fowlers now. She drove Pop to work. At the gate, assisting the uniformed officer, were two middle-echelon executives stationed there to make sure Fowler would not show up this time on a dog sled or aboard an Indian pinto, and once more be refused entrance.

This was a sort of get-acquainted day. Pop was escorted to a magnificent office outfitted with club chairs and containing a heroic fireplace. Fine oil paintings graced the teak-paneled walls. The room seemed three football downs to the nearest telephone. Sinking his heels in the Bigelow Grandeur rug, Pop thanked the studio heads for their thoughtfulness, then said, as he escorted them from the great room which would have made Ludwig II of Bavaria envious, "And now to work."

Pop then picked up a phone and asked to be connected with the Property Department. He ordered the room to be stripped, including the thick rug. Then he had an old roll-top oak desk, a used Underwood typewriter, and a clothes tree brought in. For his own decorative scheme, he had his secretary, a handsome girl, purchase the largest head of cabbage she could find at a nearby market. He placed this head of cabbage on the ornate fireplace mantel.

On Wednesday, his second day at work, there was only one executive pacing about the auto gate. But then there were also many studio employees who had reported in early just to view this eccentric writer from New York.

When he arrived at his office, Pop's secretary informed him that there was an important conference to be held "in Mr. Fowler's honor" at 10 A.M.

Everyone who is important in Hollywood is usually late for everything but studio conferences. If it is a party, each in order of stature arrives proportionately late. The top box office attraction is allotted the final arrival. Only then are other members of the party allowed to leave for home, or relaxation elsewhere.

An important executive stared at the dial of his diamond-studded wrist watch for the dozenth time. He snubbed out a gold monogrammed cigarette in an outsized jade ash tray. "Where the hell is this Fowler, anyway?" he shouted to his subordinates.

At this moment, Pop dashed in. He was nattily attired, like Jimmy Walker. But instead of pin-striped cuffless trousers gracing his legs, Pop held same folded over his left arm. He rushed over to the head man and flung the trousers on the solid mahogany conference table, saying, "Have these cleaned and pressed by to-

morrow morning!" Before the startled mogul could gather his wits,
Pop had vanished.

After having met a collection of starlets with their executive es-
corts who came up to his table in the studio commissary that noon,
Pop retired to his office to create an untitled three-stanza poem:

> See the newest starlet
>   With her gems and furs and cars.
> Her pelvis is a parking lot
>   For aging movie tzars.
>
> They sleep in one another's arms,
>   Yet dream two worlds apart.
> She of an impresario,
>   And he of an auburn tart.
>
> The pair should never married be,
>   Enduring daylong screams,
> And then leave off their wakefulness
>   To cheat all night in dreams.

This was mimeographed by Pop's admirers and read everywhere
in Hollywood.

"Mr. Fowler!" cried the executive of the jade ash tray, "we
brought you to Hollywood to write motion picture scripts, not
poems!" Pop disarmed the executive by agreeing. He promised a
good start on *State's Attorney* by the end of the following work day.
When the executive, now tranquilized by Pop's mild and coopera-
tive attitude, departed, he turned at the office door and said, "I'll
bet you wrote that last poem about C— L——!"

The following work day came to an end and Pop personally delivered the first thirty pages of his script. After reading it, his
newly found executive friend rushed to Pop's office to exclaim,
"This is great, Gene! Can you keep it up?"

"If everybody leaves me alone," said Pop, "I can complete the
entire script by the end of next week."

"Actually," the executive confided, "we only expect three pages
a day from our writers."

Pop chuckled, then said, "Well, I felt I owed you something."

Word had filtered about that Pop was an easy touch for old-timers experiencing hard luck in Cinemaland. And Hollywood was a fine place for ex-prize fighters to sun out their last days as stunt men, though not such a Utopia as to support them adequately. Before long, Pop's office began to look like his old sporting department bull pen at the *Denver Post*. A collection of characters gathered there as Fowler turned out successive movie scripts. Howard Barnes, former drama critic for the New York *Herald Tribune*, told me, "Gene had a lot of work to pound out in Hollywood, but he did not wish to offend his friends in need. So on the left side of his desk he apportioned three drawers which he kept full of money. The top drawer held a stack of dollar bills. The second had a bunch of fives. The third drawer had a scattering of tens and twenties. Gene told me he left it up to his hard-up companions to pull open the drawer suited to their needs." Barnes added that nobody ever took undue advantage of Fowler's generosity.

Lew Cody was the first movie star I really met long enough to chat with. He took the family down to his home on a desolate sand bar facing the Pacific Ocean some miles north of Santa Monica. It was a hideaway called Malibu Beach. Lew's house was built to resemble the upper decks of an ocean liner. He had a wet bar with a huge fake telephone and a "hot" silver dollar screwed and electrically wired to the mahogany counter top. When one surreptitiously tried to pick up the silver dollar, Lew would flip the electric switch and give him a cautionary jolt.

Later the actor brought us to a small circus under tents. When we arrived at the sideshow, Jane asked Pop where the wild man in the cage came from. Pop whispered to Cody, then answered his daughter, who had never seen a "geek" before: "This gentleman is one of the critics of the medium for which I now write."

When Rex Ingram was directing Barbara La Marr in *Black Orchid*, Pop was an occasional visitor on the set; not to visit with the director or the star, but to play with Joe Martin, a one-hundred pound chimpanzee who was one of the principals in the cast of characters. The chimp was fond of Ingram, who affected Foreign Legion garb and carried a huge six-shooter in his sash. The animal also loved Barbara La Marr, and when he saw the screen villain abusing her in a scene, he leaped from his chair between Pop and the director, charged the villain, threw him down and began to throttle him.

Pop rescued the "heavy" with difficulty and Ingram gave the chimp a severe lecture. To teach Joe Martin a lesson, Ingram fired his big six-shooter near the animal's feet. Joe screamed and scrambled up a parallel standard.

Next day, the ape fawned over Pop inside the sound stage. He draped one long muscular arm about Pop's shoulder—but meanwhile frisked Ingram (who was sitting once again next to the chimp) for the six-shooter. The astounded Ingram suddenly found himself face-to-face with this gunman ape, who also menaced other members of the cast and crew. Failing to coax the beast into returning the gun, the properly uniformed Ingram led a retreat. The ape sat playing with the pistol, putting it in his mouth like a lollipop, then pointing it at anyone who came near. He then chose to run amok through the studio. Work was suspended for the day. This was costing the company thousands of dollars in lost time. Police reserves arrived, but it was finally Miss La Marr who, by throwing kisses, finally lured Joe Martin within range of a cowboy who tossed a riata about the ape's neck and retrieved the gun.

Pop was delighted when his friend Charlie MacArthur arrived in town to write a movie. The two celebrated the Scotsman's arrival with a couple bottles of Vat 69. MacArthur suddenly remembered he was to be the guest of honor at the home of Lady Furness, and asked Pop to accompany him. A butler admitted the two slightly spiffed gentlemen as Lady Furness approached. MacArthur was the first to kiss her hand. Then he turned to Pop and said, "Gene, I would like you to meet Lady Furness."

Pop bowed low, kissed her hand, then said, "Yes. Lady Furness . . . Tell me . . . Have you been stoked lately?"

Exiled now to a dark corner of the outside terrace, MacArthur was complaining about his present writing assignment. He said: "One thing that smothers art, especially in Hollywood, is the fact that the writers are not allowed to write what they want to."

"You are mistaken," Pop countered. "Hollywood authors can write anything they please, providing it is not good."

Pop completed his film assignment in the early spring and traveled back to Fire Island to consult his builder friend Nate Woodhull about constructing a new summer home in Seaview, a neighboring village separated from Ocean Beach by a six-foot-wide cement sidewalk. While Pop sat on an old ship's keel section on the beach front, designing the house floor plans on the back of a large cedar shingle, Woodhull ordered two boatloads of rough pine lumber. Construction began immediately. Pop worked along with the carpenters in the daytime. At night he struggled with his second novel, *Shoe the Wild Mare,* in the Ocean Beach cottage. The novel was centered around a Wall Street tycoon with a deficient libido who tried unsuccessfully to corner the wheat market and also tame an aristocratic maiden.

During these months, not being one who liked to cook, Pop lived on canned beans, clams (which he dug up with his toes in the bay), brown bread and butter.

As the foundation was laid, my father realized the house he had drawn on the back of his cedar shingle was considerably larger than anticipated. He visited his prospective next-door neighbor to ask if he might carry on with his construction. "I'm afraid I might block your entire view of the ocean," Pop warned. "If you wish, I will purchase another lot and begin again. I don't want any hard feelings."

The neighbor assured Pop that no house could be so large as to cut off his view of the Atlantic.

The neighbor began to view the construction with alarm as Woodhull ordered more supplies from the mainland. By the time the principal floor studdings were in place, the house had already reached the roof level of the man's house next door. The main floor boasted a huge living room, a large kitchen, a dining room, big sun room, a bathroom, spacious service porch, and a lanai.

When his neighbor realized the roof rafters were not being put in place yet, but rather a *third* story was being added, he became downright annoyed. The upstairs had five bedrooms, a bath and a five-by-eight-foot office where Pop would write his books. (Mother later named this the "Bread and Butter Room.") After shingles were applied to the outside walls, our neighbor realized that not only was he cheated of his Atlantic Ocean view, but that the sun would never again shine on the south wall of his cottage. Our house was the largest on the island, and we would often comfortably sleep up to twenty-two people at one time.

The last thing Pop's neighbor ever said to him was: "This is outrageous!"

Mother arrived in New York just before our school term ended in Hollywood. She sold the Ocean Beach cottage, then furnished and stocked the new Seaview home and awaited the family's onslaught. She equipped the kitchen with a gas stove, a wood-burning stove, and two refrigerators, one used exclusively for soft drinks and cooling watermelons.

By the time the rest of the family arrived, including two dogs and our parrot Chester, Pop had completed his novel and sent it along to the Liveright publishing house and was already outlining another book he wanted to call *The Loving Guru.* This one, however, never came off.

When *Shoe the Wild Mare* was about to hit the stands, Pop traveled to Manhattan to autograph some of his books. During the day, he became well oiled. Carrying an armload of volumes, Pop met artist-author Alexander King in the publishing company's main hall. He handed King a book from the top of a pile and said, "Alex, I want you to have this copy of my new novel. It will be very valuable one day because I did not autograph it." King, who had designed the dust jackets for *Trumpet in the Dust* and *Shoe the Wild Mare,* learned later that in his enthusiasm, Pop had autographed every single book of the first edition with the exception of the one he had offered the illustrator.

"This," said King, "was a typical Fowler gesture."

Inscribing my copy of *Shoe the Wild Mare,* Pop wrote: "I never learned anything well, except the uselessness of holding malice toward anyone. Fortunately, you are not a holder of malice, and therefore, I can teach you nothing."

During this time, Pascal Covici and Donald Friede established a new publishing concern. Covici guaranteed Pop a 25,000-copy first edition if he would try his hand at biography. Pop scrapped *The Loving Guru* and decided to write the life of his old friend, William J. Fallon, a famous criminal lawyer who had recently died. Pop buried himself in the Bread and Butter Room and worked through the remaining summer nights. The machine-gun rattle of his old Underwood No. 5 typewriter played counterpoint to the crashing of the ocean waves.

Four years Pop's senior, Fallon was born in New York and got his L.L.B. at Fordham in 1909. He was a State Assemblyman in Westchester County in 1913, was appointed an assistant district attorney in 1914, then opened a private practice a year later. In less than ten years, he amassed more than $1,500,000 as "the man who never loses a case." Such figures as Peggy Hopkins Joyce, Louise Groody, Gertrude Vanderbilt, Arnold Rothstein, Nicky Arnstein, Daddy Phil Kastel, Dapper Don Collins and Fuller and McGee moved through the strange background of his life. He was only forty-one years old when he died.

By the time his children re-entered Public School 99 in Kew Gardens, Pop had finished his first biography, which he named *The Great Mouthpiece*. He had completed the first draft in six weeks. And his first drafts always read like a finished piece of work. His years as a newspaper reporter had honed his mind for chronology, analysis, and a fashioning of words which suited biography well.

Covici-Friede published *The Great Mouthpiece* in a de luxe edition. This was a daring venture considering that the U.S. was in its darkest days of the Depression, and that people were not spending money on books. The Fallon work sold for three dollars and was into its second edition within weeks after it was presented on the market. It was a best seller of its time. Few law students have not read this book. Many, indeed, have said it inspired them to enter the legal profession.

"I never once said in *The Great Mouthpiece* that I knew Fallon," Pop told me. "I don't like footnotes in biographies, nor do I like, if possible, to drop names. In fact, I left out a lot of anecdotes. In the Barrymore book, where I did things for Jack, I attributed these actions to others because I did not want to appear like the male Lady Bountiful. I loved the guy. So what?"

During the writing of *The Great Mouthpiece,* Pop had made an offhand remark that he wished someone could relieve him of a vast amount of typewriting copy work. "If you want," said Mother, "I'll do the work for you."

"But you don't know how to type too well," said Pop.

"I can go to school," said Mother. "I'm not too old to brush up."

"You have to love me quite a lot to do a thing like that."

"Did you ever doubt it?" she rejoined.

But for Mother's dedication to her job, it would have been a joke to watch her drive up to the Jamaica Avenue typing school in her new Cadillac. Most of the students were in their late 'teens and early twenties, and had scraped to get the money together to take the course. Mother was forty-two. But she breezed through the course in record time and was at the head of the class both in typing and shorthand. Now she was ready to take over Pop's copying work.

Pop's next project was a collaboration with Ben Hecht on a play whose locale was Coney Island. The authors described their play as "a love-sick charade in three acts and something like eight scenes, recounting the didoes of two young and amorous souls who nigh perished when they weren't in the hay together." They named it *The Great Magoo*.

One evening during their collaboration Pop and Ben caught me with a letter I had addressed to Charles Atlas, the "dynamic tension" body builder of that day. The two opened the envelope to discover I had filled out a questionnaire for the course. One of the printed questions was: "Do you have any secret habits?" My penciled answer was, "I twist my neck." Pop and Hecht broke into laughter, but I could not understand what was so funny until some years later.

Eventually we all traveled to Ben's home, situated on the west bank of the Hudson River well north of Manhattan in Nyack. Pop and Ben buried themselves in work while Ben's wife, Rose, entertained us and brought us over to Charlie MacArthur and Helen Hayes' home down the river bank.

The Great Magoo was finished and into rehearsals by November. Producer Billy Rose said there was need of a song, and that he would engage Harold Arlen to write the music to his (Rose's) and Edgar Y. "Yip" Harburg's lyrics. The result was *It's Only a Paper Moon*. This song still remains a popular standard, as do Harold Arlen's many melody hits such as *Stormy Weather, I've Got the World on a String, That Old Black Magic,* and *Over the Rainbow,* to name a few.

A young man named Roy Roberts, who possessed a really fine baritone voice, tried out for the major singing role. When he was finished with his song, Pop shouted out from a fifth row seat, "You cannot sing the song, and what's more, don't ever sing anyplace else ever again!" Roberts, undaunted, went on to Hollywood and fame as one of the finest character actors in motion pictures and television. Roy told me this story.

The Great Magoo opened at the Selwyn Theatre on December 2, 1932, but lasted for only eleven performances. It was too daring for its time, for one thing, though its uninhibited dialogue would hardly raise an eyebrow today.

Fire Island was more beautiful than ever during the early spring of 1933 as Pop walked on the ocean front sidewalk with Gene, Jane, and me. We circled the sidewalk convergences where the seagulls dropped clam shells to crack them open, then eat their contents. Pop's hands would clutch our smaller palms sporadically as if he were trying to make up his mind how to tell us something. He stopped walking and asked us to listen to some new sound borne on the air, then put his arms around us and said, "I love you."

We knew that Hollywood called again and Pop would leave us for many months. At the boat landing, he looked off at the wild flowers and said, "It's nice here in the spring. Many who come here just for the summer don't even know the huckleberry, the beach plum, and the dusty miller have such lovely blossoms." He kissed us, and the boat took him away. We had done this often, but we never got used to it.

When he left for the Coast this time, he was to become entangled in an infatuation which could have ended his marriage and the hugging of his children.

Chapter Thirteen

*HOLLYWOOD IS A PLACE WHERE YOU
HAVE A CHOICE OF
RIDING IN A ROLLS-ROYCE, OR
BEING RUN OVER BY ONE.*

GENE FOWLER

On his second term in Hollywood, Pop's screen-writing career was guided, on the business side of it, by one of the new powers in the motion picture industry. The late Myron Selznick, brother of producer David O. Selznick, had conceived the idea that the talent agent should no longer be classified as a mere "flesh peddler" abused by the studio executives and barely tolerated by their underlings.

Then in his early thirties, Myron Selznick acquired wealth and power by signing up many of the top actors, writers, and directors, and then putting the big squeeze on the studios for more money for his clients and more respect for their agent. No agent had ever held such power over the studio heads.

"Myron acquired his empire out of revenge for the way the industry had forgotten his father, Lewis J. Selznick, one of the founders of the motion picture industry on the West Coast," Pop told me. "Myron raided studios for talent much after the fashion that William Randolph Hearst raided newspapers. He would call people such as William Powell or Kay Francis on the phone and ask them outright how much they were making. Then he would ask if they would be interested in having their salary doubled, or tripled. They could not help but sign with Myron on these terms."

Others to join the Selznick stable were Clark Gable, Myrna Loy, Spencer Tracy, Leo McCarey, and a host of the top talent available.

Through the efforts of Selznick's chief lieutenant, E. O. "Noll" Gurney, Pop's weekly salary was raised to $3000. When Pop was asked by his studio to stay on for a second assignment, he said he would do so only if he was given a raise in pay. "One dollar a week raise is what I want," Pop said.

"But this is ridiculous," said the executive. "One dollar a week raise for a six-week job. This request is too bizarre. I'm afraid we can't do it. If a thing like this got out, imagine the trouble I'd have with my other writers!"

"A dollar a week more, or I'll not work," Pop said.

"No," the executive replied. "Think of the bookkeeping nuisance, making a check out for $3001!"

"I will call Myron," were Pop's last words. "He'll take care of the matter."

It so happened that Selznick was in London on business. But this did not thwart Pop. He put in a telephone call to his agent at the Grosvenor House in London and explained the matter. Selznick considered my father's request most reasonable, and proceeded to deluge the studio executive with cablegrams and long distance calls until he won the dollar a week raise.

"Myron was a dedicated man of principle," Pop told me. "For the $6 he got me, it cost him $1700 in communications to consummate the deal."

During the following two weeks, Pop's producer made a habit of calling him in the middle of the night at his hotel to "talk over the script." My father could be temperamental. In Hollywood, without the presence of Mother to listen to his woes and settle him down, his temperament came to the fore quite often. During one of his producer's nocturnal telephone calls, Pop exploded, "The Prince of Wales is in town and he just usurped my suite! I'm going to have to move elsewhere! I have made arrangements with a private airplane pilot to fly me in daily from a house I have rented in Santa Barbara one hundred miles north of here. And there is no telephone!"

This eliminated the late-hour telephone annoyances for the remaining weeks of his contract. Each day at the studio conference now, Pop's producer would ask, "What kind of trip did you have in today, Gene?"

"It was foggy along the coast as we headed in," Pop would ad-lib. "We had to climb to 7000 feet because of the overcast. Quite bumpy landing, too."

"I don't like your taking these chances every day in the air like this," said the producer. "You're valuable to us, you know."

"It gives me a chance to commune with nature," Pop rejoined.

What his producer did not know was that Pop had taken residence in an apartment directly across the street from the studio under the title of Horace J. Witherspoon, Jr., Eccentric Polish Juggler.

One night when Pop was looking forward to a good night's sleep, directors Gregory La Cava, Leo McCarey, and Raoul Walsh cornered him for a night on the Sunset Strip's newest glamour gambling palace called the Clover Club. The rugs were thick and the main gambling room was crowded with fat men and beautiful women. Director Walsh could not help but stand out in a crowd because he wore a black patch over his missing right eye.

Years ago Walsh lost his eye while directing and playing the lead role of the Cisco Kid on location fifteen miles outside of Cedar City, Utah, in a two-reeler titled *In Old Arizona*. The film he sent back to Hollywood was so exciting that the studio insisted Walsh expand the picture to a "five-reeler." Then the sound equipment broke down, and Walsh called for a driver to spirit him to the nearest telephone in Cedar City to have new equipment flown to him immediately. His choice of drivers was poor. This one was a cowboy who apparently handled a steering wheel in the manner that he tried to break a wild bull. Along the way, the cowboy chauffeur drove at break-neck speed through a pack of jack rabbits. One of the rodents was thrown against the windshield, which shattered. The accident damaged Walsh's right eye, which was eventually removed by surgery, and Walsh engaged Warner Baxter to play the role of the Cisco Kid in his place. Baxter was acclaimed for his acting as Cisco, which in later years was quite annoying to the star, who considered that character as one of his lesser dramatic roles.

This night at the Clover Club, Walsh got lucky at roulette. His system was simple: Pop closed his eyes and pointed to a number which he played. A loser on the other side of the table, a successful producer accompanied by his mistress, howled that "This Fowler person should not be allowed in here unless he wants to make some bets for himself!"

La Cava took this as a "hey rube" call. Soon Pop, La Cava, Walsh, and McCarey were standing back-to-back. They presented such a fearsome quartet that no one dared approach them. One rather plastered fellow, however, turned and tore the front of a lady's sequined dress. This was enough to cause the fists and bottles and handbags to fly.

Pop and the three directors came out unscathed but the next morning was something else. Pop was rarely late for a day's work after an evening on the town. He did not show up several times when he suffered the "flu," recurrent attacks of malaria (a disease he contracted while boating through the Panama Canal), or the after effects of a tooth extraction. But he considered an attack of booze not to be an excuse for missing work.

This morning found Pop one hour early at the studio. Before he began his productive writing, he would always "warm up" with any subject that came to his mind. This time, he felt a poem coming on. And to insure his anonymity, he usually signed these poems, which were destined to be widely circulated, with the name "Ned Gimp." His warmup this morning remains one of his classic take-offs on Hollywood, and specifically on the producer who was at the club with his mistress.

THE FACE ON THE CLOVER CLUB FLOOR

Come, rear a stained-glass window, sirs,
In yon cathedral apse
In mem'ry of the men we love—
And the ladies, too, perhaps—
Those gallant sprites who spend their nights
In wine and shooting craps.

Dids't see the blue-blood knights errant
Of Sunset-on-the-Strip
In rendezvous, while bon mots flew,

And many a deathless quip
Was born from brains whose labor pains
Would sink a battleship?

And dids't thou glimpse, among his peers,
P. Bruno Nessbaum, Third,
A blade of guile, a juvenile,
Who, princely, has preferred
To drink and wink and slink and think
Of love in ways absurd?

Discreet and suave his manner was
Beside the gaming wheel.
His speech was pure, his glance demure—
When suddenly a squeal
Uprose and died. Then someone cried:
"Young Nessbaum's copped a feel!"

Director Igor Stuffertitz
(Whose mistress is so chaste)
Roared: "Nessbaum's gone too far *this* time!
I'll teach the rat some taste.
The goddam churl! To grope my girl
With holds below the waist!"

The babe who'd suffered Nessbaum's nip
Of the place whereon one sits
Was Francine Slade, a maid of trade—
Before she'd played some bits
And sold her nights and boudoir rights
To the great von Stuffertitz.

Von Stuffertitz was born to rule,
And ladies were his fancy.
He'd made the grade with Francine Slade
With gold—not necromancy—
And any stooge that touched her rouge
Was taking quite a chancy.

There was a lull, a murky calm,
That naught but storm asserted.
The ladies' room was like a tomb,
And the gents' can was deserted.
The wiser hams took to their gams,
And yelled: *"I never flirted!"*

A candid cameraman revealed
A lens beneath his sox.
The chatter queens of ink latrines
Prepared to pen their knocks.
The columnists wrote down the lists
Of those who'd had the pox.

In Hollywood, all feuds are waged
With manners fine and mellow.
The overt act must rest with tact
Upon the code duello—
A *charlotte russe* thrown in the puss,
Or a schnozzle full of jello.

Some dastard flipped a *petit four*
That sideslashed Nessbaum's ear.
The caviar, the chutney jar,
The bones of Chanticleer
Caressed his tail. A champagne pail
Became his lavaliere.

The sluggers and the bouncer boys
Began to clout their neighbors.
The croupier knelt down to pray
And broke his leg, bejabbers!
He sank in Scotch up to his crotch—
His heart resigned its labors.

Those goodly folk of Hollywood,
The glass of all mankind,
The flower, indeed, (perchance the weed)

Of beauty, and of mind,
Fought fair and square to tear the hair
Of ladies from behind.

They threw the flasks, they threw the kegs,
They threw some hot zucchini.
The champagne corks, the knives and forks,
The cocktails of Martini,
Bashed in the teeth and gums, beneath
Rare bridgework by Cellini.

Torn sables, marten, fox and skunk
Were tossed about this villa.
And one poor miss showed that-and-this
In a closeup of chinchilla.
Old Stuffertitz collapsed in fits—
An ermine muff his pilla.

Meanwhile the cause of all this brawl—
Or double-cause, I ween—
The Nessbaum jade and Francine Slade—
Were nowhere to be seen.
Now where were they? Why, in the hay—
New lovers of the screen!

When he completed this effort based on Robert W. Service's
epic, *The Face on the Barroom Floor,* Pop looked down from his
studio window and across the street where he spied a man in black,
rubbing his hands in front of the local morturary. My father opened
his window to shout, "Hah! You didn't get me *this* time!" Then he
settled down and turned out twenty pages of dialogue for the studio.

Meanwhile Pop was undergoing an emotional storm, one of the
most critical of his life, a disturbance which began shortly after he
met a leading motion picture star early in the spring of 1933. He
was forty-three, as handsome and virile as any male star on the
screen. He was also alone in Hollywood. She was in her twenties
and also married. There was a deep involvement on both sides.

The infatuation, among other things, brought an attempt at
blackmail. On the last day of his assignment Pop received a letter
from the young actress' husband demanding $5000—otherwise the

husband would tell my mother about the love affair. Pop called the husband to ask if his wife was aware of the blackmail attempt, and instead was told, "I have your addresses in Richmond Hill and on Fire Island. Pay up, or I'll let the whole thing out to the newspapers."

Pop suggested that they meet face to face and have it out, but the man hung up.

He knew it wouldn't be long before the gossip reached the Hollywood columnists, then the wire services, then the front pages all over the country.

"I've got to get out of town," he told Myron Selznick. "Can't I take a slow boat from Los Angeles, through the Panama Canal, and on to New York? When I reach home port, Myron, the scenario will be completed. I give you my word."

"I understand, Gene," said Selznick. "Your terms will be met."

Within three days, Pop boarded an oil tanker with his Underwood No. 5 and was off without reporters discovering his whereabouts. This only heightened newspaper interest. Now there were front-page headlines:

AUTHOR GENE FOWLER MISSING

When Pop's ship docked in Havana, Cuba, he discovered there was an international incident in full bloom. He learned that his actress friend heard of his shipping out and had flown to Havana to be with him. The day before his cargo vessel dropped anchor, the actress, to pass the time, had been out sailing. The small boat capsized in an unseasonable wind. The Cuban who was at the tiller swam toward shore for help as the actress held on to the overturned hull. The boatman was killed by sharks. The actress was not rescued for many hours. When she was brought to shore, she was suffering from severe exposure and sunburn. Learning of this when he landed, Pop telegraphed New York for money to insure the deceased Cuban's family an income for several years.

Now it was time for Pop to face up. He telephoned Mother in New York and told her everything, including that he was being blackmailed by the actress' husband.

"Now that I know," Mother said quietly, "there is no need for you to be blackmailed. That is far worse than anything you could do."

The tanker sailed from Havana that afternoon. Pop remained, however, to be of assistance to the actress and await the money, which finally arrived that night. The money was offered to the dead man's family and also to certain government officials who insisted they be paid for their services. This was an obvious shakedown. It would be several days until a settlement was made.

Mother and the press were under the impression that Pop was aboard the tanker when it docked in New York Harbor. She and a number of newspapermen and publicity men from the studio waited anxiously for Fowler to disembark . . . but there was no Fowler. The ship's captain came down the plank to say he thought all concerned were aware that Pop was to take an airplane to New York directly after "a certain Cuban matter is settled."

The reporters and a radio man with a microphone surrounded Mother and began firing questions, which she fielded with complete composure.

The radio man asked if this was the first she had heard of the actress' friendship with her husband. "Of course not," Mother replied with a smile.

She was told that the actress had been quoted as saying she was in love with Pop.

"I am patient with those who say they are in love with Gene," Mother said. "But I'll be a tiger if they interfere with his talent."

The radio man was amazed by the frankness of her replies, which were going out over the airwaves across the country, and made so bold as to press his luck further: "Is it true that Mr. Fowler is being blackmailed?"

"If it is true," she answered, "and this woman is only good enough for a blackmailer, then she's hardly good enough for Fowler!"

Then Mother turned to all the reporters to say, "I don't know what all this fuss is about. My husband and I are very much in love."

Pop arrived home downcast and bewildered. Mother took us all to our new Seaview home on Fire Island and went upstairs to the Bread and Butter Room with Pop, then locked the door. When they emerged two hours later, Pop had lost his cowed expression. "I never want to see that beaten look on your face again," Mother told him. "It is not your nature. Now, why don't you get to work on your new book?"

While in the Bread and Butter Room, Mother told Pop that it was time he started writing the book he always wanted to do about Denver and the *Denver Post* publishers, Frederick Bonfils and Harry Tammen.

Pop hired two trusted reporter friends who were out of work to comb the back issues of the *Post* and collect names and dates relating to the stories he began to put together for this book, which he titled *Timberline*. He paid his friends each $300 a week for two weeks. When they finished the job, he gave each a $300 bonus. This was the beginning of a pattern Pop set by investing heavily in research for his books. In two instances, the novels *Salute to Yesterday* and *Illusion in Java,* he paid out more than he eventually made from royalties.

Pop lived by night, pounding his typewriter. When dawn arrived, he went to bed and Mother got up to spend six to eight hours transcribing the pages into their clean final form. After about five hours sleep, Pop would arise, eat a meal, edit his copy, then the entire process would be repeated. After eight weeks of this strict routine, the book was completed. Mother suggested that Pop dedicate *Timberline* to their friend Thomas Meighan, then *the* matinee idol of the movies.

Pop sent the *Timberline* manuscript along to Pat Covici, then a partner in Covici-Friede.

The Great Mouthpiece was still on the best-seller list at the time Parliament cigarettes first came on the market with the recessed filter tips. On top of the box was printed *"Mouthpiece."* My brother showed this to me one day and added, "You see how important Pop's book is now?"

I looked at the word *"Mouthpiece"* and asked, "Did they name the cigarette after Pop's book?"

"That's right," said Gene. I asked Gene if I might have the box of cigarettes so I could show it to all my friends in the village.

I arrived home that evening for dinner a very puzzled boy because I had shown the new cigarette box to at least forty of our neighbors. I could not understand why some laughed, and others just offered me a blank stare. Nor did I understand why Mumsie would not believe my story when she took a whip to me for having caught me with cigarettes in my pocket.

Timberline stayed on top of the best seller list for nearly a year. Pop was offered a Hollywood assignment, but he was reluctant to accept. The third time she saw Pop hang up the telephone, and the cowed expression return to his face, Mother said, "For Heaven's sake, Gene. If you want to talk to that actress, please don't do it behind my back. Just have her call here directly. I won't object. And for that matter, if you're still all bothered about this thing, why don't you go on out to Hollywood and get her out of your system?" So he accepted the studio offer.

Pop got the woman out of his system a few weeks after he arrived in Hollywood. As writer John Lee Mahin later observed to me, "When you're given permission, it's no longer any fun."

Pop's letters to Mother seemed gayer than usual, almost as if he were trying to conceal his loneliness for her and the family. In one, he wrote, "About Miss Bunny, my secretary in the hall. [He put her at a desk in the hall to act as receptionist.] She can't take shorthand or type. The studio sent her to me from the casting department." Mother did not write often. She did, however, keep him informed about the health of the children. Jane and I were unaware of what was going on, nor did we understand why we could not travel to Hollywood with Pop as we had in 1931.

Another of Mother's correspondents was Damon Runyon. Mother, perhaps, was closer to the Runyons in the early New York years than anyone. So now, when Damon wanted to unburden himself of his woes, he would write to Agnes Fowler. Damon was confiding to Mother this time that his daughter Mary might get married against his wishes:

[Mary is] dragging a very mild looking little youth of some 23 long, hard years, who was presented as the fiancé. He is a sports writer, no less, and of the opposition in Washington, being one of Roy Howard's fledglings. Isn't that treason, or something? . . . We leave tomorrow for Miami. Damon, Jr. got home yesterday from Riverside Military Academy at Gainesville, Georgia, and this school moves to Miami every winter, or rather to Hollywood [Florida], just outside of Miami, which is why we sent him there. He is as tall as I am, and the three months he has been down there in Georgia has done him a world of good. . . .

Damon went on to tell Mother how much he loved his son, and how he hoped the two of them would get along together "when the boy grows up."

During Wilson Mizner's last illness, when he was living at the Ambassador Hotel in Los Angeles, Pop thought it might cheer him if he sent the great con man a gift. "I heard that opium addicts, when they ate at all, were fond of bananas," Pop told me. "I did not bring him a mere bunch of bananas. I brought an entire stalk of them, some fifteen dozen, done up in a bright gift package with many ribbons and everything.

"Billy was so delighted with this gift that after I departed, he had a crew of bellboys suspend the bananas from the chandelier. Now as you undoubtedly know Hollywood hotels have ceilings less sturdy than those in New York where the heavy snow falls. Well, the weight of the banana-stalk wrenched the chandelier out of its socket like Painless Parker used to yank a bicuspid. It caused a short circuit, and nearly burned down the hotel."

Mizner had telephoned Pop to report all this. "And I was happy," Pop said, "because the last thing I ever heard from this peculiar, gifted, and slightly larcenous six-foot, four-inch man was his bass laughter. Two days afterward he was dead."

The jest has been attributed to many other persons, but, when an oxygen tent was placed over Mizner, he said, "This looks like the main event."

"I was told by Anita Loos and Mark Kelly, friends of Mizner," Pop said, "that one of the old padres visited Billy on the day that was to be his last. The priest did some adroit beating about the bush and then said, 'Billy, isn't there something you would like me to sort of straighten up for you?' There was a pause. Then the fifty-eight-year-old Mizner said, 'I know what you mean, Father. You'd like me to square up according to the Book.' There was another pause. Then Billy added, 'Now I ask you, what would be the good of my telling you something that in a matter of hours I'll be telling your boss?'"

This was to be the beginning of Pop's increasing loss of old friends. He was depressed and began writing completely serious letters to Mother. None had the masking hilarity of the previous missives. In his anguish, Pop bolted away from Hollywood once again. Ben Hecht and Dorothy Parker, presently on assignment at the same studio, also left suddenly because of a disagreement with their respective producers.

Pop took off for Cheyenne, Wyoming, where his close friend there, Sheriff T. Joe Cahill, offered to put him up at his house. Pop insisted on a cell in the local jail where he could think and finish his scenario. Although he received his mail at the Plains Hotel (because he did not wish her to worry about where he was taking his accommodations), he wrote Mother the following from his cell:

You have beauty inside, and it can not fade . . . Look forward to quiet old age with more writing and less stewing . . . When you are hurt, I am hurt . . . I have just passed from a rather funny youth into another age —a kind of change of life . . . When you suggest I do not like being mothered, you are crazy. I dote on it. Thank you for being so patient . . . So tired of Hollywood and all that it means . . . I like to study people while they think I am dumb. I get their real inside then . . . I have yelled out loud that I love you and only you, and my family! . . .

Shortly thereafter, Mother telegraphed the following to the Plains Hotel:

DARLING BOY. WELCOME HOME. HAPPY YOU ARE COMING TO ME. HAVE JUST BEEN DYING ON THE VINE. LET'S FORGET EVERYTHING AND START ALL OVER AGAIN. AM PLUGGING HARD FOR YOUR SAFE LANDING. WIRE ME FROM CHICAGO. ALL MY LOVE AND KISSES.

After finishing his movie assignment in the Cheyenne jailhouse,

Pop made up his differences with the producer who had caused him to seek solitude while he worked on the script. Not only that, but he was given a boost in salary.

Before that reconciliation took place, however, he had written an angry 800-word essay on Hollywood's many faults, a copy of which fell into the hands of a friend on the staff of the Hollywood *Reporter*. The denunciation was published after Pop had cooled off, causing him a certain amount of embarrassment. "When you make a mistake, son," Pop told me later, "just remember that you can't dream back your teeth."

The diatribe published by the *Reporter* read:

. . . I leave for Fire Island to be with a grand entourage of goats, a parrot, two dogs, a frog, three utterly incorrigible brats, and a wife, who gives me her word of honor that I never have bored her . . . It is a fine thing to leave without bitterness or screaming, as I am afraid so many have done. In my days of romance (Chapter X, Breasted's *Ancient History*), I made it a practice to shove off at high tide. In romance or life, Fowler takes parachute jumps . . .

I doubt if any Hollywood writer ever received better treatment than I. And as to the pay, I should be arrested for taking so much. And still I cannot stomach the game. It may well be conceit, or perhaps a dash of paranoia, but Fowler refuses to send his talent walking the streets, winking at intellectual boatswains, or letting uncouth chefs make an avocado salad of his bosom.

Many of the finest men I know live and thrive here. To them, greetings. Here also are credit-grabbers, buttock-surveyors and fabulous fakers. Why not? Every man to his game. There are handicaps, also, that would defeat any sincere artist; such as the stupidity of censorship and the timidity of the local overseers of the industry . . . Fowler will not continue to contribute to stories that start with great health and end up with diabetic sugars.

It is not all Hollywood's burden. Let us admit that civilization has foozled; that men are pop-eyed with fear. Until men quit singing "Mammy" songs while they are simultaneously kicking their mothers in the teeth, I shall have no faith in them. Until there is not one single hungry child in the world, I shall not admit to our humanity.

And as for the basket-weavers and peanut-munchers of the land—the boys who are supposed to be the movie audience—I am not sorry they get such a poor product from our punch-drunk cameras. My only regret is that the pictures are not *worse*.

Gene Fowler

Pop came home, and it was wonderful to have him around the house again. Every day he was there to play with us and to read to us. Then he began work in the Bread and Butter Room on his fifth book. This time it was about an actor who became the silent motion picture comedy king. His name was Mack Sennett. Pop titled the book *Father Goose* and dedicated it to his new friend, comedian W. C. Fields. In later years when Mack Sennett fell upon hard times, or, rather, when hard times fell upon him, Pop assigned all dramatic rights of this book over to the former king of comedy. This gesture kept Sennett hopefully alive for many lonely years as he worked on plans to have the story of his life presented in the medium in which he once flourished. He died recently at the Motion Picture Home in Calabasas, California, still making vast plans for this opus which never came off. "A poor man can die happy," Pop once told me, "if he keeps his mind filled with great plans, even though they might have been hastily constructed with papier mâché."

Chapter Fourteen

LIFE ITSELF IS A LOTTERY,
BUT CHARACTER IS A FIXTURE.

GENE FOWLER

Pop had one more Hollywood assignment. He was to collaborate on an original screenplay for Twentieth Century Pictures. He was reluctant to travel to the Coast this time, even though Mother was to accompany him, because he learned his collaborator was to be a woman. He was far from being a woman hater but he believed that women were out of place in all but one profession. Reflecting upon his trepidation before he met this woman, whose name is Bess Meredyth, Pop said, "I felt trapped once again." Then he added, "Oh, well, I am worrying too much about something that has not yet taken place . . . and *worry,* my son, is the most worthless commodity known to man."

Pop met Bess Meredyth at the studio in Hollywood two days later. He was surprised to see that she was only about five feet tall, and a most attractive girl. Pop came home to Mother that night to say, "This Bess Meredyth. She has brains," then added, "We're going to do the story of Phineas T. Barnum."

Bess Meredyth inspired Pop to take a new interest in the writing of motion picture scenarios. "She taught me a lot," Pop said. "This woman who wrote the original silent screen version of *Ben-Hur,* starring Ramon Novarro and Francis X. Bushman, would show me how to put down dialogue that was not as fatuous as the usual junk that was being turned out."

Pop called her "Bessie," this lady who had been married to the suave European-born actor Paul Lukas. Their son, John, is a highly successful television-motion picture writer and director today.

While working on the last draft of the Barnum movie, Pop and Bessie would knock off work sharply at 4 P.M. to have tea. This was a hangover from the *Mirror* days. "And if you could have seen the collection of busted knuckles holding on to little cups," Bessie told me, "you would have laughed yourself to death. There were Jack Dempsey, the old fighter Frank Moran, Mickey Walker, the 350-pound wrestler Man Mountain Dean, Jimmy McLarnin, Fred Perry, and a few who *could* hold the teacup, like Harry Brand, Mark Kelly, Dr. Harry Martin, and actor Donald Crisp."

The screen play was completed and titled *The Mighty Barnum*. Wallace Beery starred as Barnum. Adolphe Menjou, champion of the double-breasted suit, played Beery's partner, and others in the cast included Virginia Bruce, Janet Beecher, and Rochelle Hudson.

Pop turned down a second assignment during the latter part of March 1935, but offered to read and edit a screenplay by a new writer named Samuel G. Engel before he and Mother took the plane to New York to make plans for our extended boat trip. Let me quote Engel's evaluation from a letter he wrote my mother recently:

Of the many instances I can recall wherein Gene gave me a warm, heartening pat on the back, there remains, vividly, one such act for which I shall remember him always with affection and gratitude . . . I was trying to break out of my cocoon as a junior writer and earn my first full screenplay credit. I had written a script for Darryl Zanuck on sort of a trial basis. Darryl liked it, but felt it needed the more certain, tried, experienced hand of an established writer of Gene's calibre. Darryl gave my script to Gene, who read it, and at a story conference later that week, in my presence, Gene said that he thought it an excellent job, and that he didn't think he could improve it sufficiently to warrant his undertaking the assignment. He said it in his typically honest, frank and confident manner. The result: my career was launched.

Another example of Pop's working for a young author was Al Stump, who wrote the Ty Cobb biography, *My Life in Baseball*.

"Ty was considering several writers for his book," Stump told me at a book club luncheon, "when, for no reason I knew of, because I didn't know your father, Gene wrote to Cobb recommending me in glowing terms for the job. I know it was Gene's letter which turned the trick for me."

When Pop finished the *Barnum* assignment, he and Mother prepared to take the family on a three-month tour of Europe, North Africa, and Asia Minor. On the morning of April 2, the family sailed aboard the American Export Line's ship S.S. *Exeter*. On our first evening's deck walk, Pop held my hand and Jane's as we peered inland past the lightship. He pointed out a covey of electric lights and said, "That's Fire Island. I think my heart will always be there."

The morning of the fifth day, Pop was on deck early to point out the San Salvador Islands. They were only a collection of barren gray rocks, but were the first European land we had seen. It was dark when we anchored off Gibraltar. We joined passengers to go ashore and travel through the hewn tunnels of the great cannon-fortified Rock. Inside the tunnels were rubber-encased steel communication cables along the walls. Gene told me, "These cables hold the whole Rock together. If they ever get loose, the whole damn thing will crumble right down to the ground."

Naples the first time around was uneventful. Our ship moored there only long enough to allow us a trip to the Isle of Capri and to see the Blue Grotto. We departed the following day for Alexandria, Egypt. Unfortunately for the Italians we would have at least a month studying their rate of exchange. When we returned, Mother and Mumsie would be able to rattle off corresponding values in their bargainings.

When we docked at Alexandria, however, my parents were to fight the local tradesmen with their English pounds and piasters. Anxious to get into a battle with a rug merchant, Mother spoke in terms of English numbers instead of Egyptian denominations. An Arab merchant insisted he be paid "500" for a Bukhara rug measuring about six feet in length. Mother, however, was unmerciful with the turbaned salesman and got him down to "150." Happy to set her feet on land once more, Mumsie shook the thin merchant by the shoulder and said: "I won't give you any more than a thousand."

Our ship sailed on without us as we departed Alexandria for Cairo via train. It seemed that Pop had waited a lifetime to travel to Egypt where he could put his study of hieroglyphics to work. We registered at the Continental Hotel, where we had a huge sitting room on the third floor flanked by four bedrooms, two on each side. On hand to see that all went well was our guide Asher ben Garbi. He was dressed in what looked like a daring silk evening gown of white with maroon stripes. He also wore a soft red fez.

We had been away from home for some time now, and Pop asked Asher if he could get us a can of American fruit. "We'd like to ice it and have a snack before we lie down for a rest."

Canned fruit in America of the depression years was going at about six and eight cents a can. When two butlers arrived at our suite with a champagne bucket, Pop poked around the shaved ice to see a small tin which contained Dole pineapple squares. The headwaiter ceremoniously took out an anchor opener and pried open the lid. We all sat around as Pop meted out four squares of pineapple each. We ate the delicacy, picking up our shares with quill toothpicks. The bill for this morsel was one pound. (The pound was $5 at the time. It broke down to $2 for the pineapple, $3 for the ice.)

The next day Asher called for us with two chauffeured limousines and we traveled out to contemplate the Cheops pyramids and the Sphinx, the nose of which, Pop insisted, had been blown off by one of Napoleon's cannon. We rode camels. There was a native who brewed Arabian coffee at the top of the Great Pyramid, but Pop passed up this pleasure, reminding us of his fear of heights.

We spent the following night in a line of six tents where we had all sorts of food wrapped in grape vine leaves. There was a belly dancer, too. The top of her skirt was just about as low as a skirt could go without dropping off during navel maneuvers. Then Jane leaped up and improvised a dance. Just as she finished, an uncommonly strong breeze came upon us. This so impressed the native crew that they declared my sister possessed unearthly powers.

Yet another day we visited King Tutankhamen's tomb. But Pop spent most of his time in King Tut's gardener's burial place, deciphering the hieroglyphics there. When he emerged, he turned to Mother and said, "You know, Agnes, this gardener had an extremely interesting life. There was a passage of word pictures just past the entrance to his tomb which tells historians more of how Tut came to the throne and married Princess Ankh than I saw in Tut's tomb itself . . . And the gardener had an interesting formula for fertilizer."

"You came all the way to Egypt to tell me this?" Mother said.

Asher, however, was impressed by an American who had a great knowledge of his country. From then on, the rest of the family returned to the Continental Hotel as Pop and Asher conjectured on various facets of Howard Carter's book on King Tut.

Pop returned to the hotel somewhat elated because he deduced from his studies that day that King Tut had died at an early age because he was a hydrocephalic. "Asher had never considered this," he told Mother.

"You came all the way to Egypt to tell me this?" she repeated as she busied herself with packing our suitcases for a trip down to Luxor, where Pop would become lost in the Temple of Karnak.

It was 135 degrees Fahrenheit at Luxor. I developed a case of "Egyptian Belly." My fever rose to 107, but it dropped back to normal the morning following the visit of a local doctor who made me swallow a troche (a small two-sided bun with medicine therein). My grandmother, Mumsie, was less interested in my critical condition than she was in the Moslem physician wearing his red fez. Unaware of certain Mohammedan customs, she spoke sternly to the doctor: "Can't you take your hat off when you're inside, like other gentlemen do?" He must have realized that she was a woman of conviction, for he took the fez off.

Pop and Gene left us in Luxor to travel down to Aswan where they viewed the great dam at the second Nile cataract.

We had a private airplane which flew us from Cairo to Jerusalem. The young, inexperienced pilot became lost on the way, and Pop, applying his outdoor lore, suggested that he follow one camel caravan trail to another.

The most refreshing discovery in Palestine came when our new guide halted our three limousines (the third carried baggage alone) at Jacob's Well where we took our first draught of pure, cold water since we had left our ship.

Later we bathed in the Dead Sea, having motored to the spot

where it was said Christ had been baptized by John the Baptist. We were warned by our Christian guide not to make the Sign of the Cross. "There are many Arabs about who might take offense," said our guide. After I had baptized myself in the River Jordan, I went farther downstream, where I offered Arab children money to allow me to baptize them. This started a small riot, if a riot can be called "small." Had not my sister been educated in the modern dance, we all might have perished. As the parents of the newly Christianized children descended upon us, my sister, who was fifteen at the time, took careful aim and began to score with high kicks on the whip-bearing male Arabs. She never missed. Gene was boxing. Pop was wrestling. Mother and Mumsie were knocking off fezes with heavy handbags.

Our guide in the meantime began to attract more adversaries, who had chosen to take him on after a tussle with the crazy Americans. He was wielding his camel whip with great dexterity. As the odds overcame him, we swiftly took up a collection of silver among ourselves, then began to toss it all about and into the river. The Arabs, in a body, began diving into the holy water for the coins. We took advantage of this truce to beat it in our mechanized caravan.

Within a week we were back to Naples. To accommodate the souvenirs we were buying and stealing along the way, Mother went into the leather trading district and purchased various-sized suitcases and a trunk.

Following a talk with Mother, Pop told her to go to bed, and he would counsel his children about stealing. He started off in our bridal suite living room beneath a beautiful imported Dresden glass chandelier with, "Now listen, kids . . . This thieving has to stop."

"They've been stealing *us* blind," Jane averred.

"You can't say that isn't true," said Gene.

Pop stared at this exquisite chandelier and continued. "It's the principle of the thing," he said. "We are on foreign soil, so we must conduct ourselves in a most polite manner."

"Mother took off with a big piece of sandstone in Egypt," Jane insisted. "And you were the one who told her to do it just because there was a hieroglyphic on it."

"Let us hear no more about that," said Pop as he placed a foot-stool directly beneath the chandelier, stood upon it and reached up. "Are Mother and Mumsie asleep?" He detached an exquisite glass stem decorated with delicate flower buds from the chandelier. He removed his undershirt and wrapped the piece of glass in it. We made room for the latest booty in a suitcase that held about a dozen stolen hotel ash trays. Then Pop turned to us and said, "It's getting late, kids. Go to bed. We're off to Rome tomorrow . . . And not a word of this to your mother."

Pop decided to cancel the train tickets, and we motored up through Florence, where he laid a wreath of poison ivy on the tomb of Machiavelli. Then we went to Venice, and back to Genoa where we boarded the S.S. *Excalibur*.

We had a single wild afternoon in Málaga, Spain. After consuming much of the local wine, the males of the family sought to purchase tools to disassemble a small roller coaster Pop thought he had bought from a concessionaire. Returning to the amusement park after much looking and haggling, we attacked the miniature roller coaster with wrench and screw driver, intent on removing it to the ship, piece by piece. Its owner exploded with purple-faced objections, and a policeman had to be summoned to arbitrate. It developed that the roller-coaster owner thought Pop was an eccentric American millionaire, and that the large sum of money he had been given was to buy rides for the American and his sons, not to pay for the whole contraption.

Somehow we got back to the United States without being stoned, lynched, or even arrested.

We entered Customs in New York with two extra trunks and seventeen suitcases, one of them containing nothing but a magnificent collection of hotel ash trays. Pop later figured that the trip had cost him $25,000, not including the wear and tear on his nerves.

Chapter Fifteen

*YOU HAVE TO LIVE A LONG TIME TO DISCOVER
A LONG TIME IS NO TIME AT ALL.*

GENE FOWLER

When the family moved from one coast to the other, it was always at the end of spring or the end of summer. New Year's Eve was the middle of our transient fiscal year. Pop and Mother would fly to one coast or the other while Mumsie, Gene, Jane, Chester the parrot, two dogs, and I made the trip in a new Cadillac we usually purchased in Los Angeles just before the drive back to Fire Island.

Those cross-country treks were far more taxing and dangerous twenty-five years ago than today. If we made it across in four to five days without creating work for a fender straightener, we considered ourselves fortunate.

In speedy succession, Pop wrote two pictures based on Jack London's books, *Call of the Wild* and *White Fang*. The first starred the late Clark Gable, Loretta Young, and Jack Oakie. "It so happened," Pop told me, "that I had not read *Call of the Wild* at the time, so I asked one of the studio book readers, Mrs. Frankie Neill, to tell me bits of the story, but not too much of it to get me confused." If one read the book, then saw the picture, it would be obvious that with the exception of Alaska, a dog, and a load of snow here and there, the two stories bore little resemblance to each other.

After this box office hit featuring a dog, the next film introduced a new star, Michael Whalen, who rightfully resented playing second fiddle to a white police dog co-star named "Fang." This opus, however, met the fate of most sequels. The day trade paper reviews termed *White Fang* a fiasco, Pop was walking to the studio commissary with Harry Brand for a spot of lunch. A mongrel dog, chained to a nearby post, began to growl at them. Pop stopped, turned slowly and pointed a long finger at the threatening canine, who began to look as though suddenly hypnotized by his stare. "One more growl, and I'll write a motion picture about *you!*" Pop warned.

We had taken residence in a West Los Angeles house. I signed up the first day Emerson Junior High School opened. Gene and Jane enrolled at Beverly Hills High School, but were caught shortly thereafter by a sleuth who followed them home one day to discover the family did not live in that exclusive little city. Pop called his long-time friend, the late Marion Davies, to ask if one of her several Beverly Hills homes was available for rental. Marion asked when he wanted to move in. "Right now," said Pop. It was a Thursday when Gene and Jane had been discovered to be non-residents.

"You can move in Monday, in time for the kids to get to school," said Marion. She had three decorator crews work twenty-four hours a day until a home was ready for us in the 700 block of North Bedford Drive in Beverly Hills. When we moved in, Marion was on hand with Thomas Meighan to give us a house warming. (John Barrymore referred to Thomas Meighan as being "the only gentleman actor I ever knew".)

"No rent," said Marion. "Consider yourself my guest. I'll even give you the house if you want it."

"I can't do that," said Pop. "What if we grew to hate each other? We'd never live it down."

Many years later when Pop had lost the desire to complete his final book, Marion Davies visited him at his Brentwood home and offered to buy a good-sized newspaper for him. "Just take it, Gene, and do whatever you want with it. If you really don't want to work any more, sell the thing. It's a present from me to you." This brought Pop out of the doldrums and got him back to work again.

The only exchange of harsh words I had ever witnessed between

Pop and Mother was during a Saturday outing in 1936 when we drove past the old Gilmore Field (which today is the site of the Columbia Broadcasting System's Los Angeles television center). Approaching this spot near Fairfax and Beverly Boulevards following an excursion to the ostrich and alligator farms, Pop spotted the semi-rigid blimp *Volunteer* floating in for a landing. It looked to me like a giant bee that had overeaten and was coming home to suffer through a bellyache.

"Let's take the kids for a ride in the dirigible," he said to Mother.

"Over my dead body," said Mother. "Those things aren't safe."

The air did not get too blue, but Pop was determined to take Jane and me up in the silver bee. And when we returned to the car, Mother had her lips pursed. As we drove home, Pop finally blurted out: "All right! If you want to be mad, I can be mad, too!"

Now we all were silent.

Mother told me later that she and Pop never stayed mad for more than a few hours. "We'd give each other the dirty look, then eventually break up in laughter, and the bad feelings were washed away."

Another summer passed on Fire Island, but Pop did not make any attempt to start a new book. Then we returned West in the fall to rent the late actor Roland Young's home on North Linden Drive in Beverly Hills. Once, while being interviewed for a newspaper feature, Young was asked if he had any unusual fixtures in his exquisite home. To this, Young answered tersely, "Yes, Gene Fowler."

I reminded Pop of this quip, and he said, "When I paid my entire ten months rent all at once, Roland was so shocked that we got together to become fast friends."

Pop often yearned to get away from this tinsel town without actually having to fly somewhere. He came to know homicide detective Joe Filkas of the Los Angeles Police Department. Filkas is a tall, powerful, lantern-jawed man who used to punch a heavy boxing bag fifteen three-minute rounds each day just to keep in shape. The two, along with Filkas' partner, Sergeant Baker, and Pop's crony, Dr. Samuel Hirshfeld, would prowl many nights in an automobile they nicknamed "the Kitty Car." The car had a siren, hidden red light, and a loaded sawed-off shotgun in a sling just above the driver's seat. Filkas understood Pop was not a mere seeker of thrills; rather, he knew that Fowler wanted to relive the old days during the '20s in New York. It seems that Pop was always harking back to those times when he was happiest.

Pop and Filkas brought me along one night when I was in my fourteenth year. Another friend, Allen McNeil, a former professional fighter who had since turned film editor and put together many of Hollywood's better pictures, also came along that night.

Our Kitty Car idled through streets where girls waved enticingly to us from several windows directly above a porch with magenta-colored electric lights. A call came over the short-wave radio. Sergeant Baker flipped on his red light and the siren began to scream. Filkas explained, as we sped down the street, that we were going to a place a few miles away where a murder had just been committed.

As he piled out of the car, drawing his revolver, Filkas told me to "take down the shotgun and shoot anyone who looks like he's running away." This Filkas was a pretty relaxed character, and I carefully studied what he had told me, then I decided not to touch that damned big gun.

Time passed very slowly until Filkas showed up holding an elderly man by the wrist.

Sergeant Baker radioed in that a sixty-eight-year-old named McMannus had presumably murdered his wife. Pop was administering first aid to McNeil who, somehow, had suffered a bloody nose. Filkas laughed uncontrollably. It seems that when the four broke into the murderer's apartment, the first thing the suspect did was to size up the men, then walk calmly over to McNeil and punch him squarely in the nose. McNeil, a veteran of many professional prize fights, complained, "If he wasn't such an old bastard, I think I'd of killed him."

When the fingerprinting and picture taking were over, Pop sat on a wooden bench with the elderly wife-slayer. As Pop talked with him, the desk sergeant answered the telephone to tell a night police reporter about the case at hand. The newspaper would cover this man's moment of homicidal insanity in a paragraph which would probably be lost in overset.

Pop asked Filkas if it would be all right to take the murderer McMannus out for a glass of beer. "It'll probably be his last."

"That's a hell of a request," said Filkas. Then he chuckled. "Go ahead, then. I have to make out a report anyway. But see that we get him back. No tricks, Fowler."

"I'll have him back in a half hour," Pop promised.

Pop ordered two schooners of beer in a bar two blocks from the old First Street Station which has since been replaced by a sterile-looking civic building. "The way you walk," Pop said to McMannus, "it seems to me that you must have been athletic at one time in your life."

"I came in third in the Boston marathon thirty-five years ago," said the murderer.

"Now that's a coincidence," Pop offered. "I used to know Edward Payson Weston, the champion pedestrian who walked from New York to Philadelphia."

The old man's eyes brightened as though he had managed to forget he had just killed his wife. "Mr. Weston was my idol," he smiled.

"Just why did you kill your wife, Mr. McMannus?" Pop asked casually. "Two more beers, bartender. And give us a little bourbon on the side."

"We were married many years," the old man replied. "We always slept in a double bed, Lucy and me. It was really a very narrow double bed, and I'm a light sleeper. Once I'm awakened, it's just impossible for me to get back to sleep." Then he asked: "What did you say your name was, young man?"

"Thanks for the 'young man' compliment," said Pop. "Fowler. Gene Fowler."

"Well, Mr. Flower," McMannus continued, "Lucy and me slept in this double bed for all those years. She is . . . or was . . . very fat . . . ate chocolates in bed all the time . . . I guess I never got used to being knocked out of bed when she had her nightmares . . . Just knocked out of bed about most every night . . ." He stopped and sighed, then tears began to well in his eyes.

Three hours later, Filkas and two uniformed policemen finally located the pair. The uniformed men seemed a bit miffed. But Filkas, understanding that Fowler was a pixie, and knowing that he probably had a confession by proxy, led McMannus back to the station. He staggered along First Street saying, "Lucy? Where's my Lucy? It's awful late, and I shouldn't be out this time of night. I gotta buy her a box of candy."

McMannus was eventually placed in the psychopathic ward at General Hospital to spend his remaining days calling for his wife to come pick him up and take him home.

Chapter Sixteen

WE ARE NOT ALL GREAT MEN,
BUT WE MUST ALL BE DEDICATED.

GENE FOWLER

There were two letters spanning eighteen months that touched on John Barrymore's role in our lives. The first was one from Pop to myself. It was dated September 23, 1943, and read in part:

I shall have finished the editing of the book about our great friend by tomorrow. This is my last hour on Fire Island before taking the boat across the bay. I wanted to write to you from this place which has so many first-rate associations for both of us.

I came here as a young man, shot with dreams, desires, and a modicum of whiskey. Now, I sit in my crow's nest overlooking the beach-grass, the sand, the water. And the sea is still the same, ageless and embracing. Only man changes, never the sea. The hurricane which drove across the island still is evidenced by the scars in the dunes, and a far-off house or two tilts like the hat of an actor taking his last bow. There have been shore-changes, but the waves roll in still the same. And all this reminds me of two things: Byron's apostrophe to the sea in *Childe Harold,* and my own life-long philosophy—"What of it?"

Everywhere I turn in this large, empty house, I find reminders of a happy time when we were all young together. I can hear the laughter of my children. A whistle which you used as a life guard lies near me. I'd like to blow on it. I think I shall.

Let us stay young inside, for the inside of us counts most, although the world passes judgement only on our *outsides.* This may well be my last journey here, so, until the boat comes, I shall look out at the grass rippling in a West Wind, hear the locusts sing of frost, and admire the autumnal complexion of the poison ivy.

The second letter was from a Yank somewhere in occupied Germany. It was nearly Christmas in 1944 when this boy wrote Pop the following:

Please don't think I am forcing a prolonged correspondence upon you just because you were kind enough to answer my letter about the Barrymore book that I found in a ruined French château. My reason for writing right now is this: you told me when I caught up with some captured Rhine wine in a German château to have one for you; and who ever thought I would see the day, along with a goodly number of other Yanks, when it was easier to find champagne to drink than water? Of course most of it is 1937 vintage when the natives' feet were clean and the corks well in . . . I just wanted to begin to tell you how eagerly we Yanks drank in all of the Fowler words about John Barrymore in *Good Night, Sweet Prince*. You brought us a part of America no other propaganda could send.

When Pop spoke to me in later years about Barrymore, he voiced various emotions about this man who had never really found himself. Once he said, regarding Barrymore's retiring after his one-hundred-and-first performance of *Hamlet* (when the Edwin Booth Society warned Jack that their idol performed only 100 Hamlets, and Jack said: "Then I shall perform 101!"), "Jack grew tired of being masterminded by managers, and left the stage."

Once Barrymore, artist John Decker, and Pop were talking with three other intellectual gentlemen, two of whom were physicians. One of the learned doctors said that there was no such thing as a true aphrodisiac. The second physician agreed with this and said that the old stories about love philters, etc., were so much bosh. Then Barrymore offered, "You are mistaken, gentlemen. There is only one superior aphrodisiac, and it works." The third intellectual opposite Pop, Barrymore, and Decker (a mere Ph. D.) asked in a somewhat patronizing tone, "Well, well, Mr. Barrymore, and would you please give us the name of this aphrodisiac?" To which Barrymore replied: *"Women!"*

Before Barrymore died, he had fallen into bankruptcy, but once again bailed himself out. Pop claimed the only reason he hit debtor's prison in the first place was that he would sign anything before reading it. As a case in point, Pop rushed up to Jack's fifty-five-room home on Tower Road which afforded a magnificent view of Beverly Hills. Pop unfolded a large scroll and tossed it at the actor. "Sign this immediately!" he insisted. "Please, Jack, there's no time to lose. It means my entire future if you don't sign it right now!"

Barrymore trusted Pop, so with an "Of course," Jack asked, "Is this a petition, Gene?"

"That it is," said Pop. "Please sign it immediately so I can get it down to my lawyer before I'm thrown in jail!"

"In that case," said Barrymore, "we shall do it in all haste." He accepted the pen thrust at him and affixed his signature to the bottom of many, many signatures at the bottom of the document.

As Jack blew the ink dry, Pop stood to his full six-feet-one and asked, "Now, you silly bastard, do you know what you have just signed?"

"Does it make that much difference, you un-named son of the Grecian seas?" Then Barrymore perused the document and asked, after realizing its complexity, "Just what *did* I sign?"

"The Declaration of Independence, you dull fellow," said Pop.

Barrymore began to roll up the parchment, then said: "Why not?"

"One time Jack's extraordinary wit turned an embarrassing question into a quaint tale without drooling a lot of fake modesty," Pop told me. "Jack was too great an artist not to know his own mental power, but he was extremely modest and reticent about it.

"Ashton Stevens, our late friend, and the best drama critic Chicago ever spawned," Pop continued, "asked Jack in an interview what he considered the greatest piece of acting he ever did. It is a common question of interviewers, and is always a poser. Here is how Jack got around it:

" 'You see,' said Jack, 'I had been on a spree, and had just been fired as result. I found myself in Atlantic City with a large hangover and some small change. My aunt had given me a beautiful pair of lapis lazuli cuff-links, which I proceeded to hock. Then I wandered along the Boardwalk, and stopped in front of one of those fresh fish joints where they serve you a sort of pink soup made from shrimp. The thought of the pink soup was rather horrible, and I was just pulling myself together for a short walk to the nearest bar when a guy bumped into me, shoving me toward the fish joint. When I turned back to bawl him out I was aware now that he was a sailor, so I took the hint and went in for the sea food. Here I ordered the pink soup. As I meditated over it, my old friend John D. Williams must have got bumped in too, for he appeared through the haze and sat down with me. He said I was just the guy he wanted to talk to. He said he had a new show trying out in Chicago, and the leading man had been drinking and he needed a prize replacement. Here, I thought, comes the lecture; but the hunch was wrong for Williams continued to tell me that the part was made for me. Then he asked it I was doing anything at the time. I smiled a No sweetly and casually, like the poor devil in *Dinner at Eight*. The fellow asked me, "What is your salary now?" and I turned on the elfin smile. I was just about to start the sibilant "s" that begins the "sev" in "seventy-five dollars a week" when Williams interrupted. "Would five hundred do for Chicago?" I gulped, then said that it would. And the way I said it, and the way I restrained myself from diving into that pink soup, was the greatest piece of acting I ever did!' "

When Pop began to take on the writing of *Good Night, Sweet Prince,* his actual working title was *The Grampian Hills*. He extracted this title from a letter which Jack had written me a few years before his death:

Soon I trust we will all be tending our flocks together on *the Grampian Hills* where the cows *really* come home!

Then when Pop completed the manuscript he decided on the final line of Horatio as the title. But the publishers were against it. So was one in that organization against Pop even writing a book about a "drunken old actor." Pop did not care about this eleventh-hour opinion; he was mainly interested in the title. Mother, who had actually given the title to Pop, encouraged him to stand his ground.

"They're paying you to write the book," she said. "At least they can accept our title." So it stayed to become one of the most apt and compelling book titles of its time.

He had begun planning and thinking about the book even before Barrymore, his health declining rapidly, was removed from his huge and almost empty house to what proved to be his deathbed.

One evening as the month of May had about run its course, Pop wrote this note on the back of a large envelope of the Frank Perls Art Gallery. He left it on the desk in his library. It read:

Agnes Dear,

Your pious husband is on his way to Hollywood Hospital once again to see John Barrymore dying. But I have it on good authority, it is not John, but I whose death rattles are about to sound across the moors. Thine (as usual) Pop.

During the hospital death watch, Pop sat with several newspaper reporters. A man who claimed some sort of medical degree entered the sitting room opposite Barrymore's last resting place to aver: "Just give me three minutes with Mr. Barrymore. I can give him a muscular adjustment, and he will be cured!"

Having imbibed severally with the reporters, Pop stood up to speak with this intruder. "Do you know at this time that Mr. Barrymore has many tubes in his body and is unable to receive your adjustments?"

"It makes no difference. I am a physician. I can heal him if I am given the chance!"

Pop considered that this man was causing too much disturbance, and though at least ten years older, took him by the scruff of the neck and turkey-walked him to the stairs and booted him on his way. Pop hollered after him, "Physician, heal thyself!"

Lionel arrived as Pop put in a local telephone call to John's daughter by Michael Strange, Diana. Lionel went into Jack's room as Pop spoke over the phone to Diana. "Get out to the Hollywood Presbyterian Hospital right away," Pop instructed Barrymore's daughter. "I believe your father is dying."

"I can't possibly do it," Diana countered on the other end of the phone. "I have a very important appointment."

"So has your father," said Pop. Diana, in any case, was too late. Lionel came out of Jack's room and said: "It's all over."

A nurse later reported that Barrymore, after Dr. Hugo M. Kersten had introduced alcohol into his veins, had rallied and said to her, "All right, darling. Hop in."

Now Pop entered the sick room with artist John Decker. It was 10:15 P.M., May 29, 1942. Barrymore's last words were directed to my father: "Is it true that you are the illegitimate son of Buffalo Bill?" His face puffed up for a few seconds, then he breathed his last, mumbling, "Mumm-mumm, Mumm-mumm."

Dr. Kersten reentered the room as Decker picked up a piece of manila wrapping paper and began to sketch the actor's face in death. Dr. Kersten felt for a pulse. There was none. He went out to the nurse's desk to write the following report after filling in the date and time:

The immediate cause of death was myocarditis. The recent contributing factors were chronic mephritis, cirrhosis of liver, gastric ulcers.

The fact that Mr. Barrymore survived this attack for more than a few days, instead of hours, following his collapse of Tuesday, is more of a tribute to the patient's amazing vitality than to any medical science practiced in his behalf. Perhaps this unexplained vitality had something in common with the several other matchless qualities of this talented and courageous artist. As his physician, called upon several other occasions to minister to him when his condition was, to say the least, critical and alarming, I was compelled to wonder at the recuperative faculties of the man, and to marvel at a spirit and will that belied his sixty years.

In exploring his physical history, and taking into account his chronic carelessness in getting proper rest, or observing even a semblance of diet, I also became acquainted intimately with the man himself, his fine mind, his opinions, his philosophies. I found that his great personal strength and courage, even his foolhardiness, cloaked, in fact, the gentlest sort of soul; tolerant, generous, without conceit, and almost childlike in honesty of thought. It is not for a medical practitioner to say that these qualities have any bearing whatsoever on a man's physical fortitude at the threshold of death. Yet, who knows?

At the bottom of a carbon copy of this statement, Pop wrote in a confidential penciled note to me:

Will: The doctor, a splendid man, wanted to know how he might best word a statement. I wrote the above, hoping to give something which I felt was true, and which might be the beginning of the salvaging of Jack's reputation. The doctor did not want to take the credit for this, but I insisted, saying that it would be quoted the world over. It was.

A newspaperman is seldom remembered for a good piece written on a deadline. The man who wrote the finest account of Barrymore's funeral was James Lee of the Los Angeles *Examiner,* which began:

With the oldest and the most majestic drama of all, the sacred rites of the Church, John Barrymore's body was entombed yesterday.

The good that he did, the notes of tenderness and romance and comedy, too, that he struck with his singular genius, still live and will not be forgotten.

This was evident in the tears of those who love him. It was apparent in the gentle touch of the hand of his elder brother, Lionel Barrymore, upon the orchid-covered casket where the holy water glistened. . . .

There were only seventy-five invited guests in this cemetery on the east side of town, seemingly far removed from Hollywood and the scenes of Jack's capricious life. Outside, however, were about two thousand of his fans who knew him only from the other side of the proscenium arch, on the motion picture screen, or over the air waves. His fourth wife, Elaine Barrie, was the only former wife to appear at the funeral. Jack's sister, Ethel, had been unable to obtain airplane reservations to attend; Dolores Costello, his third wife, had taken suddenly ill and could not be there; his first wife, Katherine Corri Harris, had died some years before; his second, Michael Strange, was in the East, and also too ill to attend.

The pallbearers, besides my father, were W. C. Fields, John Decker, Edgar J. Mannix (M-G-M studio executive), and C. J. Briden and Stanley Campbell, Barrymore's two make-up men.

Listed as honorary pallbearers were Edward Sheldon, Charles MacArthur, Herbert Marshall, Roland Young, Thomas Mitchell, Alan Mowbray, Ben Hecht, Arthur Hopkins, George M. Cohan, Herbert Bayard Swope, and Bramwell Fletcher.

Among the invited guests were Louis B. Mayer, Clark Gable,

Errol Flynn, Fredric March, Spencer Tracy, Norma Shearer, Harpo Marx, Earl Carroll, Edmund Lowe, Anthony Quinn, Raoul Walsh, Frank Craven, William Powell, Ronald Colman, Cecil B. de Mille, to name a few.

In the closing paragraphs of his story, James Lee wrote:

It could not be denied that the solemnity of the occasion was marred by the disorder of the throng outside the chapel when the services had ended.

Women twittered at sight of the mourning stars. Amateur camera enthusiasts elbowed for focusing positions. Girls in their teens and some of their elders broke past the barriers to gain vantage points.

But never in all his eventful life was John Barrymore a solemn fellow. He met such situations with a grin and with easy grace.

Perhaps he would have wanted it so.

Jack's death occurred during World War II, and from a Japanese internment center at Manzanar came a floral wreath from his close friend and gardener at Tower Road, Mark Nishimura. The Japanese was reported gravely ill.

Pop was assigned, along with Attorney Gordon Devoy, to be co-executors of Barrymore's will. After having read the bankruptcy transcript, my father answered a letter from one of Jack's various former attorneys, a gentleman who had filed a creditor's claim with the court referee, stating that his own client had been left out of the will. To this Pop replied:

I have read the John Barrymore bankruptcy transcript and believe I have as good a grasp of it as could be expected of a layman. Of course, lawyers appear to fall into a tradition of words that seem to be designed exclusively for the discouragement of the English language. I have often wondered if this were less than accidental. No one, including the American Courts, knows what the hell is being said at all. But these robed Blackstones, having been learned counselors themselves, pretend they know what the salad of words means, and proceed to add such speech-confusions and bewilderments as they are capable of, throwing their own well-manured phrases and ambiguous clauses into the salad bowl, further confusing the issue.

Of course, we occasionally chance upon some low fellow, such as the late Supreme Court Justice Oliver Wendell Holmes, who actually *could* be understood by such persons as ourselves. The wonder to me is that Mr. Holmes was not disbarred, or drowned in a deep cesspool, for having the audacity to have written clearly and simply and in good English. All this is a preamble to a brief report on my reading the transcript . . .

Never in my career, both as a savant and common drunkard, have I come across so much fertilizer. You will please understand that I do not refer to your own comments in court, or to the remarks of your advisers. Some of these men, other than your seconds, seem so mixed up, either feloniously or not, that I am led to speculate on their private behavior, and to wonder how in hell they can order a piece of pie at a drive-in and make themselves understood . . .

Possibly the higher courts can understand the speeches. I hope so. Then again I hope not, because it will be a further degradation of our language. My suggestion is that most lawyers return to school and *stay* there!

My one hope is that the wrangling over the decent bones of my friend John Barrymore will cease.

With the highest personal regards,

Gene Fowler

When Barrymore's private possessions were placed on the auction block, Pop presided as the legal onlooker. What was left of Jack's fortune was not too interesting to the average bargain seeker. There were crates of fishing tackle, ancient wooden figures, inexpensive pictures, a set of dominoes, a few sketches rendered by Barrymore himself, three sets of Spanish bronze stirrups, a collection of well-lived-in Sears-Roebuck furniture which did not even get an opening bid of $10, and two shrunken human heads which Jack had given me on two separate occasions. The heads were purchased by Edgar Bergen, who placed them in his guest room to frighten any relatives who outwore their welcome.

Pop bought an old wooden English chair (Jack's favorite), his sword used in *Richard III,* and a painting which Jack had executed over a map of the southern coast of Florida.

Now Pop set about the task of writing the life of John Barrymore. "Everything, as usual," he told me, "was against me. The war was on, and there was a paper shortage. If the book was any kind of success, there would not be pulp available to make paper for an abundant supply. But then," he philosophized, "this was a labor of love."

During the writing, which took nine months in all, Pop was plagued by ill health. He had been in correspondence with Benjamin Shalett, M.D., a famous New York dietitian. The two had become friends when Dr. Shalett had put a lot of meat on Fowler's frame, which had become alarmingly thin following successive attacks of malaria.

Dr. Shalett was not only his dietitian, but an eventual confidant during the writing of *Good Night, Sweet Prince*. Pop answered a letter from Dr. Shalett which asked about the condition of his health, after reading in a newspaper that he was ill:

I can't say that I was surprised at your prompt response. I did not know that the matter got into print, and in fact, I tried to keep it to myself . . .

I have been working extraordinarily hard night and day trying to meet an almost impossible deadline. The book is going to be about a thousand pages long, and you can readily see, what with the research and the writing, that it is a superhuman task . . .

I am supposed to have a duodenal ulcer and chronic appendicitis, and perhaps a slightly congested gall-bladder. I have not had time to get X-rays . . . I have worked with the God-damnedest bellyache for six weeks. I have been doing no drinking; in fact, I have had six brandies in a year come this May . . . I think the vagus nerve and the emotional short circuits or deadlocks are indeed the answer . . . The doctor wanted to operate on me, but Agnes would not hear of that . . . There is no tension there now and no pain at all. Of course, the belly pain may have been "referred" but my ache seems to come at an hour and a half to two hours after eating. . . .

During the writing of *Good Night, Sweet Prince*, Pop began to experience nearly unbearable chest pains. Perhaps he found more solace in writing than the average person does in medication.

At any rate, the book was born and it was a resounding success. What Pop had to say about John Barrymore seemed to be accepted by the public. This was his greatest writing success. His publisher had to buy up another publishing firm to use their government paper allotment in order to fill the staggering demand. This book received the greatest acclaim from Yanks overseas of any work printed during World War II. "The only thing that topped this for me," Pop said, "was that it was translated into Braille."

The critics, who were often at odds with the Fowler approach to biography, were generally exultant this time. Claudia Cassidy of the Chicago *Sunday Tribune* on January 9, 1944, wrote the following:

If ever a man had the right biographer, it was John Barrymore in Gene Fowler . . . It is a fabulous story told with the full throated ease of infinite pains, deep understanding, acutely personal knowledge and the ability to write the way John Barrymore could act. [Fowler offers] with a stinging wit and a lyrical overture, his stubbornly understated insistence on what was to him a psychic manifestation of Barrymore's death, and there is a poetic division of the biography into four cantos, with affectionately revealing titles, 'Songs of the Morning,' 'The Sun on the Meridian,' 'Golden Siesta' and 'The Stag at Eve.'

Writer-actress Patricia Collinge stated in *The New York Times* that it had a meticulous regard for truth that made the biography a "four-dimensional image of the man." She added:

. . . No facets of his subject—and they were many—have been left unexposed. If some appear tarnished, that is how they were. If at times the gutters were as familiar to John Barrymore as were the heights, his loneliness in each is faithfully recorded . . . When the story is told and that last poignant page read, John Barrymore emerges whole and in dignity. . . .

On the other hand, Edmund Wilson in his scholary work, *A Literary Chronicle: 1920–1950,* made a candid appraisal of Pop's style upon putting down his views of this book:

His [Fowler's] notion of syntax and the meaning of words is . . . of the vaguest. When it is a question of anybody's conduct, the word "behaviorism" is always summoned: "After the passing of his grandmother he entered upon a bouncing behaviorism" . . . The language of Mr. Fowler has no structure and no harmonics. It is something that is exhaled like breath or exuded like perspiration. And yet the fuzzy, raffish style of this book has its special appropriateness to the subject: it is a literary equivalent for the atmosphere in which the events take place . . .

Gene Fowler, with his word-slinging jargon and his husky-throated, sports-writer humor, is the right person to tell this story which might otherwise never have been told. . . .

Wilson also remarked that Barrymore was "a great man with the women."

"Regarding the bedroom," Pop later told me, "this was exactly the opposite. Because of his legend, and notwithstanding his handsomeness, Jack always felt an inferiority in the boudoir. He had a trick with the ladies, though. At the climactic moment, he would let out a great scream. He would so shock a strange bed partner, that she would often wonder the following day exactly what *did* happen."

An actor friend of mine, Charles Tannen, once told me that Orson Welles had loudly criticized Pop for having written a book about Barrymore and completely ignored even an opinion regarding the *Hamlet*. The exclusion of Jack's *Hamlet* attitude in the book was a constant burden to Pop. But he philosophically kept this secret throughout his life, only writing of it to one person, Dr. Harold Thomas Hyman, author of many medical books, including an encyclopedia on medicine. Dr. Hyman wrote a letter to my father from his Park Avenue office directly after the book was published. He was the first to inquire regarding the absence of comment on Jack's *Hamlet* in the book. It was a lengthy letter, and I refer only to the last three paragraphs therein:

You have built the book, as I see it, up to and away from the *Hamlet*. You have faithfully recorded the reaction of many people to the *Hamlet*. You did not, however, make clear, at least to me, just why the Barrymore *Hamlet* was so important and why it is as vivid to me today as when I saw it so many years ago, and that despite the fact that my memory has been fouled by the other *Hamlets* such as Gielgud, Evans and Leslie Howard. I almost got the impression that you had not seen it yourself and, hence, were unable to evaluate its importance.

Not the least of Jack's achievements in his *Hamlet* was his psychoanalytic concept of many of the incidents. Part of this was his extraordinary intuition, but part, which you fail to mention though I think I wrote to you, were his many conferences with Pearce Bailey or Edward Zabriski, I cannot remember which. For example, the bedroom scene

with his mother was deliberately played for incest. This was in keeping
with his concept of the role of the Ghost, whom he regarded as his
father image and a villain—not with the affection which you have stated.

I hope you will forgive my bluntness in calling these things to your
attention but I am sure you, as an artist and a biographer, could not
wish a friend to be other than frank. The rest of the book is so very good
that I cannot refrain from an expression of an addition that might make
it that much finer. . . .

Pop worked at his gardening for a week, considering all that
time while digging and planting how he would answer this learned
doctor who had written three books on psychoanalysis. Finally,
on January 13, 1944, Pop sat down and spent an entire afternoon
putting together this answer. Unfortunately it is necessary because
of the libel laws that I drastically edit my father's reply. The answer,
in cautious part, follows:

It ordinarily is a sad, and, for an author, futile horseplay to try to
explain a published book. To attempt to add to or subtract from it now
would be rather like an accused surgeon telling the coroner why he had
amputated a healthy right leg when it was the left one that was gangrenous.

I wouldn't discuss my own recently born work with most persons,
partly because I am done with it, thank God! after nine months of precarious going. I am not like Lot's wife. Then, also, there are not many
Hymans to be met with on the pier after the ship has sailed and the
crowd has dispersed.

You have been good enough to read the book intelligently and comment upon it from the standpoint of an articulate practitioner. You
have also let yourself in for a long letter that you have not the time to
read, nor I the time to write with true clarity.

You must bear in mind that the project itself, from my standpoint at
least, was primarily reportorial, the only sphere perhaps in which I might
claim any eminence by nature or by training. Perhaps you will permit me
to postulate these two facts: I am neither a psychologist nor an expert
on the drama. In respect to the former, I have, of course, read more of
the authorities than the average layman; but, inasmuch as I am essentially a person of intuitions—with a slight dash of the creative impulse—
I always have deliberately sought to keep memory's filing cabinet free

of too much textual persuasion by the savants. Whenever I get deep, I get dull . . .

My views on psychoanalysis in general could not by any stretch of the imagination be regarded as more than the babblings of a layman. However, we have had occasional examples of laymen finding out certain facts without benefit of Krafft-Ebing or Professor Alonzo Doakes, Jr. I cannot dismiss my impression that a great deal of mental therapy has accomplished about the same sort of thing as does the psychoanalyst's couch. And before all of these, in point of chronology, the mind-over-matter Hymns of Aknaton of Egypt, who was described by Breasted as "the first individual in history," had their innings. I also believe that the age-old philosophies of the Hindus managed to achieve, and for a whole race, a serenity that offset neuroses. There is a whiff of plagiarism about Freud.

I think that, notwithstanding the brilliant pioneers among the P.A.'s, there are abroad many well-intentioned bunglers, as well as an army of burbling charlatans who have made a cult of what really should be a sound and beneficial science. There are too many dramatics practised in this cult, and too many "hams" with medical degrees in one hand and jingle bells in the other.

How . . . can I pontificate on the Œdipus Rex phase, when I have neither a diploma nor even a set of phonograph records containing the Freudian correspondence school course? How also can I, who seldom go to the theatre (except backstage to drink with my pals) present myself suddenly as a rival of the late Archbishop [Alexander] Woollcott? Except for a short season, during which I was assigned to sit in for Alan Dale while he was having his prostate removed, I probably have not been a member of a playhouse audience for more than 100 times in my life. (Yet I saw *seven* of Jack's *Hamlets*.) I have attended numerous rehearsals while a play was being created. I have sat with many playwrights while they were incubating. I have known numerous actors and actresses, not a few of them intimately. I even helped write a flop of a play. But the theatre itself seems to me so puny as against the hourly drama of life itself that for me at least it becomes an anticlimax. How can it be otherwise for one whose theatre has been the court room, the operating chamber, the Death House at Sing Sing? Selah.

The audience for the most part seems to me, the reporter and observer of the realities, a drooling, program-rattling, asinine mass of strangers who have paid a stud fee to enjoy a vicarious hump. True, I am interested in the better literature of the theatre, but largely as literature, just as I am interested in people of the theatre mainly as people.

. . . I brought into my narrative a gallery of expert witnesses. Just as an attorney for the defense does in a capital case.

. . . it was apparent that the incestuous motif [in *Hamlet*] was solidly lodged within the Barrymore *Hamlet*. Still, I ruled out his pre-play conferences with psychoanalysts. I had to do so for two principal reasons: first, all the competent testimony, gained at some pains by me, pointed to the fact that Margaret Carrington was his principal and only *real* adviser in regard to this role. And even she merely dispelled the smokescreen and opened the channel through which he moved into navigable waters and by virtue of his own intuitions and first-hand experience with situations.

You must remember that this man had one outstanding faculty—to make *anyone* to whom he spoke or *listened* feel that that person was the only one in his immediate confidence, the only one to be entrusted with the helm. I sensed this fact early in my long acquaintanceship with him. And he knew that I was wise to this artful dodge. He even made Einstein (believe it or not) think that he understood the broad elements of his theories, just as he made Dempsey think that he knew every nuance of pugilism. So, when any of your confreres tries to tell you that *he* shaped Jack's *Hamlet,* do not laugh too loudly, but please believe me, they are talking via the sphincter muscles.

As to his reported hatred of his father, I, as a layman, would not presume to debate that point with the scientists. Personally, I don't believe it. It may be argued that he hated his father because of a fear that his sire might have passed on to him a blood-taint, or bequeathed some other curse that promised eventual mental disintegration. It may be said that a hatred arose from the experience wherein Jack (and this is between physician and patient) was taken to bed by —— —— —— and given the works. These two "situations" are imbedded in the text, *if you look for them.*

There not only are libel courts, but there is a greater court, in which the biographer and friend must decide whether or not to hurt the living or degrade the dead. I had to make such a decision several times. For example, I chose to "let lie" the Thaw case (so often discussed in print, but never with the real, amazing background revealed) in which Thaw *shot the wrong man,* Stanford White.

As an indication of Lionel, the brother's sagacity and wealth of mind, I quote what he said to me while I was gathering material from him:

"Too bad we are not all dead; then you would be free to write a *real* story."

Jack concealed from me little if any of the tragic thread that was woven into the golden cloak of his genius. In fact, he was quite frank in discussing certain dark urges he had had, such startling revelations as I do not wish to discuss in a letter.

I eventually, as reporter, had the choice—even as a non-psychologist—of describing fully his affair with a woman who afterward became the wife of ——, and I assure you it is something that Dostoyevsky could have cast into a great novel. The employment of this grim saga would have made my book undoubtedly a sensational, and perhaps even a valuable case-history contribution; but it also would have crucified ——, a great person and my friend.

. . . A certain hesitation caused me to leave out many revealing anecdotes in which I myself participated. I am so God-damned weary of reading the works of glib exhibitionists, who put themselves in such a fine and important light at every turn, that I did not choose to be enshrined in that category.

Here is something that I left out, Harold, partly because I did not want my book barred from the libraries, nor did I want to destroy my protagonist's character utterly in the opaque and intolerant public mind. I think you will be interested in it, inasmuch as you are a connoisseur of Hamletiana. I also think it was one of the shrewdest questions ever asked by a reporter of an actor. I shall first state most of the queries I one day put to Jack in this regard, as nearly as I can record them, and then give you the gist of his answers, together with the one direct quote that I distinctly remember verbatim. My son, Will, was with me.

QUESTION: Do actors have a subconscious, or an unconscious, when they are on the stage reciting? By that I mean . . .

JACK: (*interrupting*): I know perfectly well what you mean, you inquisitive police reporter bastard! Does the actor think beyond the line he is saying? Does he have a mind within a mind, or rather a mind within another mind?

QUESTION: Yes, would Barrymore on the stage, when reciting, say, a Shakespearean line, at the same time think as Barrymore, as Shakespeare, or as *Hamlet*?

JACK: It all depends upon my mood during a particular performance. If I was "into" the part (which I was during the first weeks at least) I thought as *Hamlet*.

QUESTION: All right. Could you now, years afterward, re-create the subconscious flow of ideas, associations or back drop thoughts while you were declaiming in the presence of your stepfather, whose name escapes me?

JACK: Yes, I could, and, if you will wait until we have this can of beer, I shall do it. If the dear old schoolteachers who used to come to the Sam Harris theatre knew what was going through my mind while I was saying my lines, well, they would have run screaming into the street, either to escape what was going on, or to hunt a sailor.

QUESTION: Now give me, not *Hamlet* externally, or merely in a thespic Shakespearean scene, but repeat as nearly as you can *Hamlet's* stream of consciousness or unconsciousness, the associations of ideas, when in the presence of his stepfather on the stage.

JACK: It wasn't merely when I was in the presence of my stepfather. It was *most* of the time. The thing I like best was the second soliloquy, which closes with my determination to put on the play for the king. That is the soliloquy I remember best, and I can best remember what went through my mind while reciting it.

[Note: The circumstances and import of the above reconstructed conversation were perfectly clear in my father's mind, although the words were reassembled from his memory only. The conversation occurred at a sanitarium in West Los Angeles in 1937 when Pop and I visited Jack. It was a time when Barrymore was having his first marital troubles with his fourth wife, Elaine Barrie. He was drinking only one or two cans of beer at most a day. The first line of the following answer is verbatim, and Pop put that part in quotes.]

JACK: That dirty, red-whiskered son-of-a-bitch! That bastard puts his —— in my mother's —— every night!

Now in like language, he held forth for perhaps two minutes on his own (——— — — ——— —— —— — —— —— — —— ——— ———). The language was obscene, yet one began to forget its actual filth as against the powerful and unique performance.

Pop's letter continues:

I think I saw beyond the shattering violence of these words, and, with a reporter's intuition, found at least part of an answer that satisfied my frequent curiosity as to the subordinated thoughts of actors while speaking their lines.

All this may, I concede, substantiate your position that Jack hated his ——. It may well be that his stage stepfather was a symbol that replaced a symbol, and that he had had similar thoughts about —— when —— was alive . . .

. . . I, as a reporter, cannot go beyond this. If I had the answer to "What made Barrymore 'tick'? or his *Hamlet* 'live'?" I also could tell you what sleep is, and what electricity is.

. . . He thought that he had come most fully into the character-mind of *Richard, III*. He himself placed *Hamlet* second, not only as to the quality of performance, but also as to the amount of subconscious surges experienced during the rendition. Indeed, he added, he was "more of Richard than of any other character" he ever played. I do not agree with this, of course, nor indeed may you. Perhaps he was so closely akin to *Hamlet,* by force of circumstance and mental similitude, that the naturalness (to him) of the part outweighed the conscious striving he had exercised in preparing for his short-lived Richard.

He said that, not only did he think as Richard when on-stage, but even off-stage, and also had dreams pertaining to Richard rather than to Barrymore. Suppose you wrestle with that one. I am out of hammerlocks.

I must say, as a rambling addenda, that while Jack was giving the private *Hamlet* second soliloquy, translated by him into obscene and ghastly, incestuous terms, it became a most startling and compelling performance. The man's whole manner changed. He seemed to be staggering beneath the reality of an unholy burden. He revealed to his listeners the hidden urges. I must admit that I at once had recourse to a double whiskey (which I refused to share with Barrymore, a fact that caused him to denounce me for "coming in on a pass and occupying an aisle seat under false pretenses").

Dr. Hyman's immediate reply was:

I have never been more highly complimented than by your extraordinary letter of recent date. Were it not so highly personal, I should return it to you and ask you to publish it. It is a document that unites the combination of integrity and facility of expression which you possess as a person and as an artist, though you will probably smile at my use of the term.

I am so completely persuaded that you are right about the Barrymore matter and I am wrong that I am now, in retrospect, somewhat awed at my audacity in presuming to express *any* opinion to you.

I shall indeed look forward to spending some time with you when you arrive in town. I would like very much for you to read the Chapter I have written on Psychiatry . . . I think you will find that our experiences and opinions have been very strikingly parallel. If you are not coming soon, I will mail the manuscript to you. . . .

The publication of the Barrymore book also had its humorous aspects. "With the exception," Pop told me, "that I paid our actor friend's former personal secretary and business manager, Henry Hotchner, $20,000 cash for the use of a sea log Jack kept while aboard his yacht and pining for Dolores Costello. Also, for the record, I assigned twenty-five per cent of the book's profit to Hotchner. But then, I'm just a crazy artist."

Shortly after the book had passed the quarter-of-a-million sales mark, a letter appeared in a Denver *Rocky Mountain News* column. It was addressed to that paper's Molly Mayfield, asking for Pop's address. It read in part:

. . . My husband was somewhat of a playboy before we married, but during the last 25 years has become a stalwart citizen . . . I guess if you chose one word to describe him it would be "conservative." That is WOULD HAVE BEEN. He read Mr. Fowler's book and the anecdotes about John Barrymore delighted him so that he said one night, "You know, honey, I've just been wasting my time! I used to be full of fun and frolic, but look, I've gotten old before my time!"

. . . Since then he's done everything he could think of to out-Barrymore Barrymore—except annex an Elaine. The other evening when we were night clubbing, my husband reached over and up and snapped a waitress' garter and she let out a yelp that brought the manager and if it wasn't for my husband's hitherto sterling name we would have been evicted . . .

I don't believe he will be able to emulate the late Mr. Barrymore in his drinking habits—but he did try. That was a week ago. We played bridge with some friends, and when we finished, our host suggested a night cap and brought the bottle and glasses out.

My husband said, "May I pour my own?" Well, he poured his own, three-quarters of a glass full, then took the jigger and measured out a jigger-full of soda water. Then he was all-of-a-sudden ill. And this humiliated him.

Well, I've only listed one or two incidents, Mr. Fowler, but, believe me, I would like you to meet my husband and see the results of your handiwork. If Mrs. Mayfield will publish this and thereby act as a go-between, I will be grateful. I also have hopes that when my husband reads this, or hears of it, he will see himself as others see him and not as you saw Barrymore.

Fed-Up Wife

The latter part of a letter my father addressed to Molly Mayfield, which was ensconced in a special box atop a page in the *Rocky Mountain News,* gave solace to the Fed-Up Wife:

Many persons have imitated the late Mr. Barrymore, both in a professional and personal sense. The results usually have been futile and-or disastrous.

Mr. B's fellow actors have assumed his nasal overtones, his grimaces, his rolling consonants, his steamboat engine penultimates, and only a caricature was born. Again, in reference to emulation of personal whimsies, his victims have taken to the bottle and the moonlit rendezvous and found themselves soon thereafter in police cars en route to the iron pergola or, at times, receiving the knuckles of a husband or lover on the chin.

I believe that Fed-Up Wife's mate merely is undergoing a passing phase of lunacy that seems to attack us males as we come cheek-by-jowl with middle-age. We gentlemen apparently have two times in life that must be weathered adroitly. When we are 15 or 16 we are balmy and jittery. When we come to 50 . . . well, the best thing for us to do (we males) is to pretend that we are on our death-beds, and make believe that everyone must tip-toe about and converse with us in discreet whispers.

My dear Fed-Up Wife, please pay no attention to the whoopings and bellowings and prancings and curvettings of your stimulated husband. He will trip over his own didoes. Then you will be able to toss a riata about his aging ankles, throw him for keeps, brand him, and he will be a better though sadder male.

Of course, let us not overlook the possibility that we have here another potential Hamlet. If so, don't hesitate to shoot him on sight. Yours truly, Gene Fowler.

In addition to *Good Night, Sweet Prince,* Pop had written another, more clandestine work inspired by Barrymore.

During his last days at the studios, Barrymore confessed that he had given all he could offer to the movies, adding unhappily that since he left the stage, "I am still a ham. But I am not about to be accepted as a dying cinema hero at this time. Let us go out and have a bit of the cup, and I shall listen to *you* for a change."

Crowded into a corner booth at Bob Cobb's Hollywood Brown Derby restaurant with Barrymore, Pop called for paper and pencil.

"It was late afternoon, just before the supper crowd was to arrive," Pop told me. "I was well into the mood to write a poem about what Jack and I knew he would eventually become: a dying ham. His line memorizing had been effected. Just one simple scene that day. There were forty-three takes and it was still not right. Finally Jack asked that someone print the principal lines on a blackboard and hold it up so he might read it on the sly. 'An idiot board,' Jack called it. Today the idiot board is an integral part of the television acting profession. Barrymore was its inventor."

As Barrymore brooded and sipped his whiskey sour, Pop started to write. Bob Cobb joined them. Barrymore interrupted at intervals. Pop stopped his writing and looked up at Jack with a benevolent glance, then went on. Within fifteen minutes, Pop had completed this poem, which heretofore has been unpublished, excepting for an enormous mimeograph circulation.

TESTAMENT OF A DYING HAM

On the eve of his self-immolation—
By means of a rafter and strand—
A Hollywood mime of a happier time
Wrote his will with a resolute hand.

To the fair-weather leeches who bled me,
Who helped me to scatter and spend,
Who flattered and licked me, but soon enough kicked me,
Who fleeced me while calling me friend . . .

To the wenches who trumped up a passion
And held a first lien on my cot,
To the simpering starlets and gleet-ridden harlots
Whose sables were masking their rot . . .

To the preeners who haunt drab parties,
To the crackpots in snobbish undress,
To those bogus upstarters who flip off their garters
To pay for a puff in the Press . . .

To those impotent, credit-mad authors,
Whose skulls with manure are be-crammed,
To those clap-trap extollers and stinking log-rollers
Who mince in the waltz of the damned . . .

To the venomous merchants of slander—
A conclave of pandering gnomes—
Whose seedy portmanteaus are bulging with cantos,
To poison the air of your homes . . .

To the parasite rabble of agents,
Who nibble like rats at the yield,
To those scavenging cravens, the ten-percent ravens,
Who croak o'er a gilt battlefield . . .

To the poseurs who simulate talent—
The nances, the Lesbian corps,
The cultists, the fadists, the blustering sadists,
The slime of the celluloid shore . . .

To the mountebank clan of producers,
Who hang their dull stars in the skies,
Who rifle the pockets and gouge the eye-sockets,
But never look higher than thighs . . .

Witness:

I leave them the curse of the dying;
I leave them their own fetid crowd;
I leave them the voices of midnight;
I leave them the hope of a shroud:
I leave them the groans of the fallen;
I leave them the culture of swine . . .
All this, but another—bear witness, good brother—
I leave them the fate that was mine.

Chapter Seventeen

I AM A BETRAYED HOBBYHORSE.

GENE FOWLER

There may have been certain drawbacks to being born a child of Agnes and Gene Fowler, such as shuttling between the coasts and getting accustomed to new schools, but it was never dull inside the family circle. A boy who has Jack Barrymore as his friend and confidant and W. C. Fields as his capricious Uncle Claude is not likely to think of home as "the last place to go." It may seem that Barrymore and Fields, as two of the most notorious roisterers of their era, were a little sophisticated as playfellows for a growing boy, but my parents never considered their influence harmful. Nor do I. I could only wish two such kindly friends of the family were available for my own children.

One thing Barrymore and Fields had in common, aside from their partiality to alcoholic beverages, was particularly enchanting from a child's point of view. They never talked down. Both of them wrote or spoke to me as if I were their equal in age and experience.

On the screen, W. C. Fields, demonstrating the misanthropy which he raised to a comic art, pretended to dislike children. In one classic scene, which he played with more than usual relish, he was permitted to kick one of the reigning child stars of the day, Baby LeRoy, a comeuppance he maneuvered so adroitly that audiences actually cheered when they should have been shouting for the Society for the Prevention of Cruelty to Children.

To the Fowler children, Uncle Claude, as we called him, never

15. The desk upon which Pop wrote, in longhand, *Salute to Yesterday*, *Illusion in Java*, *Good Night Sweet Prince*, *A Solo in Tom-Toms*, and *Beau James*. He surrounded himself with mementos such as the John Barrymore *Richard III* sword, a New York Giants' baseball jacket presented to him by John McGraw, John Decker self-portrait and even a Norden bombsight (atop the elephant's foot).

Photo by Will Fowler

16. Westbrook Pegler (right) poses in his Tucson, Arizona, ranch home with Pop (second from left) the day "Peg" blasted Pop in his nationally syndicated column for "going too easy" on the character of New York's mayor, Jimmy Walker, in Pop's book *Beau James*. My brother, Gene, Jr., stands at the left. Peg's late wife, Julie, is seated between Pop and Peg. In spite of the Pegler blast, which was printed internationally, Pop first told Time, Inc. reporter Jim Murray: "My friendship with Peg has nothing to do with what he prints about my work."

Photo by Reginald Russell

17. Comedian Joe E. Lewis (third from left) said he wished he had the "stand up come-backs" Gene Fowler was able to cotton out of left field. Mother is at the left, holding on to Pop's arm. At far right and taking up most of the picture is Pop's long-time friend, restaurateur Bernard "Toots" Shor. "Toots" was like a kid of mine," Pop told me. "Maybe that's why I dedicated the Durante book to this guy who never seems to overlook a friend in need." *Photo by Bill Mark*

18. Comedian Red Skelton poses, cross-eyed, with Fowler in the latter's Brentwood, California, workroom. It is 1945, two years after Skelton adopted Pop as a sort of Father Confessor. *Photo by Will Fowler*

19. Pop and restaurateur Dave Chasen look over W. C. Fields' racing form card at the track in Tijuana, Mexico, in 1946. The following day, Uncle Claude's nose exploded because of too much exposure to the sun while deep-sea fishing. It was one year before his death. Pop was the only writer he truly respected and even adored. I was the only child he ever liked because, at age eleven, I drank martinis. In this photo Fields raises his eyes to Heaven for a winner.

20. Non-extant portrait of Gene Fowler by artist John Decker. Because Mother disliked this picture she had it destroyed in 1942. Over it was painted a snow scene.

21. A study of the Fowler laugh. It was 1950 when Pop was writing the Jimmy Durante (right) biography, *Schnozzola*. The two are sunning themselves in Durante's Beverly Hills patio.

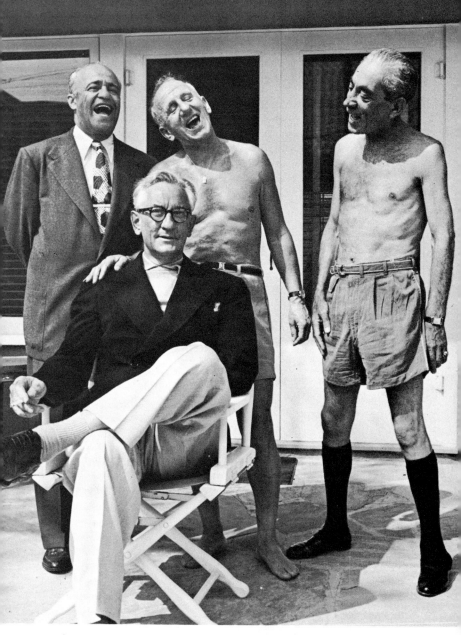

22. The names: Clayton, Jackson, and Durante, were the biggest during speakeasy days. Now here are these three, photographed by Johnny Florea, in 1950, as they sing the praises of Fowler (seated). From left to right standing are Eddie Jackson, Durante, and Lou Clayton, shortly before Clayton's death.

23. Here is Pop with the Dean of all sports writers, Grantland Rice (left),
Director Gregory La Cava, next, and Pop's adopted son, Richard "Red" Skel-
ton. It was 1953. Note the John Barrymore deathbed sketch above them, by
John Decker.

24. Last portrait taken of Gene Fowler in his workroom. It was 1959, the author was sixty-nine and working on his last published (yet unfinished) book *Skyline*. *Photo by Frank A. Brown*

25. June 1960. Last picture ever to be taken of Gene Fowler. He sits by his fish pond, holding his seventh grandchild, my daughter Jenny. I took this picture just five days before Pop's death.

unleashed his waspish temper. Not that Fields was stickily sentimental. One night a young man called at his house claiming to be his long lost son. Fields bolted down the rest of a martini in his glass and roared at his butler, "Give the young man an evasive answer. Tell him to go —— himself!"

I don't know just how Fields rated among my father's friends. I once asked Pop who his best friend was, and he replied, "It might be the time, or the day. It might be the one I am thinking of or writing to. It may be the one I am with." But I know Uncle Claude rated very high.

He and Pop delighted in exchanging press clippings telling of various untoward events, generally those which appealed to their sardonic, and occasionally morbid humor.

One note from Uncle Claude to Pop began, "I am enclosing a copy of Ciba Symposia. The Siamese twins on the front page of enclosed who have been so successful both here and in Europe have decided to split. I heard the left one said to the other a few nights ago at Murphy's, 'You go your way and I'll go mine.' I think it is a shame as they have been very close for so many years." The letter ended with, "I hope Charlie Chaplin's picture is as bad as the critics say it is . . . *Yours for fair play and justice. . . .*"

Another enclosure to Pop contained only a clip from a Hollywood trade paper. The headline, telling of the possibility of 20th Century-Fox Studios handling some of English producer J. Arthur Rank's products read, *20TH WILL HANDLE SOME RANK FILMS.*

Uncle Claude also sent a cartoon cut from Robert Ripley's daily newspaper feature. It displayed a cross-legged tot smoking a huge cigar. The caption read: "Baby Carl Yenson, Age 2, Smokes 10 Cigars a Day . . ." Under this, Fields penned to Pop: "Dear Nephew: Those kids of yours are just sissies. Love, Uncle. . . ." The meaning of this jibe may be deduced from this passage in Robert Lewis Taylor's *W. C. Fields:*

. . . Fields threw his best literary effort into his letter writing, which was marked by . . . majestic hyperbole . . . "Dear Dago," he usually addressed missives to Gregory La Cava, and in one of them, in 1937, he spoke of dining with Fowler and his "unholy family." Fowler's youngest

son, Will, Fields said, smoked black cigars and drank whiskey until it
ran out of his ears. His daughter, Jane, chewed tobacco, and spit tobacco juice on Fields' clean shirt front, and the elder son, Gene, "tried
to roll me for my poke."

Pop and I visited Uncle Claude at his De Mille Drive home the
day of his release from a hospital. His enforced rest there was the
result of a broken neck. While walking downstairs with a martini
glass balanced on his forehead, he had slipped and tumbled the
rest of the way. During his stay in the hospital, he refused a neck
cast and lay motionless on a lead pillow for the weeks it took the
fracture to heal. Home once again, and overjoyed to have Pop as
his first visitor, he demonstrated just how he had been injured. At
the top of the stairs, he placed a filled martini glass on his forehead
once again as Pop pleaded with him not to tempt fate a second
time. At this, Uncle Claude superbly navigated his descent. At the
bottom of the stairs, he reached up for the glass and tripped over
an Oriental throw rug, again fracturing his neck. This time he was
fitted with a brace, but refused to return to the hospital.

Fields would rarely arise before 10 A.M. He made an exception
to this rule on New Year's Day, when he traveled in a large automobile trailer to the Rose Bowl football game with a select group
of friends. For these occasions, he would meet us all in his front
yard long before sunrise, having stayed awake all night, batting golf
balls off into the dark from his lawn.

On one New Year's Day before dawn, La Cava, Leo McCarey,
Fields' trainer Bob Howard, Pop, and I discovered the comedian
clenching a half-drained martini glass in one hand and gripping a
golf club in the other. Whenever irate, Uncle Claude would speak
with exaggerated slowness, chewing each syllable. "Those dratted
. . . canines . . . The interlopers . . . I'll have a bill . . . placed
in the . . . State Senate . . . banishing the four . . . legged beasts
from Southern California. . . ."

"Don't you believe," asked Pop, "your rantings are unfounded
regarding man's best friend?"

"Best friend, hah!" said Fields. "Look at what one did to my
new bed of pansies!" In what was left of the moonlight, Pop could
see that the pansy bed had been uprooted. (Uncle Claude was an

ardent lover of flowers, and spent much of his time planting and pruning.) "Drat . . . *drat!* I hate all forms of dogs!"

"But why?" asked Pop.

"Why?" Fields rejoined, "because they lift their legs on flowers!"

The Covici-Friede firm had been dissolved when Bennett Cerf convinced Pop he should publish *Salute to Yesterday* with Random House. Inside the front leaf was printed the following quotation:

In the aging heart there resounds the echo of far-off romance. Eyes tired with life see once again the sweet, green fields of youth. Within the parenthesis of a dream, youth and love are everlasting. Before the night's long sleep, there comes an illusion in autumn.

The signature below was that of Pop's father, Charles Francis Devlan. Pop had really written these few lines himself, but the quotation was a tribute to his father, who had died shortly before publication of *Salute to Yesterday*.

I acquired respect for what we today call extrasensory perception. One night in 1937, shortly after Pop had sent in his final draft of this book, he awakened from a nightmare. He walked downstairs to the kitchen for a glass of milk and some soda crackers. Being a light sleeper, I was awakened by his outcry. I looked at my clock, then got up to follow him to ask, "What's the matter?"

"My father just died," he said.

Pop had neither visited nor corresponded with his father, who was living in Denver with his second wife, for several years.

Three hours later, I answered the front door to sign for a telegram. Pop reappeared to read the wire which informed him that his father had just died. Calculating the hour of death by Rocky Mountain Time, we judged that the wire had been filed just a few minutes after Pop had awakened from his nightmare.

Pop dedicated *Salute to Yesterday*, the story of a newspaper's mining editor, to Random House senior editor, the late Saxe Commins. When Uncle Claude read the book, he sent Pop a wire reserving the main character, Captain James Job Trolley, for himself in the movie version.

Salute to Yesterday was acclaimed by the critics as one of Fowler's finest works, but the book-buying public thought otherwise. It remained on the best-seller list only three weeks, then disappeared. It was retitled *Onward Trolley* in England, however, and achieved a fair success.

During this time, Pop was difficult to live with. He complained he had spent too much time on this work, the first draft of which he wrote in holograph. For the first time, he had discarded his typewriter. He told me later that "When I write in longhand, I feel closer to my work. When I type, my thoughts sometimes seem to go ahead of what I am putting down. But using the pen, I am able to keep mind and hand pretty well together."

Now Pop decided to write a historical novel, the subject of which had to do with the feuds of Wyoming cattle and sheep herders. He shot a telegram to his rodeo-promoting friend T. Joe Cahill, asking if Cahill might find him lodgings in Cheyenne while he made notes for this book he planned to call *Powder River*. He added in his wire to Sheriff Cahill: . . . AND THIS TIME I REFUSE A JAIL CELL.

His research done, Pop returned to Beverly Hills and completed the first draft of *Powder River* in nine weeks. Mother had an itinerary made out for an extended Matson Line cruise of the Orient, during which Pop planned to put the finishing touches on his book. As a reward for Gene's high school graduation, he, too, would accompany them.

During the second day at sea, when Pop wearied of rewriting, he sauntered to the ship's library to pick out an Erle Stanley Gardner mystery. Rummaging through the limited collection, Pop was taken aback to discover a volume titled *Powder River*. He pulled it from the shelf and thumbed through the pages. It was a story about the cattle and sheep herder feuds in Wyoming. He replaced the book, went to the stateroom, and tossed his entire manuscript and notes through an open porthole.

While on the voyage, Gene met a girl who was returning to her home in Australia. Her name was Jane Siebert. The two fell in love, and this kept Pop's mind off having given his nearly completed book "the deep six."

After landing in Tokyo, a Japanese official asked Pop why he was taking this trip. Pop answered: "I am writing a novel about Java." All at once he thought that this *was* a good idea. He had spent two days in Java already, and would be returning for another day in that country before sailing home.

On their return trip, the ship's newspaper reported that a hurricane had "ripped the length of Fire Island, New York, sweeping scores of houses out to sea." Pop sent his mother-in-law a wireless. In Beverly Hills at the time, Mumsie had already received a telegram from Mrs. Nate Woodhull that our house had remained in good condition. In her usual frugal way, especially after learning of the high wireless rates, Mumsie sent back the message: ONE WINDOW PANE BROKEN.

On their return to California, Pop had Mother purchase a four-unit apartment house south of Olympic Boulevard in Beverly Hills. "We must economize while I write this book," he said. One apartment was too small for a family accustomed to spaciousness. A fifth unit was then constructed over the garage for Gene and myself.

Pop attacked several legal-sized yellow-lined paper notebooks with his Parker pen as Gene sent streams of love letters to his girl in Australia. Miss Siebert eventually traveled across the Pacific and their wedding occurred shortly after Pop completed his book, which he named *Illusion in Java*.

This book tells the story of a youthful musical genius living in a small village. His name is Ajax, and he plays the bonan in the community gamalon. Although another critically acclaimed success, and a book-selling failure, the publication of *Illusion in Java* brought a letter from Pulitzer Prize Poet Robert Silliman Hillyer, then Professor of English at Harvard University. Hillyer informed Pop that this book was now his prime selection for the teaching of the novel in his classes.

When 1939 came around, Myron Selznick had a contract drawn under which Pop would perform a "doctoring job" on a script Metro-Goldwyn-Mayer was unable to have brought to a satisfactory conclusion by its salaried writers.

"Why stick me with this kind of assignment?" Pop asked Myron.

"You're the only one who can pull the story out of the ash heap," said the agent. "Anyway, I'm setting a precedent . . . $5000 a week. No Hollywood writer has ever been paid this much. No one in the world!"

"One condition," Pop insisted.

"What's that?" asked Myron.

"That I am paid $1000 at the end of each working day."

"What's this all about?"

"I wish to be considered as a day laborer," said Pop.

Pop was paid $1000 at the end of each working day for a period of one year. When he felt Fire Island calling, he was given a stag party by Selznick at which time he was presented a two-foot-high silver loving cup for "sticking to the job without once getting into serious trouble with studio executives."

Accepting the trophy, Pop stated that he *did* get into trouble just once. "I was called up to Mr. ——'s office one day after having inserted a limerick referring to this executive in a suggestion box. I entered Mr. ——'s plush office and refused a seat. I just stood and listened to the tirade. Then, when I thought I had heard enough, I turned to leave. 'Mr. ——,' I said, 'when I entered this office, I noticed the shoes of Irving Thalberg [the late production genius of M-G-M] just outside . . . Do you know they have not been filled as yet?'"

On his trophy was engraved a lengthy Latin phrase sprinkled with English words. Being a Latin scholar, Pop surprised his friends with the translation: *"For meritoriously being listed by the Department of Internal Revenue as the tenth highest salaried worker in the United States . . ."*

Pop earned a quarter of a million dollars that year . . . at the day laborer's daily rate of $1000.

Before the party broke up, Pop asked Metro executive Edward J. Mannix, "Eddie, why did you keep me on so long just doctoring scripts?"

"Because," said Mannix, "this was the most valuable task you could have performed for us. Most any gink can write himself into trouble, but it takes a craftsman like you to fight the thing out of a corner. You actually saved us a couple of million dollars."

About this time a controversy erupted in several magazines over whether or not the notorious outlaw of the West, William H. (Billy the Kid) Bonney, was left-handed. What caused the controversy was this:

In 1939, Pop wrote *Billy the Kid* as a vehicle for Robert Taylor. During the writing stages of the picture, after Taylor had been assigned to play the title role, the actor tried his best to master the "quick draw." The dejected Taylor gave up and came to Pop with his problem. "Gene," he said, "I just can't seem to draw a gun worth a damn this way."

"What way?" asked Pop.

"Right-handed," complained Taylor. "You see, I'm *left-handed*."

"Then let's create a legend, say Billy the Kid *was* left-handed. When Pat Garrett kills you in the picture, we'll have you attempting to draw with your *right hand* . . . And thanks for a good ending, Bob."

Pop handed Mannix a poem. "I wrote this on company time," he said. "That Bob Taylor picture inspired the story I really wanted to write. It has a whiff of a Robert W. Service style, but this is how I meant it."

Mannix took the paper and read the finest poem my father had ever written, *The Cowboy's Lament,* to which Pop signed his favorite alias, Ned Gimp:

THE COWBOY'S LAMENT

> Don't call the cops, Bartender,
> Or strike me with you fist.
> I'll pay you for my whiskey when I can.
> First listen to my story,
> Then ring if you insist—
> Oh! God damn old Bessie Bond, the courtesan!

> Oh! Bessie Bond, the shameless courtesan.
> She's been the death of many a healthy man.
> She demands the biggest fees, sir,
> Then spreads the French disease, sir.
> Oh! God damn old Bessie Bond, the courtesan!

> I was but a country bumpkin
> When I rode the prairie trail.
> My tutor was a cowboy, Dirty Dan.

He lured me to the city
Where he found some love for sale—
Oh!   God damn old Bessie Bond, the courtesan!

Oh!   Bessie Bond, the smirking courtesan.
To ruin country lads is just her plan.
She pets them like a mother,
Then does that dreadful other—
Oh!   God damn old Bessie Bond, the courtesan!

Ah, how I rue the moment
When upon my boyish cheek
I felt the perfumed tickle of her fan.
I thought that she was playing—
(Till my leg fell off next week)—
Oh!   God damn old Bessie Bond, the courtesan!

Oh!   Bessie Bond, the vicious courtesan.
T'was she who wrecked the noble Ku-Klux Klan.
Each Knight who flipped her garter
Became a crippled martyr—
Oh!   God damn old Bessie Bond, the courtesan!

I had no one near to warn me—
I was innocent and proud—
The perfect tool for such as Dirty Dan.
He led me into pastures
Where the fields with sin are ploughed—
Oh!   God damn old Bessie Bond, the courtesan!

Oh!   Bessie Bond, the vengeful courtesan.
Her doctor is a downright charlatan.
He made of me a cynic
As I crumpled in his clinic—
Oh!   God damn old Bessie Bond, the courtesan!

My other leg has withered;
And my arms went down the drain.
My ears now look like mildewed flakes of bran.

> My sinuses are lacking,
> And I've soft'ning of the brain—
> Oh! God damn old Bessie Bond the courtesan!

> Oh! Bessie Bond, the hateful courtesan!
> I wish she'd thought to take some Salvarsan.
> For, once you're in her clutches,
> You're bound for slings and crutches—
> Oh! God damn old Bessie Bond, the courtesan!

> There's not much left, Bartender,
> As you can plainly see,
> Of what was once the semblance of a man.
> Don't telegraph Headquarters,
> But dig a grave for me—
> Oh! God damn old Bessie Bond, the courtesan!

> Oh! Bessie Bond, the spiteful courtesan.
> Inter me in the ground near Dirty Dan,
> And carve upon some stones, sir,
> To mark my tragic bones, sir:
> Oh! God damn old Bessie Bond, The courtesan!

It was difficult to predict where any member of the Fowler family might be any given week.

The Beverly Hills High School band and orchestra had just won the national gold medal at the San Francisco World's Fair under the baton of George W. Wright. I came in second with my tuba solo, playing *The Flight of the Bumble Bee*. I know I missed out on first place because my girl friend was present and to impress her, I played the last passages of my solo triple fortissimo instead of the directed pianissimo.

Gene was now a film editor at 20th Century-Fox, and was living with his bride at the Beverly Hills apartment, although Pop had sold the place.

Mother and Jane were stopping off in London on a tour which was to be cut short because of the outbreak of World War II. Jane later enrolled at National Park College in Washington, D.C.

Pop was alone in the Seaview house. He was resting, and it

would be four years before he would publish another book. He was lazy when he had money.

After returning from the San Francisco Fair, my grandmother and I took an apartment in Beverly Hills. It had been planned that we would stay on there until a piano composition I had written was broadcast on the CBS radio network by Lud Gluskin and his orchestra. Later, with the specific aid of composer Harry Revel, this piece was put out by Jack Robbins, a leading musical publishing firm of the time.

I dreamed of Fire Island, and felt left out because I had not been asked to join Pop there.

Finally I received a telegram which read:

DARLING SON. YOU HAVE BEEN SUCH A FINE SPORT AND SUCH A GREAT GUY THAT I CAN'T BE WITHOUT YOU ANY LONGER. I WANT YOU AND MUMSIE TO COME TO FIRE ISLAND AS SOON AS CONVENIENT.

Film editor Al McNeil came along with us, but was thrown off his feed when he discovered that the colored lady cook Pop had engaged was a professional embalmer.

Mother was worried about gathering war clouds, but wrote little of it in her letters to Pop. She was a natural gossip columnist, and could have run a close second to the old pro, Louella Parsons, who once worked for Pop on the *American*. In one of her letters aboard ship, Mother wrote:

Tomorrow evening Jane is playing "straight" for a cowboy rope thrower. Believe it or not, he is "ze" Frenchman, about 28 or 30 . . . Yes! There is a *queen*. She is Peggy ——, a model for *Vogue* and *Harpers* magazines, and I think the "blues singer" from the Troc in Hollywood. She has the men drooling. There are always about ten with her every hour of the day, and maybe night, too . . . The women have a disdain for her . . . The Turkish gentleman who is on the make for Jane (and he is as old as you and I, and has three grown children) refuses to visit Second Class with us . . .

Next day:

Jane and I had breakfast in bed. She decided not to be a stooge for the French rope thrower. She passed the buck to me. She is always a little bewildered at the actions of men . . . Jane met a very nice chap today. He is a dancer. His lady partner is with him. They have been dancing at the Waldorf, and now are going to London . . . A nice old gentleman, about 65, noticed Jane in her Chinese dress. He said she was beautiful, and that he was a painter, eventually traveling to Pasadena to paint a rich lady's portrait. He is from Belgium. He wants to paint Jane on the boat, but I think he better wait. Maybe he's not 65. He acts like a clumsy 25 . . . We still have some of your flowers. I guess flowers keep better at sea than any place else . . . Goodbye, and thanks for a grand trip. I love you so much. . . .

Shortly thereafter, Pop received a cablegram from Mother:

CANCELLED PARIS TRIP. SAILING SOON AS ACCOMMODATIONS AVAILABLE. WILL ADVISE. CONTACTED AMERICAN CONSUL. MEANTIME SAFE. DON'T WORRY. LOVE. AGNES

Except for Gene, who was still working in Hollywood, the family was together at Fire Island when the news came over the radio that England was at war with Germany.

"Look around our home, children," said Pop. "This is the beginning of the end of expensive times. Thank God we've had a good time together. We've seen much of the world, and more, we've been happy." Shortly thereafter, we returned to Los Angeles.

On October 4, Uncle Claude wrote my sister a letter:

Some months ago I met your drunken father in a beer parlor where I had gone to hear the results of the baseball game. He informed me that you had married. I was stunned . . . Knowing you as a smart girl, I could not understand how you could let me slip through your fingers. I had bought you a mink coat and a string of black Romanoff pearls as an engagement present.

Last night I again met your Da-da and was he ga-ga! I checked up again with him and I find it is your brother Gene that has married. This is all too late for I have given the mink coat and the pearls and the cabochon ruby to a titled Ethiopian lady in appreciation for her assisting my chauffeur in washing the cars. I might add that I also had purchased for you some Royal Catherine of Aragon cigars and 80 pounds of Jolly Tar Chewing Tobacco. When you next return to our Hollywood, what about a little swing-around—a day with the bangtails, lunch in the stand, dinner at Dave Chasens and after that, a trip through Chinatown?

An old-fashioned hug, a hearty hand-clasp, and my warmest love. From Mid-Fields, The Cinema Thespian!

Pop had a talent for shutting his children up while we were in the middle of a noisy discussion. He would demand in stentorian tones, "Hold that thought for a minute," then go on to make his own point.

This occurred one night in Chasen's upstairs banquet room. Pop had yelled at Jane and me twice. I was trying to get to the piano to entertain the guests. We shut up when Leo McCarey, the director of *Going My Way* and other cinema hits, got to the keyboard first. McCarey taught Pop the lyric to one of his songs, and we sang it through many times. Then Leo went on in his classic style to entertain all, including an impeccably dressed gentleman with smooth black hair. Exhausting his repertoire, Leo backed away from the piano and said, "That's all."

Now the dapper gentleman sat down at the piano, using Pop's words, "Hold that thought for a minute," and added, "Two hours listened to, and two hours I shall play." He did just that, and in superb style. He glided from Manuel de Falla's exotic *Fire Dance Ritual* to several Chopin etudes, nocturnes, and waltzes, then topped his concert off with Liszt's *St. Francis Walking on the Water,* an exhaustive composition which seemed to leave the pianoforte in want of repair. When he stood up, two hours later, to receive a cooling highball, he introduced himself around as a party crasher.

"I heard the piano upstairs," he said, "and I just couldn't resist coming up to listen." Perspiring but happy, José Iturbi departed as quietly as he had entered.

Pop and McCarey took over the entire first floor of the Writer's Building at RKO Studios about this time. I recently visited this workhouse, which is now Desilu Studios, as the guest of Ken Morgan, publicity director of that studio. Never return to the scene, I thought. The offices were now cut up into cubicles, destroying the splendor of years gone by.

McCarey had purchased a new Lincoln Zephyr which was guaranteed to travel one hundred miles an hour. He and Pop traveled in this bomb for a weekend at McCarey's Lake Arrowhead retreat in order to polish their latest script, which was intended to pour scorn on Hitler and his gang. When they thought they had the story in nearly complete form, they departed for Hollywood.

Leo was testing the Zephyr's speed on a long, straight stretch when Pop cried out, "There's a cow on that narrow bridge!"

The two crossed their arms, shielding their faces. A few seconds later, they found they had somehow negotiated the bridge. Pop looked back. The cow was still peacefully chewing its cud.

Still doing ninety this time, Leo suddenly saw a car pull out of a side road. It was too late to brake down. He swerved the car, which catapulted from the highway, elevated some twelve feet above an orange grove. There was a crash, the sound of tearing metal, then silence. McCarey fortunately had the presence of mind to turn off the ignition just before the grinding impact. Passersby called an ambulance.

"I woke up," Pop told me later, "with my face down in a puddle of mud. I thought my clothes had been torn from me. My back was burning, and I thought I had been on fire. I heard some voices." As he was lifted into an automobile, he whispered, "There's another man. Find him and tell him I'm all right." He passed out.

When he came to for a fleeting second, Pop observed that he was stretched out on a litter. He heard a voice say, "We thought you were dead. You're in a hearse, but don't let that worry you."

"Worry me, hell!" exclaimed Pop. "Give me a cigarette."

"You can't have a cigarette," said the voice. "You're drenched in gasoline."

McCarey lay in critical condition at a nearby rural hospital while Pop was removed to Good Samaritan, in Los Angeles, where he immediately wired his agent Myron Selznick:

HAVE BEEN IN DREADFUL ACCIDENT. SHATTERED GLASS. PLEASE TAKE TEN PERCENT OF MY CUTS.

W. C. Fields was the first to send a telegram:

GOOD PUBLICITY, YES, BUT DON'T YOU THINK YOU WERE TAKING AN AWFUL CHANCE? ONCE OVER WOULD HAVE BEEN ENOUGH. BUT WHY THREE TIMES? THINK OF YOUR MRS. AND THE NIPPERS. I LIKE THE PART WHERE YOU SAID "TAKE CARE OF LEO, I AM ALL RIGHT," AND HE REPEATED VERBATIM WORDS. WAS THAT AN ECHO? COME CLEAN. I AM OFFERED $5,000 FROM SATURDAY EVENING POST TO EXPOSE THIS HOAX . . . YOUR DEAREST UNCLE WILLIE FIELDS.

Actually, Uncle Claude spent two entire days in the hospital reception room awaiting an improvement in Pop's condition.

The hundreds of other gag wires and letters Pop took in stride, even though he had been informed by his doctors that he had suffered a severe diaphragmatic hernia. This injury eventually brought on his heart condition.

One night, after having stood as much as he could of hospital routine, Pop called his secretary Helen Dooling. "Get me out of this joint," he pleaded on the phone.

"I can't, Mr. Fowler," she cried. It was very late. "What will my mother think?"

"If I knew your mother's age," said Pop on the other end of the phone, "I might be able to tell you. Get down here immediately!"

Helen had a Model A Ford which was difficult to start, but she made it to the Good Samaritan Hospital and found Pop hanging onto a lamppost outside. "He had had nothing to drink," Helen told me later. "But he looked a mess. His hair was missing in spots. I shouted to him, after trying to decide if I should pick him up at all."

She finally helped Pop into her car. He said, "I have a feeling that I am going to die tonight, so I want you to deliver me to a saloon where there is sawdust on the floor."

Helen suggested the Beverly Wilshire Hotel, but Pop wanted to hit East Sixth Street, which was loaded with low-life bars.

They compromised and Helen drove Pop to a nearby hotel.

"Mr. Fowler was obviously under sedation," Helen said. "I didn't know what to do, since he'd said he thought he was going to die. I put his big arm over my shoulder, and we walked to the elevator entrance. Mr. Fowler said he had always been able to walk anywhere he ever went. So the both of us actually crawled up to the mezzanine where the bar was situated. His picture had been on the front pages of all the papers, so he hid his face, but, God knows, he must have been noticed by the people around, crawling upstairs as he did. We took a small table in a corner. I didn't want a drink, but I needed one by then."

Helen went on to say that she spent a fascinating two hours with this man who thought he was going to die. "Then I noticed his strength was leaving him, so we left the hotel, walking, this time, down the stairs. He insisted I leave him at the ambulance entrance, so I did. I heard him shout at an attendant that he was an expectant mother, and insist upon entrance to the hospital. I drove away."

The following day, Helen called the hospital to ask how Pop was doing. She learned that he was "in a coma, and on the critical list."

"I told Lois Short [McCarey's secretary] about it," Helen said, "only because I needed someone to commiserate with. I thought that I had about killed Gene Fowler."

Pop rallied after three days of unconsciousness and began to mend.

"I'll never forget his meeting me at the hospital entrance that night," Helen has told me. "He made excuses for his hair not being well combed because the gasoline burns had about taken it all away . . . Even the way he looked that night, I can realize now why so many women said they were in love with Gene Fowler . . . I laugh about it now, but every Friday Mr. Fowler used to hand me a check. The studio paid my salary, but he used to hand me something extra each week . . . He'd say, 'This week buy your mother some roses.' What a thoughtful guy, what a *real* man . . . When my job was finished at RKO, I was offered a position with a certain movie personality who was, I later found out, a *roué*. When Mr. Fowler found out about this, he utterly refused to let me take this job. 'Until you find suitable work for a lady, I will underwrite your salary, no matter how long it takes.'

"I'll never forget Gene Fowler. His tall figure. His countenance. His kindness. Even in the shadow of death, he seemed cheerful while waiting."

Several months passed before McCarey was well enough to return home. One of his arms was partially paralyzed. He wore a
brace for a long time thereafter. Having had a few drinks one day,
Pop decided it was time that he took Leo for an auto ride. He
drove down to the ocean front where Leo lived and knocked on
the door. Leo's daughter Mary answered, and Pop demanded to
see The McCarey. Mary, a child at the time, called upstairs,
"Daddy, there's a man who wants to take you for a ride."

"Who is it?" Leo called down from his sickbed.

"I don't know," Mary answered, "but he's dressed in a New
York Giant's baseball uniform."

Leo crawled out of his bed, grabbed his rosary, and dressed for
the ride. Downstairs, he discovered Pop wearing a Giant's wind-
breaker which that team's late manager, John McGraw, had given
him. The two went out for a ride, Pop driving about seventy miles
an hour slower than Leo was going when they cracked up.

When summer came, Pop asked Mother to go house hunting
again. She found a fourteen-room mansion in Brentwood which
had been copied after a villa on the Italian Riviera. There were
seven huge bathrooms, two of which had three steps up to the outsized tubs. Pop had a chance to see the place just after sunset one
day. There was a stand of thirteen royal palms about the circular
driveway, and a redwood tree, already about forty feet tall, had
been planted next to a curved outer wall which housed the library.
Mother, Jane, Mumsie, and myself came along. We looked like
housebreakers. Pop peered through the leaded-glass windows into
the library.

"It's round," said Mother. "Completely round."

"Let's buy it," said Pop.

Mother engaged a couple from Finland, Armor and Ella Sari.
Ella was the finest cook we ever had. Armor was a tall, husky
blond who had a habit of interrupting the conversation while serv-
ing guests. This was often a surprise to the guests, but Pop had an
affection for the fellow and enjoyed the extemporaneous remarks.

During 1940, a 14,000-ton British cargo ship of Australian
registry named *The Jervis Bay* had been sunk by a German pocket
battleship one thousand miles off the eastern coast of the United

States. In a diversionary action, the ship's captain, Fogarty Feegan, broke orders and engaged the battleship. His action, it was said, saved thirty-nine other ships in the convoy heading for Great Britain.

While lying in a sickbed, wracked with malaria, Pop was visited by actor Ronald Colman. He asked if Pop might write a poem about the brave action of Captain Fogarty Feegan, who had been recalled from retirement to serve in the wartime merchant marine. Pop's temperature was up to 104 degrees, but he asked Colman to hand him pen and paper.

Thirty-five minutes later, Pop handed Colman the completed poem, which was one thousand words long.

Before Colman read the blank verse over a coast-to-coast radio network, there had been thousands of mimeographed copies circulated throughout the United States. When *The Jervis Bay Goes Down* finally hit the airwaves, with an accompanying dramatic musical background composed by Meredith Willson, it had already been accepted by the public and a hard-cover booklet of twenty-four numbered pages was rushed through for publication by Random House, with a sale price of fifty cents. All profits, including the publisher's, went to Bundles for Britain, Inc.

The night before Pop was to fly to New York in connection with the poem's formal publication, a strange dog leaped into our backyard. Our shepherd bitch, Fang, was in heat. Pop rushed into the dog run, picked up the intruder (a large, vicious-looking German shepherd dog), and threw him over the ten-foot fence. Then he tore through the house, cursing in such an impassioned manner that the entire family was frightened by his actions.

I grabbed Pop at the front door. Although I was an extremely strong young man, Pop was much more powerful this night. I held onto his coat. He ripped it to shreds as I attempted to hang onto him. Then he dashed out the front door. The best thing, I thought, was just to follow him down the street.

He rushed down the middle of the road past Director William Wellman's home, then past Gary Cooper's house, and Fred MacMurray's. He slowed up at Saltaire Avenue, but his walking pace was still murderous. When Pop finally slowed to a calmer pace I expected him to drop dead, since he was already suffering from angina pectoris.

He had not spoken a word to me during this impromptu marathon. There we came to a halt in front of Deanna Durbin's home. He took several deep breaths before he could speak, then plucked a sprig of red vine geranium from that front garden and said, "You know, son? It takes a rather damp loam to make this flower grow really well."

Pop never explained that strange outburst but perhaps it was a symptom of the inner stresses afflicting him.

Pop was still well-heeled at that time, and since I had been rejected by the Canadian Air Force and the U. S. Marines because of a faulty right lung it was my turn to have a long trip with Mother and Pop aboard the *Lurline* to Hawaii and American Samoa. Our last stop before we returned home was Tahiti.

Before we went to the dining salon the first evening out of Tahiti, Pop said he wanted to take me for a walk. "Son," he said, "I never want to make another dollar unless it's by a book."

"I don't know what you mean," I said.

"I can't take Hollywood money any longer," he said. "I feel like a thief."

"That's all right," I said.

"But this means I won't get that big dough each week."

"I'm happy," I said. "Books last."

It was an uneventful trip back home.

Chapter Eighteen

*CRITICISM IS THE
LOWEST FORM OF ART.*

GENE FOWLER

After ten years of writing in Hollywood, Pop had earned a great amount of money only to give much of it away to old newspapermen, retired prize fighters, and various other needy friends. He had quit Hollywood at the height of his earning capacity. While he wondered what he would do next, he allowed his mind and body a recess after our Tahiti trip. Pop had always been a superb provider, so Mother just relaxed while he took his last fling.

"He'll come to me one day soon," she observed, "with a fine idea for a book, and that will be that. Then watch him buckle down. He is a boy in some ways, and right now he needs to play."

One night Pop met wrestler Man Mountain Dean at Bob Cobb's Beverly Hills Brown Derby. The well-proportioned Mrs. Dean was also present. The wrestler informed my father that his wife was the only person in the world of whom he was frightened.

"Ridiculous," said Pop.

"Show him, honey," the Mountain told his wife.

At this Mrs. Dean stood up, grabbed my father by the wrist and gave him a demonstration of the flying mare. After he landed on the Derby floor, Pop gathered himself up and said, "You know, Mr. Dean, I am afraid of my wife . . . and now of yours, too."

Sunday was a day when the family usually stayed home together. This Sunday, December 7, 1941, Gene, his wife and their infant daughter Martha were still living at the Beverly Hills apartment. By this time I was engaged to a lovely blonde named Beverly Blanchard whom I met in the Beverly Hills High School graduation procession more than a year before. Pop had planned to visit his first grandchild later in the day, but now the family was sitting in the circular library of the Brentwood home. When the flash came over the radio that Pearl Harbor had been bombed, we thought it was another Orson Welles invasion-from-Mars gag. When he was convinced the war was real, Pop's first idea was to rush to the nearest grocery and buy baby food for my brother's daughter. Prices were moderate then and Pop carried off several cases of baby food to store away in the large trunk closet off my music room. He tacked up the bill "just in case the Government wants a reckoning." The total came to $17.76, a most patriotic number.

What Pop did not know on December 7 was that Mumsie had bought one hundred pounds of sugar. She had lugged the sack into the kitchen, added water, and boiled it down into syrup. When this was declared to the ration board, the family lost its sugar stamps for the duration. There were many cold mornings when Pop used to leer at Mumsie each time he poured the syrup into his cup of coffee. Toward the end of the war, it was necessary to crush sugar crystals to get our coffee sweetened.

Pop called Lionel Barrymore and W. C. Fields on the telephone, asking what they might do for the war effort. The three met at Fields' home. Uncle Claude had also been doing some emergency purchasing. He proudly displayed forty cases of gin, three of vermouth, and eighty of Dutch beer. He claimed it would be a "quick war." Shortly thereafter, the three went to sign up at the local recruiting station. Taking one look at the three volunteers, the recruiting officer exclaimed: "Who sent you? The enemy?"

Disturbed because he had been rejected at the age of fifty-one, Pop insisted that I drive him to an after-hours drinking parlor on Sunset Strip. By 3 A.M., we were talking low over a glass of beer when blonde film star Carole Landis sat down at our table to talk. A male customer chose this particular moment to deliver an audible remark about Carole's splendid torso. Pop stood up, asked the fellow to apologize. He sneered. Pop grabbed his shirt with his left hand and a handful of pants with his right. He turned the man sideways in the air and threw his body at least eight feet before it hit the floor. Then Pop casually walked over and put the pressure of his right instep on the man's neck. "Say it again," Pop suggested but the man was not conscious.

My enlistment as a boot sailor was accepted in the U. S. Coast Guard. I became a helmsman, and it was my grave responsibility to convoy the Los Angeles garbage barges a few miles past Catalina Island. I later reflected on what advantage the enemy might have gained by firing a torpedo into one of my garbage scows. I know for certain it would have spread squeezed oranges over one hell of a lot of Pacific Ocean.

While I was still in uniform, Beverly and I decided we wanted to get married. I wrote to Pop, telling him of our intentions. To this he answered:

My dear son:

It is dangerous to go on record in regard to anything during these times, particularly in regard to the seven-league jump of matrimony. But here goes:

You are apparently firm in your resolve, and obviously very much in love. And, from all accounts, that love is reciprocated. Furthermore, two intelligent persons—with a possible reservation involving youth and the age-old anesthesia of Venus Aphrodite—are concerned in the present particular case.

There is so little happiness utilized in a world that could, and one day shall be found to possess a great, natural and available store of it, that the impulse is to seize fragments of contentment whenever it can be done. So no one is keener than I to see, know, and understand your predicament. I have not entirely forgotten my own Youth.

I do not make a habit of appearing as a Bogey Man, either to my own children or to other parents' children. And, in the final consideration of the problem, the forces of Nature will (and perhaps should) outweigh any of my rusty opinions or warnings. You have seen examples of hasty wooing and the precipitate plunge into a contract that is the most ironbound of all civilized (did I say civilized?) business arrangements. And marriage, alas, in many cases is an inescapable obligation. You have heard of the horrors of wedlock; yet, there can be, and I feel sure will be, an exception in your case, provided you will know in advance that all is not rose petals floating on cream. Examples in Reno and elsewhere might suggest that marriage is not a solemn obligation, that it can be tried, like a short session with a hop-pipe, and then put aside after a short nightmare of nausea and headache. But marriage, in its essence, is *still* a deeply-rooted institution, and should (until our economic system becomes even more deranged and imbecilic than it is getting to be) be regarded with earnest honesty on both sides of the bed.

I don't think you can be dissuaded from taking this step, and, after all, you are the best judge. Like a man being kicked in the ribs by two mules, the thing is happening to YOU, and not to the spectators, no matter how sympathetic they may be. So, if you, in your deepest heart, feel that you are prepared to take a wife now, and that you will not shrink from the obligations, which are many and oftentimes heavy; and can start at the bottom, with a wife who also has no aversions to hard work during a time of war *and its still more complicated aftermath,* then who am I or anyone else to defy an urge which an inscrutable God has placed in the souls and bodies of his children?

I try in the first stages of my reasoning to objectify the case, to state things not found in the "Lived Happily Ever After" school of thought. Then, when I have done my little urinations against the wind, I abdicate. From then on, my grown-up children must exercise their own functions and their own independent rights. I can only sit on the side-lines, hoping and praying for the best—which sometimes DOES miraculously happen.

You have the reins in your own hands now. If you say March, then it is March. You shall have all the blessings that we can give (although I have not consulted your Mother in this letter-writing) and I shall of course be very proud of such a lovely girl as Beverly. I think she has sense and can perhaps exercise certain practical restraints on your nature, a nature which I fear is not unlike my own. I never would take advice from anyone, so it is not such a pretty picture when I am suddenly found in the role of giving advice. One thing is certain: although I desperately suffer when my children meet with any unhappiness, I am never bitter about it. And you are apparently suffering now, in a manner of speaking, and I cannot find it in my nature to make a gesture of denial. You are free to act, as you well know, and God bless you both.

I do hope, however, that you will do your Mother the courtesy of consulting her thoroughly.

With all the love I have left after many battles—some of which were with myself.

Devotedly and fondly,

Pop.

Jane had already married, and now I was the third, and last, of the children to leave home. I had developed pneumonia, and while in the Long Beach Naval Hospital, my asthma history was discovered and I was given a medical discharge.

Beverly and I were married in the West Los Angeles Methodist Church on February 7, 1943. There was a flashing moment I thought the ceremony would never come off when my brother, who was the best man (and now separated from his wife) turned to me in the bridegroom's waiting room to say: "It's not too late!"

Pop and Mother were living in a Manhattan apartment, having sold the Fire Island house because it would be difficult to travel east every summer in wartime and besides all their children had homes of their own now. In a letter, Pop wrote that they were hastily packing for home, adding: "The book will be published in January, and the title of it is *Good Night, Sweet Prince*." He bypassed a $40,000 first serial magazine publication, partly because of the delay it would mean to book publication, but mostly because, as he said, "the cutting down of a good work to the popular . . . romanticism and sensationalism of a great life (and without the psychological backgrounds and explanations of a character) would, in my opinion, greatly detract from the book itself."

The day before they were to fly back to the Coast, Pop decided to walk around the streets of mid-Manhattan. For many years Mother had rebuked him for carrying his money in little wads distributed among his pockets. "Put it in your wallet where it belongs," she admonished. "One day a pickpocket will get you."

"There is never any room in my wallet," Pop replied.

The last time he took inventory (in 1936, with a policeman at hand asking to see his driver's license), Pop found in it a guest card to the Far Rockaway Elks' Club, seven ancient photographs of somebody's children (perhaps his own), a permit to carry a pistol for the year of 1922, his draft card for World War I, two ticket stubs to the *Ziegfeld Follies of 1925,* a pass to the Jack Dempsey-Gene Tunney fight in Chicago (which he told me he had searched for vainly on the night of the match, before he finally had to be ushered in on Tex Rickard's arm), a letter of introduction from Grantland Rice to James J. Farley (dated sometime in 1919), several locks of hair tied with small ribbons, a few pipe cleaners, a key of uncertain heritage, some blank checks on the Corn Exchange Bank (where he had not had an account for twenty years), a Customs House declaration on purchases made abroad in 1925, and several match-book covers containing telephone numbers. The thing looked like a Gladstone bag. Pop carried it on the right hip. It was quite a load, and many persons of his acquaintance mistook the bulge for a symptom of advanced arthritis, or a goiter gone south.

Although this bustle was something of a nuisance, Pop later told me, "it served to break many a fall after a night in a saloon."

With this wallet straining at the seams, with recent acquisitions, such as a new draft card (for older men), a Social Security card, a fresh driver's license, and another lock of hair (his granddaughter Martha's), but still no money, he went for his stroll along crowded Broadway.

When he returned to the apartment several hours later, Mother said: "I don't know, but somehow you look as if you had lost a little weight."

Pop admitted his pocket had been picked on Broadway, but with an air of victory, and enjoying one of the few moments of domestic triumph permitted a husband, he began to shell out from his various pockets his wads of $1 bills, forty-eight in all, and grinned triumphantly.

"But you've lost your Social Security card," my mother said.

"There is no security for fellows like myself," Pop replied. "I'll never need a card."

"But your driver's license?"

"I don't drive now that gasoline cannot be had in worthwhile quantities."

"But the draft card?" she persisted.

"Don't you remember?" Pop asked. "They don't want old men like me."

Mother insisted that he put an ad in the Lost-and-Found columns, and bought all the papers the following day to check on Pop's ad. It was there all right, in bold face type. It listed every single article. At the end of this chronicle, it read:

Who stole my purse stole trash. Please advise the well-intentioned fellow who picked my pocket not to return it or its contents. I am now so light of hip that I shall again take up dancing after a quarter of a century of terpsichorean inertia. Love and embraces. *Gene Fowler*.

Pop's humor was often too robust for some people. The day he returned from New York, he took a walk around the block in Brentwood, and stopped to watch his neighbor, Director Frank Capra (who had recently become a colonel in the army), striking out with a hoe at a gopher that had been dining on his victory garden. When Capra rested between attacks on this elusive pest, Pop spoke up, "My, Frank, what a thing for a colonel to be doing when there's a war on."

He returned home to write a letter to his Chicago drama critic friend, Ashton Stevens, telling about his Hollywood writer acquaintances who were coining fortunes by rolling out inferior patriotic scripts. "I suppose I should be envious," he wrote, "but I'm not. I decided a long time ago that I must make the most of the best I have, and envy no one. Perhaps you will forgive me for not crying about the woes of the world or the sorrowful comparison between the wonderful past and the hopeless present. I am not bitter because the world is not better off. I am astonished that it is as good as it is."

I had become an actor, under contract to Director Michael Curtiz. When my first picture *Janie* was previewed, Pop refused to go see it. Nor did he express a wish to see me any other time in pictures. One day he asked me if I would be interested in becoming a newspaper reporter. At the time, Beverly and I were living in a small West Los Angeles home with our first child, Will Timothy. I explained that I was beginning to get good parts and that my salary had been raised to $250 a week. He said if I took the job as a

reporter, he would subsidize me until my salary reached a point
where I could support my small family.

The following day, I went downtown to Hearst's Los Angeles
Examiner and was given a job as general assignment cub reporter
by that paper's Jim Richardson, one of the last of the rough-and-
tough city editors. I am happy Pop made this decision for me, for
the wealth of knowledge and experience one can obtain through
ten years of newspaper reporting which I eventually gained cannot
be equaled in any other place of learning in the world. And Jim
Richardson was the first person who really taught me discipline.

Meanwhile, Pop, having launched me on a new career, was beginning a friendship that proved of great value and sustenance to
him. Professor Robert S. Hillyer had decided to resign his post at
Harvard to devote his time and talents to writing. Since *Illusion in
Java,* Pop and Hillyer had engaged in a lively correspondence
which branched out into all subjects, including poetry, ancient
Egypt, the evils of moviedom, the excellence of the Abbey of
Theleme and its motto *Do what thou wilt,* and other Rabelaisian
matters. Now Hillyer was coming to California to meet Pop for the
first time.

As he stepped off the train, Bob had no difficulty in singling out
Pop by his cordial roar, combining some friendly profanity with a
Latin phrase or two. They repaired to a bar and fell into a lively
discourse on all manner of subjects, agreeing so violently it might
have been midnight instead of eleven o'clock in the morning.

That evening I drove Pop and Bob to Ben Hecht's rented house.
Ben was then occupied in a spell of film writing. On the way, Pop
warned Hillyer that "This is a one-fact town. Upon arriving at a
Hollywood party you might hear a man say with conviction: 'Roses
are red!' and that will be that regarding his entire knowledge. From
then on he will be regarded as the sole authority regarding 'Roses
are red.'"

We walked into Hecht's living room to discover several guests
drinking and talking. Pop introduced Hillyer around. Hillyer answered a host of questions, the subjects of which ranged from a
single line of verse to the cosmos in general. His answers were direct
and lucid. One musician present played a Bach two-part invention

not too correctly. Hillyer amazed all by sitting down at the piano and executing the composition quietly, modestly, and perfectly. Hecht, equally as brilliant as Pop and Hillyer on a variety of unrelated subjects, howled with delight after the one-fact guests crept away to another place to restore their egos. Pop and Ben spent the remainder of that night singing names directly from the Los Angeles telephone book as Hillyer accompanied them at the piano.

When I wrote to Hillyer recently, I asked him to give me an opinion of Pop, "the way someone else beside his son might see him." He wrote back:

. . . Gene was a hundred different guises, and all of them kind. There was a courtesy in Gene so much a part of his being that it was in his voice, his every glance. It had no connection with conventional attitudes, for it was the essence of a deep understanding or a desire to understand. I have never met anyone else with quite that quality, and the pity of it is that it is indescribable. When I was with Gene I felt that every talent or good characteristic I had was magnified a hundred-fold and that my weaknesses were negligible. I felt, as well as heard, every word, and each was like a friendly hand on my shoulder.

. . . He was modest, and in his reverence for poets and poetry he was unaware of the fact that his own nature was profoundly poetical. Without knowing it, he was endowed with so many qualities that he praised others as though they were beyond his reach . . . He never would admit to being a learned man, but I never brought up a subject in which he was not well versed. He has won a reputation for so many things that, no doubt, he possessed an eye for the significant, a gift of recording conversations as though they were taking place at the moment, and for a wild exuberance . . . His style is really, *if one takes the trouble to examine it carefully,* very quiet. That is why a noisy character like Jimmy Walker can be heard so accurately in his pages—the style does not compete.

. . . Who better than Gene could have understood my retirement from Harvard? Everyone else thought I was crazy to give up such a position and "devote myself to writing." He wrote a letter to the secretary of the Department of English at Harvard that was a masterpiece of understanding and justification. I still have a copy of it. He summed up the situation in a paragraph and in a flash of intuition illuminated my motives and my gifts. . . .

As a postscript to his letter, the Pulitzer Prize-winning poet added:

I just read this over to Jeanne, my wife, and she said it was a good description of a very great gentleman—*in the old sense*. How true!

Many of my acquaintances have asked me: "What were your father's writing habits?" Well, to start with, when composing a book, he was an extremely early riser. He would usually rise about 3 A.M. and make a pot of coffee, then allow his brain to awaken by writing an essay on the first subject which would come to mind. He called this "practice," explaining, "A writer must warm up just as a musical instrumentalist before attacking a concerto." When visiting Pat Covici's New York apartment, I was allowed to study the holograph manuscript of John Steinbeck's *East of Eden*. I discovered that Steinbeck also did his mental setting-up exercises before attacking the work at hand.

Pop's long-time secretary, a lady who was near perfect in her duties as stenographer, typist, and researcher, Miss Agnes Bane, said: "Mr. Fowler had a great temptation to look at the dictionary, but oddly enough a strange reluctance to refer to it. Whenever he opened a dictionary or encyclopedia, he began reading and often put aside an entire day's writing. I found it better that I look up a word or subject for him in order to shield him from this great temptation."

Agnes Bane added that Pop was a detective in digging up facts for his biographical writing. His manuscripts were always about twice as long as the end result in publication and with his later books he began extensive rewriting, unlike the first-draft versions of his earlier works. "His notes were voluminous, and the material he deleted from the final draft," she added, "would be ample for a second book on the same subject."

He wrote swiftly, with an upward slant, but his penmanship would have been awarded a failing mark in any grammar school. His "y's" and "g's" had no loops to them. He was unable to think about his writing unless he was working on the best bond paper, something of a luxury, considering that he once rewrote a chapter forty-three times before he was satisfied. Blank paper always frightened him.

He would finish his writing just about 9 A.M. when Miss Bane reported for work. Then he went to bed for a nap which usually lasted about two fitful hours. When he arose, Miss Bane, who knew his hand well, had a perfect copy typed and ready for his editing.

He used long, hard, sharp pencils for his editing, and could not think over a piece of work unless he held a pencil in his big hand. When the pencils were eventually sharpened down to two-thirds their length, he discarded them because by that time the erasers had been worn away. His edited copy was smeared black with deletions and corrections. Beyond added words, commas, semicolons, and hyphens, one could find marks which represented italics, brackets, two-em dashes, carets, broken letters, and many others which looked to all but the printer's eye like hieroglyphics.

Now, Agnes Bane would type a newer, and more finished copy. Then the same process of penciling and erasing would be repeated . . . unless Pop decided to start all over again.

When in the midst of creating, Pop preferred to live in solitude. If he was doing well, he was happy. And, as with most men of talent, if he was faring poorly, one had to be patient and understanding to remain within earshot. Mother was a master at handling these moods. When he experienced a few non-creative "dry" days, he often manifested his displeasure with sharp remarks. He could find fault with small things entirely unrelated to his work. This might cause him to blow up and leave the house to take a brisk walk. Mother would remain silent, or try to agree with him, unless he voiced the opinion that he would never be able to write again. This happened often. He had great doubt of himself and his ability to write. When this mood passed, he would invariably apologize and take on his hangdog look. In a matter of minutes, Mother would say something funny, or overdramatize his temperamental gushing in jest. Then they would both laugh heartily and before long Pop would be back at his desk, writing better than ever.

The only other stress which would send him spiraling when he was writing well was a phone call from some well-intentioned out-of-town friend who had just arrived in Los Angeles and thought he was doing Pop a favor by asking him to "get together for a big old time!" Pop was usually able to feign sickness, and this is why so many thought my father was in bad health most of his later years. This was not true. He merely wanted to be alone when writing. His close friends respected Pop's wishes. The ones he could not escape, he often gave in to and often got roaring drunk in self-defense. To escape the worst nuisances, Pop would just say he was not at home, and bury himself in his garden.

He told me once that he figured his well-intentioned acquaintances took at least four books out of him.

Pop never wrote for publication while under the influence of alcohol. He did, though, get off a few letters and essays while half, or completely, looped. He once handed me a page which he wrote while all the way in his cups. In my opinion, it is a sample which outshines the work of many famous users of the free association technique. Above this, he wrote: "Will: This was scribbled when I had had a bit too much of the mash. Shows how a man should not depend on himself to write when 'stoned.' "

It follows:

COLERIDGE: Was it always the narcotic or did you walk with some inner Aristotle among the weed-grown marshes? Is delirium a breaking flywheel? How does the mind move? We speak of the mind working. It does not work. It *functions*. Like a liver? Like a heart? Like a team of horses at a wagon? Like a siphon? If the mind could be seen through some organic window a thousand, thousand empires of religion would fall. Charlatans, preachers, psychologists, mumblers, playwrights, poets, lovers, all would perish. Stoned to death. Stoned by one another. This will be the true end of the world. When the mind finally is seen and read for what it is. A barren earth. That's why it was hidden, like a sealed-in part of some expensive motor. To be seen never. Not to keep it free of dirt. But to keep its secret. What a calamity, O men who seek to plumb the workings of the mind, if ever you come upon a Rosetta Stone of psyche! If ever you interpret truly the mind and display its gears and rods and pistons and fuels. Ye seek the secret. Ye court the dawy, davy, dippy, day. Sic.

When the mind leaks little leakings of its fluid unconscious, it is not true that one feels with the fingers. If so, the night would feel soft to a corpse's hand.

Pop was preparing notes now for an autobiography which would cover his life up until he left Denver to travel with "Nellie" the corpse to New York and fame.

While Pop was filing papers in his large brief case, Mother was brewing tea for an actor's representative and a youth who looked remotely like John Barrymore. Pop came downstairs to talk with this young actor who was partaking of brandy "because," Pop told me, "I guess the lad thought that's what Jack would do at tea time."

"Good Night, Sweet Prince is the perfect vehicle for my boy's movie debut," the agent told my mother who remembered well that Barrymore had not been too well housebroken in his latter years.

"Oh?" said Mother.

"No doubt of it," said the agent as he began to build up his sales pitch. "My boy can do *anything* that John Barrymore could ever do." He was beaming now.

"That's what you think," said Mother.

"What do you mean, Mrs. Fowler?" asked the suddenly reticent agent.

"He can't pee on my sofa and get away with it!" she declared.

Mother is gifted at unhorsing braggarts. One time she caught an emaciated actor, who also thought he would eventually play the role of Barrymore on the screen, sleeping one off in Pop's bed. She studied the snoring thespian, then ripped off the blankets to cry, "Get out of my house, you bum! This is not *Inner Sanctum!"*

Pop and Mother journeyed to Denver where he would expand his notes on the autobiography, which was published as *A Solo in Tom-Toms*. When their train came to a stop at the station, his old friend Chief John Healy of the Denver Fire Department was there with that city's finest piece of equipment—a shiny red hook-and-ladder full seventy feet long.

Dorothy Collins of the *Rocky Mountain News* asked Mother, "What is it like to be married to a madcap, hard-working genius?"

"It's fun," she replied. "It's mad. It's a lot of laughs, and it is also pretty wonderful because he never forgets the little things—is never temperamental." Mother bent the truth slightly about Pop's lack of temperament. She added: "My first year of married life was pretty rough. But I learned one thing and that was never to tie Gene down. He just isn't that kind of man. When Gene stays out with the boys too long, and then comes and says, 'Mother, can I come home?' I always ask him, Where *else* would you go?"

When Miss Collins asked Mother whether she had any desire to write, she said, "Oh, no! That's why Gene married me."

Pop wrote a by-line story for the *News,* this time in the third person, telling of his return home after many years. In it, he remarked:

Mrs. Fowler (who actually deserves a monument) is diplomatic. It has been her practice of late to humor her spouse in all his delusions. When he took her to revisit Red Rocks, the site of their marriage years ago, they discovered a great stadium there, and he insisted it had been erected in his honor. She quietly passed along the word to Chief Healy (Fowler's boyhood hero) and through a reportorial colleague of Fowler, Lee Casey, to Mayor Ben Stapleton, former Governor Ralph Carr, Night Club Proprietor Jack Kanner, Bartender Billy Gallagher, Deputy Chief of Police Rugg Williams, and other amiable citizens—a quiet word that Fowler deemed the *Red Rocks* masterpiece a personal monument.

Almost dazed by happiness and gratitude, Fowler confided in T. Joe Cahill of Cheyenne that he thought the monument should have been raised to more deserving men of Denver, perhaps to the late Judge Ben B. Lindsey. Cahill said nothing at the time, but afterward took Chief Healy aside to whisper to him: "Thank Heavens this fellow isn't a native of Cheyenne! He'd probably move into the State Capitol, thinking we had given him a town house.

After a week in Denver to refurbish his memory, Pop's goodbyes at the station were a little like that of Napoleon's when he shoved off for Elba. Chief Healy, unworried about train schedules, insisted upon pausing in the bar of the Union Depot to take aboard a martini. With many a fine curse, the Chief refused to say goodbye. He simply turned his back and walked away. "I thought for a moment that he was going to cry," Pop said later, "but he happened to spy two nuns who also were getting on the train. I am sure he did not know either of them, but he whacked one of them on the backside, a highly un-Catholic thing to do, and said, 'God damn it, Sister, I love you!'"

Al Birch, Pop's city editor on the *Post,* later wrote that "the old Chief, after the train began to pull away, started to walk down and over the ties, waving his hand and calling Gene's name over-and-over-and-over again. It was like seeing with your own eyes the parting of the Old and the New."

Years later, after Chief Healy had died, Pop said, "I cannot get used to the fact that I now look outside my home and find no fire trucks there. It's like . . . well, I think I shall have to put the torch to my house so that I can hear the fire bells ring and see the boys come up with the apparatus. I really believe that such an alarm would in some telepathic manner be communicated to Chief Healy, and he would send his fine Seagrave truck on the way across the mountains to my burning house."

When he returned home, Pop was unable to get down to serious work on *A Solo in Tom-Toms* for several reasons. His visit to the old home town, where the *Denver Post* and *Rocky Mountain News* had treated him so regally, had left a feeling of sadness that pressed upon him. He had me drive him down to Los Angeles' Skid Row where he drank with the men who wanted nothing more than a glass of anything alcoholic and the promise of a warm bed.

Shortly thereafter, Pop sent W. C. Fields the following:

Dear Uncle Willie:

Thank you for your note. I am passing through a period of slight melancholia, and my recourse to the bottle only heightens it. I hope to see you soon in your old Crow's Nest so that we can sit and look out on the world and despise it thoroughly. Meantime, the best to you.

Pop was stalling, as this note indicated, on getting to work on the new book. Beginning a new book, particularly in his later years, always stirred up in him currents of self-doubt and uneasiness. At this time, too, my brother Gene, a lieutenant in the U. S. Army Signal Corps and stationed at Astoria, New York, was about to remarry and Pop wanted to attend the wedding. Gene's bride-to-be was Marjorie Johnson, the daughter of Nunnally Johnson, an old friend of the family, a former New York newspaperman, a brilliant wit, and presently a motion picture writer, director, and producer.

Regarding this alliance of the Fowler and Johnson clans, Lucius Beebe, an old friend of both men, wrote in a *Holiday Magazine* article published shortly before Pop's death:

Nunnally Johnson is probably as great a repository of Fowler lore as Fowler ever was of the saga of W. C. Fields. Back in 1944 Fowler's son, Gene, Jr., who was then a soldier in service, married Johnson's daughter Marjorie and the ceremony was performed by Judge Ferdinand Pecora, a celebrated jurist of the time, at the Plaza Hotel in New York. While the judge was muttering the sacred words, Fowler and Johnson got to musing over the number of firkins of whiskey they had jointly helped put away over the years. It led Fowler to the interesting observation: 'If your daughter and my son ever become parents,' he remarked in a stage whisper, 'the result will be not so much an offspring as a blend.' Fowler and Johnson today are grandfathers of two blends. [The blends are Gene Nunnally, and a daughter, Kim.]

There was yet another reason why Pop did not get to work on his autobiography immediately. This had to do with politics. In 1944, he had agreed to report for the Hearst papers the Republican National Convention in Chicago. In the midst of this reporting, he quit cold, returned home and finally began work on his book. He never gave any reason for throwing over the assignment.

Politically Pop had always considered himself a grass-roots Republican, a partisanship stemming mostly from his great reverence for Abraham Lincoln.

Although he did not consider himself politically minded, Pop did express himself on the subject once, during the Dewey-Roosevelt campaign of 1944, when a Democratic campaigner (Harold L. Ickes) aroused his anger by his remarks about Lionel Barrymore and his wheelchair, which seemed uncalled-for to Pop. He unburdened himself in a letter to Westbrook Pegler which found its way into print:

I have often been asked why I have not taken more interest in politics. My reply to this is not to be classed either as philosophical or deathless.

Instinctively I always felt that something was wrong with politics, and that those who participated in the social science quite often were somewhat less than honest or admirable persons. Even when I became old enough to attend Fourth of July orations, and after I had grown intelligent enough to escape them, the promises given and the boasts made seemed to be bombastic monstrosities.

Then, when I observed, as a reporter, many unholy things happening, peculiar things with precincts, cities, states, and occasionally the great nation itself being robbed and desecrated, I had less stomach for politics than ever. It was argued that I should busy myself, together with others, to help purge this condition. But I think that the well-meant crusaders always try to purge from the wrong end. It seems to me that the procedure properly should begin with the re-writing of our history books, the re-teaching of decent thoughts, the endorsement of tolerance and decency in minds that are young, rather than with the ineffectual discharge of popguns at the politicians when those corruptionists are old, and their eyes glued upon religious images.

I vote, and I prize my vote, as every citizen should. I vote according to my own light and my own conscience, as I think every citizen should do. I do not try to enforce my vote or my way of voting upon others, any more than I would call a man who does not like licorice a scoundrel or a Fascist because I like licorice. It is not my nature, perhaps because I am usually a minority man, to join the loud campaigns, or march in a parade just because it is fashionable to do so. I carry but one torch, perhaps a dim one, but my own. I believe in the vote. I believe in the Country.

When he arrived at a true start on *A Solo in Tom-Toms,* Pop was visiting his friends Noll and Mabel Gurney at their desert cottage sixteen miles outside of Palm Springs. Noll and Mabel were wise though to leave him strictly to himself, never talking to him until dinnertime, and then only for about an hour. Pop had told me once that "what the world in total fails to comprehend is that a person of any creative faculty is out of answers for a time following a mental gallop." To ask simple questions of such a man, he went on to say, is just as outrageous as it would be to force one's way into the dressing room of a recently knocked-out champion to ask the dazed fellow: "Would you run out and get me two packages of chewing gum and a set of false eyelashes?" When Pop was preparing himself for the writing of a book, he found he was utterly incapable of making any outside decisions unless he abandoned his work completely.

In November, just before he sat down to pen the first chapter, Pop wrote me a rather relaxed letter, casually mentioning that he had been toying with the frequently suggested topic of his memoirs:

When a writer sits down to his memoirs, he is, in fact, putting himself on a pension. He is taking from the closet an old coat that has been worn by him all too long, and he proceeds to sew upon it a few patches and mend the seams. The garment never again can impress anyone as being new, and the man who refinishes it knows, if he has any sense at all, that it doesn't even fit. For his literary belly sticks out beyond the limits of a once-trim waistline.

It was always difficult for Pop to write about himself. He was truly a modest man, and, at any rate, found other people more interesting than himself.

When one reads *A Solo in Tom-Toms,* he will note that the book generally follows the pattern of his own life, detouring often to the great characters he knew during his days in Denver. The only excuse for this was that the persons about whom he wrote had much to do with the molding of his life. Pop thought that he never could have lived anywhere else in his youth than in the untamed town of Denver. In later years, he had to laugh at his naïveté, for he had thought that the mass behavior of that city when the century dawned, and for sometime thereafter, was the norm for the entire world.

In a sense, Pop waged a mighty battle of Fowler versus sophistication. He once told me he knew that a man who dared laugh or pursue his own simplicities was bound to be kicked to death. "But that does not deter me," he said. "I shall wobble about like the great Chief Healy, no longer able to climb ladders, but still absorbed by a daffy dream that people are stupid yet wonderful." That was in 1944, when he was only fifty-four years old, but preferred to be considered "an old man."

Pop sent an early draft of *A Solo in Tom-Toms* to his Denver friend Lee Casey to see how Casey thought the work was going. He was disturbed about various cynical views Pop usually wrote into his early drafts, but most always blue-penciled after he had purged himself of this cynicism. Casey pointed out certain characteristics in Pop's earlier writings and related them to parts of the present book:

. . . You have allowed those inferior to yourself to determine some of your judgments. I think that, in the earlier stages, you let Damon Runyon cloud your thinking and, a bit later, Ben Hecht.

Runyon—I don't mean the newspaperman, but the writer of stories and books—is, of course, obvious, smoothly cynical, with a sentimentality that is palpably bogus. Hecht, many levels higher, appealed to your streak of cynicism and to your delight in burlesque—a delight which, although it certainly should not be suppressed, just as certainly needs no encouragement.

. . . You let yourself be beguiled into writing about people not actually as you saw them with your very discerning gaze but as you were influenced to see them . . . Your imagination is so vivid that metaphors rush into your mind and sometimes, because of the very luxuriance, seem forced. . . .

Casey went on to write that this was not true in *A Solo in Tom-Toms*. "Here you show moderation, restraint. You show, too, self-discipline. So this one will not be merely one of the great American books, but one of the great books."

If Casey was right, I do not know. I believe *A Solo in Tom-Toms* is my favorite Fowler biography.

It was Pop's tendency in other books and in the first draft of *A Solo in Tom-Toms* to set down a great mass of material, including anecdotes which were of value as such but did not contribute to the advance of the narrative. When he wrote about himself, this tendency was proof of modesty. He took more time on this book than on any other until *Skyline,* the uncompleted, last portion of his autobiography. H. Allen Smith once told me: "Any man who is able to set his entire life down in but a single volume is a dull person."

Inasmuch as he was wrestling with an assortment of heart attacks, duodenal flareups, and exhaustion, Pop had started taking sleeping pills in 1943 while writing the Barrymore book. Perhaps the habit that continued for nearly three years did not approach in its intensity those of De Quincey or Coleridge, but he found it a hard one to break. So in 1946, while in the midst of writing his memoirs, Pop decided, book or no book, he would have to deny himself his nightly pills. He was not the kind of man who could taper off on anything. He had to quit cold.

A week after Pop had begun to withdraw from sleeping pills, my night city editor, Pat Hogan, and I took him out for the evening to help him forget his struggles. We ended up in the desolate *Examiner* city room at 4 A.M. where we kibitzed a floating poker game and drained the corners of our last bottle of bourbon. Pat Hogan was napping now, and as some dream reached its climax, he fell over backwards, splitting his scalp on a steam radiator. Before we walked a few blocks to the Georgia Street Receiving Hospital to get the night editor's pate stitched, Pop wrote the news bulletin front-page box for the morning edition.

I stood by Hogan until his scalp was joined by a surgeon's deft hand. When we sauntered from the treatment room, Pop was emerging from another. His eyes were watering and red. While Hogan was being attended to, Pop had requested that he have his stomach pumped. A staff physician obliged. "I guess I can't drink that lousy blended bourbon," Pop said with a sickly smile. "If I don't get any sleep tonight," he added, "I think I'll move to Australia because I've already counted all the sheep in America twice!" He did sleep after I delivered him home. It took him three days to recover from the stomach pumping, but he then went back to work on the book, and he was able to sleep once again without the aid of pills, or sheep.

A short time later the same thing happened to him as befell Pat Hogan. That was when he decided that Red Skelton needed a chaperon on his honeymoon.

Pop had met the comedian about two years earlier when Skelton appeared unannounced at the door of the Brentwood house. He was carrying a copy of *Good Night, Sweet Prince,* which he shyly requested to be autographed.

I happened to be at home at the time and admitted him, shouting upstairs to Pop, "Hey, come on down. Cousin Delfred's here."

"Who did you say?" Red asked in bewilderment.

"Cousin Delfred," I said. "He's our drinking cousin."

Pop came right down, hauling on his dressing gown. He and Skelton hit it off at once; in fact, they soon became like father and son. Until his death Pop counseled Red at every stage of his career. They were so close that, I must admit, I was more than a little jealous of the affection Pop gave him.

When Red married his second and present wife, the former Georgia Davis, a tall and beautiful redhead who was then an aspiring actress, in March of 1945, Pop accompanied them to Chasen's for the nuptial dinner. Pop got to celebrating so hard that he decided it was only fitting that he go along with Georgia and Red on their honeymoon. Instead, he fell backwards off his chair, striking his head on Chasen's fireplace. Taking this as an ill-omen, he announced, while being patched up, that he wouldn't go on their honeymoon after all. . . .

Pop did not mention that the previous week he had entered Chasen's establishment, carrying an exotic meat-eating plant. He had ordered a top-round steak for himself, medium, then called for raw ground meat for his little plant which looked like a nodding jack-in-the-pulpit. During the evening, Pop fed his quiet little plant small balls of fresh meat, and had continued to talk to the plant as if it were a friend who might later condescend to pick up the check. Even Chasen broke up when Pop insisted that the plant be served a finger bowl.

Pop went on in a letter to me:

I have decided against all odds to surrender in a manner of speaking and put over the publication of my book until next spring. A combination of mental bombings turned my work into another Coventry. But I shall carry on and rebuild and reshape this work, which must be a best one for me.

Speaking of my own son, Will, whom Pop affectionately called Tiny Confucius, he continued:

If he wonders if I have reformed, tell him no! Say it to him with thunderous overtones . . . Tell him that his grandfather, who is not celebrated as the holiest of men, hopes at least not to get out of character, even on the death-bed.

In a more serious vein in a subsequent letter he wrote:

. . . I still dream of art, although it is a rather untimely thing to do. And I still desire and hope and wish to write of Faith, although it is not an age of Faith. And I look upon art as a priestly vestment, and not a crying-towel. Whatever I am in fact or by reputation, and however lax and remiss I may be as a person among persons, I have within me a Faith that sustains me. Faith in my Country, notwithstanding the lard-assed politicians and dung-grabbers. Faith in the destiny of mankind, though a million, million years must go past before people will learn to give and forgive, to live and let live, and NOT merely get and forget, grab and be grabbed, slave and be enslaved. We shall now read the Sermon on the Mount. Then let us all go out and crucify somebody. It is the thing, you know. And we must be in the fashion. Balls!

Displaying a renewed love for the newspaper life, especially after having been re-introduced to it through my *Examiner* friends, such as Hogan, Jim Murray, Clarence "Gus" Newman, Joe Santley, Mickey O'Donnell, and my weekend city editor, Harry Morgan (the first man to give me an opportunity to write a few small stories for the paper), Pop concluded:

By this time you should be enjoying your status as a newspaperman. It will bring you a resourcefulness and a quality of self-reliance in the yon days, when you and she are old, Magee. No great sums of money, perhaps. No immediate recognition, maybe. But you are in the grand-stand seat all the time, and you see the plays and misplays of the world's men, and once in a while there is a great pitchers' duel or a home run to be seen with the bases loaded. The bases, yes, and alas, sometimes the dice also. . . .

Chapter Nineteen

*DEATH WAS INVENTED TO
KEEP PEOPLE FROM BECOMING CONCEITED.*

GENE FOWLER

A Solo in Tom-Toms hit the best-seller list early. It was a natural following *Good Night, Sweet Prince*.

The jolliest venture occupying his time now was the formation of a Pallbearers' Association. The motto was *Never Stand a Friend Up*. When word of the association reached H. Allen Smith, he insisted that Pop write to him regarding the bylaws. Pop wrote:

We are planning to issue a booklet, privately printed, entitled, *The Pallbearers' Guide*. Several of our leading pallbearers, among them Gene Buck, Jack Dempsey, Thomas Mitchell, W. C. Fields, Rube Goldberg, Grantland Rice, and myself, believe that pallbearing is fast becoming a lost art. A six-man team—or, in the case of a gangster's funeral, a twelve-man team to carry the bronze casket—should move with precision, grace, and confidence, and give the spectators a better show than they are now receiving when just any old six or twelve men, chosen at random, stumble over one another or play tug-of-war with the remains. Pallbearer Goldberg is the founder of the Frank Campbell Country Club. It is a delight to see him perform at his usual position amidships during the obsequies. Grantland Rice also is an excellent pallbearer, a "pro" long known for his military manner and his ability to look straight ahead and not lose stride when some amateur treads upon his heel. Gene Buck is internationally celebrated because he brings so much color to the game. He can sob without messing up his uniform, and wears such an expression of sincere distress that sometimes he is mistaken for the corpse. It would not be the modest thing for me to discuss my own abilities as a pallbearer. Nevertheless, the fact that I am in constant demand shows that I am no tyro when toting that pine or mahogany barge . . . In passing—and I do not mean to make a pun— I wish to say that I always appear among the six or twelve at the port bow. This is a sort of stroke-oar position. The importance of it cannot be overstated. The bearer on the port bow sets the pace, which never should appear hurried, but actually should be swift, so as to get the damn thing over with.

Pop also wrote that he was contacting several leading pallbearers such as Herbert Bayard Swope, Gene Markey, Bill Corum, Mike Romanoff, Toots Shor, Paul Gallico, and Grover Whalen for big-league ideas. He went on to explain:

One of our western correspondents, Harry Brand, a professional at the Pierce Brothers Town and Country Club, has come up with an idea that promises to be one of the greatest contributions of all. In collaboration with the makeup man at 20th Century-Fox, Mr. Brand has devised an artificial "Lump in the Throat." So many pallbearers become calloused by frequent public appearances during an influenza epidemic or an earthquake, that they are unable to cry—washed out as it were— and the spectators do not like this at all. With the inexpensive Brand device, a pallbearer need not chance being thought cynical.

Pop signed the letter: "Author of How to Make a Hole in One."

At the time Damon Runyon was waging his all but hopeless fight for life, Pop had thrown himself into gardening so violently that he prepared beds for dahlias, roses, and tuberous begonias in a vacant lot adjoining the rear of his Brentwood house. He acquired this huge parcel shortly after a city inspector had caught him dumping refuse there.

"Whose lot is this?" the stony-faced inspector had asked.

"I don't know," said Pop.

"Then get that trash off in twenty-four hours or I'll have to fine you."

A month later, Pop was reproved again by the same inspector who seemed to take a sadistic delight in catching him at the offense. He demanded, "Whose lot is this?"

Pop smiled, then scattered his wheelbarrow load and answered, "Mine."

He had purchased his private dump for $50,000.

World-famous nurseryman Paul J. Howard once observed, "The only man I ever knew who could make a flower bloom where it's not supposed to thrive was Gene Fowler. His garden had actually been loved into being."

Now, at this time, a young man who wanted to become a writer sent Pop a letter about this way. One of the things that worried the fellow was an injury he had suffered during the war. His trachea and larynx had been crushed with the result that he was unable to speak above a whisper. Pop answered:

Don't regard your vocal accident too seriously. Whatever you do will be done the better if you have some handicap. I certainly have several myself, and you must remember that many writers and others sat in wheel chairs or lay in bed or hobbled on crutches. It is much better to lose your voice than your sense of humor or your feeling for your fellow men. Persons of this category are the real cripples of this world.

Undoubtedly Damon Runyon's tragedy was on his mind when he wrote that.

In a letter from Runyon to Pop, the Demon wrote that on his return to New York from Hollywood he had undergone a second operation on his cancerous throat. He made light of thirty-five days of X-ray treatments. During that period he led a dual existence, living at the Buckingham Hotel by day and by night sleeping at Memorial Hospital for the convenience of his doctors. Runyon mentioned that he was working on using his voice to some extent, but that it was really difficult. "Still, I have several friends who had this same operation who can talk better than I could when I had my voice," he wrote, referring to the technique of controlling saved-up air in the lungs, then letting it out through the mouth to form words. This did not work for the Demon, and he eventually gave up the exercise.

In this letter, he gave some news of his and Pop's old friends; men such as Wild Bill Lyons, Sid Mercer, and Jack Miley, three cronies who had recently died. He wrote of Dan McKetrick, and fight promoters Jimmy Johnston and Mike Jacobs, fighter Johnny Dundee, Walter St. Denis, Toots Shor, Ward Greene, Bill Corum, and other mutual friends of the big city whom he knew Pop would be interested in hearing about. At the end of his letter, he wrote: "Write me if you get the urge. I love you and yours, and you know, the fact that we rarely communicate in nowise lessens my affection."

From then on, Pop and Damon wrote frequently and lengthily to each other. One of Pop's letters was five-thousand words long.

On December 10, 1946, Al Santoro, then sports editor for the Los Angeles *Examiner,* called Pop to say, "Damon is dead. Would you like to write something about him?"

"There is nothing to write," Pop said after collecting himself. "He was a patron for a lot of us guys now growing old, including your young Vince Flaherty. Runyon was like a baseball scout; he was always scouring the tall uncut. He brought a lot of great newspapermen to the attention of editors, and probably the only black mark is Fowler."

When Pop lamented the loss of a friend in his later days, he would walk into the garden to meditate. At the Barrington Avenue house, he had a one-man park, a place in the shade and only large enough to seat a single person. That day, after he was informed of Runyon's death, Pop disappeared into his one-man park, only to emerge in his work clothing when a rubber-neck bus stopped in front of the house. A tourist craned her neck from the bus to ask my father, "Does Lana Turner live in there?"

To this, Pop answered, while taking off his straw hat, "Madam, if she did, do you think I would be out here?"

Pop never toyed with ideas for the subject of a book. He searched. Should he write about Damon Runyon, a man he knew so well? "No," he decided, "I'll do it later; include him in my memoirs."

Jimmy Walker, the late Mayor of New York, answered Pop's search in a providential way when he was chauffeured in a black Cadillac up the oval driveway of the Brentwood home just before the summer of 1946. I was visiting Pop, this time with Beverly and our two sons, Will and the recently born Michael.

I answered the doorbell to find a thin, impeccably dressed gentleman who introduced himself as Jimmy Walker. Pop came to the door, but the former New York Mayor refused to enter the house. He claimed he did not wish to disturb anyone inside. I laughed to myself, wondering if he might be wary of the possibility of a hidden microphone. He and Pop stood and talked for about five minutes in all, or maybe ten.

It was then that Walker asked Pop to write his biography. "I'm in poor health," Walker said, "and there's little time left," adding, "I had a good time, though."

"There should never be a law to deny a man a good time," Pop replied. "We're meant to have a good time if we can."

"How will you handle my heavy drinking, if you write the book?" asked Walker, "I don't believe I was an alcoholic, though."

To this, Pop answered, "An alcoholic is a man you detest because he drinks almost as much as you *used* to."

"The Church claimed that I committed adultery when I married my second wife," Walker added.

"As for what you call 'adultery,'" Pop continued, "it was always my axiom either to enjoy it or to cease."

Jimmy mulled this over for nearly an entire minute, then said, "Will you write my story, Gene? If you don't—and I'm pretty smart about choosing my biographer—I want no one else to do it . . . Will you? I'll be gone before you put down the first word. . . ."

Pop smiled, then said, "I will. You have my hand on it, Jimmy." They shook hands, then the former Mayor of New York stepped into his Cadillac and disappeared into a gentle fog that was rolling in from the Pacific Ocean. Pop was never to see Jimmy again, for his visitor died a few months later.

Artist John Decker, a former German baron who spent several years as a British prisoner of war on the Isle of Man, was not only an artist's artist, he was an actor's actor, a man's man, and a rogue's rogue. Decker and his wife, Phyllis, a lady with a picture-book face, lived a few blocks from Pop's Brentwood house. John entertained his friends in a modest old rented English-style cottage, the living room of which was his studio. He boasted the tallest and most prolific avocado tree "in all of Southern California."

Decker's Bundy Drive home was the meeting place of artists who neither played poker nor sat transfixed listening to one of their own latest phonograph recordings. None looked upon the other in envy over the recent purchase of a $13,000 automobile. Here minds met, not to brag about their achievements, but to find sanctuary; here such men as Pop, Barrymore, Thomas Mitchell, Henry Clive, W. C. Fields, Roland Young, Anthony Quinn, and Ben Hecht, to name a few, sat and just had a good time.

The first time my father met Decker was in 1932. Pop had a hangover that was being appraised skeptically by his cinematic collaborator, Rowland Brown, himself a teetotaler who nibbled on cookies. The two were en route to the movie studio that day to compose a scene for one of Jack Barrymore's pictures. Pop chanced to see "in Gower Gulch" a harried gentleman in a condition similar to his own. The man was hatless. A bluejay could be seen swooping down again and again as if to gather hair from his head for upholstering its nest.

When Pop told Barrymore of this first meeting, Jack said, "Decker, no doubt." He added, "Aside from his art, which I admire no end, I find him enchanting because he dislikes sunsets and his mother. And I believe we both owe him a great personal debt for exhuming that museum piece, Sadakichi Hartmann."

Sadakichi Hartmann, one of the other members of the Bundy Drive group, was the author of *The Last Thirty Days of Christ*. He damned near got thrown out of the country for this anti-religious work. He had also been an art critic of parts, a poet, a dancer, a secretary for Walt Whitman, and an all-around savant. His half-German and half-Japanese ancestry did not enhance his popularity during World War II as he sat out his time on an Indian reservation near Banning, California.

Although his successes were part illusory and all in the past, Sadakichi was often an honored guest at the Decker studio. He was a man of individual thinking. "The elements," he would say during an asthmatic seizure, "are a matter of indifference to me. I *defy* them! *Hah!*"

Sadakichi had fathered thirteen children and given each the name of a flower. Still, he decried parenthood and frowned upon all sentiment. Once he said to Barrymore, "Your father Maurice was a sublime actor. I cannot say the same for his stupid younger son. *Hah!*"

Jack, instead of becoming annoyed, replied admiringly, "What a *divine* part you would be for Lionel!"

Pop recounted another instance of Jack's aplomb during the shooting of one of Barrymore's latter-day movies: "A group of club sisters came to the Barrymore set to watch the actor at his labors. During the taking of a scene, the fumes of a noonday beer got noisily in the way of his diction. The man at the sound-control earphones winced, then advised the director, because of the detonation, to reshoot the scene. Barrymore, with the quickest eye that ever scanned a blackboard or anything else, observed the look of disapproval on the faces of the visiting club women. Then, after the second take was accomplished without maltous interference, Barrymore summoned up such an encore to his earlier eructation as to cause the visitors to glare and to say among themselves, "Disgusting!" and, "How dreadful!"

"The actor crossed over to the critical ladies," Pop concluded, "bowed elaborately, then said to one of them, 'What did you expect to hear, Madam, *chimes?*'"

During the telling of this story, and after Sadakichi rebuked Pop for not having purchased a coffin for use as a desk, "until the eventual occurs," Thomas Mitchell arrived to prescribe a drink for Sadakichi. Actually, Tommy was there to discuss a small head of Christ by Rembrandt he was about to purchase. Then John Carradine, the gaunt one, joined the group, and it was decided to give a performance of *Macbeth*. I was sent out to search for several volumes of Shakespeare and returned with six copies of the play in various editions. Sadakichi played the title role, and Barrymore was Macduff. Decker was a competent, although slightly baritone Lady Macbeth.

The performance was a memorable one, but somewhat handicapped by the fact that no two versions of the borrowed *Macbeth* volumes were in close agreement as to cues and text. Sadakichi also insisted upon improving on some of the speeches of the Bard.

At the close of the performance, Jack announced, "We at last have been given, in the performance of Sadakichi, a *Macbeth* that was slightly private, but nonetheless the most magnificent of all time. Even George Bernard Shaw, had he been present, nibbling on a head of cabbage or some other article of his diet, would not have written a letter of protest."

Sadakichi replied to Barrymore's tribute, "I still think your father was a better actor than you are. *Hah!*"

Something of the fine flavor of the Bundy group was lost when Decker moved his studio to Alta Loma Drive in Hollywood. This was a modern structure, financed by actor Errol Flynn, who falsely claimed to have stolen John Barrymore's body from a Los Angeles mortuary the day after the latter's death. As Decker's better canvases began to sell, it was all work for him. Newcomers imported by Flynn began to join the group and usually, at the end of a drinking evening, ended up in a brawl with the police taking over. The charm had certainly left. In the interim, too, Barrymore had died.

One evening, while drinking absinthe, which Decker had acquired from some extra-legal source, an actor friend, who had openly been poking fun at a newcomer for not knowing his Shakespeare, talked himself into one of the greatest straight lines I have ever heard. He averred, "Ernest Hemingway impresses me as the greatest author America has yet produced."

With deft timing, while all had suddenly become silent, Pop said, "Ernest Hemingway impresses me as a man who would walk up to the Grand Canyon . . . *and yearn to satisfy it!* . . ."

Decker was capable of painting anything. Pop's friend Philip Paval spoke of a time when Decker had an exhibit. "Arthur Miller, the art critic," said Paval, "came around and looked at all the paintings. There was a little drawing under the mantelpiece, and Miller said, 'Well, there's one guy that nobody can copy—Daumier.' But John had copied Daumier's style so exactly in this drawing that Arthur Miller the art critic had made a mistake. And John said, 'Look at that, the son-of-a-gun, thinks he knows anything and *I* created it!'"

Decker told Pop he had been an expert not at copying but of creating canvases of Daumier, Gauguin, Van Gogh, a few Florentines, and even a Rembrandt that today hangs in a European gallery with the stamp of authenticity upon it.

After Decker died in 1947, following several weeks of stomach hemorrhaging, we laid him out in a coffin at the Alta Loma studio next to an unfinished still life of a beer mug and some fruit. As we played a recording of John's reciting a passage from Rostand's *Cyrano*, a portrait of Jack Barrymore came unhinged and noisily fell to the floor. It startled the assemblage, which included casket-bearers Tony Quinn, Dr. Frank Nolan, Vincent Price, and Gordon Levoy.

On November 12, 1946, W. C. Fields dictated his last letter from Las Encinas Sanitarium in Pasadena, California. It was to Pop:

Dear Nephew:

This Gideon J. Pillow friend of yours is not a "Pillow"; his proper name is "Wetblanket."

Agnes is still in the will and shall remain there until after I examine my Christmas tie.

Your loving Uncle, Claude.

The signature was labored. The "e" in Claude did not quite make it. And "Mr. Pillow" was Death, the one he usually referred to as: "The man in the red pajamas."

Uncle Claude died on Christmas Day, the holiday which Fields abhorred most. When I waltzed in to the *Examiner* with a grand hangover at 7 A.M., I was greeted by Leonard Ribblett, then assistant city editor. I had seen a story of Fields' demise smack on the front page bearing my by-line. Pop had phoned it in earlier, saying that "my son, Will, who is not with me at the moment, wrote this wonderful story. I thought I would phone it in to you while he is reveling." I hated to take credit for this fine obituary. Shortly thereafter, I got loaded with Gus Newman and Jim Murray, and told them I had not really written this story. They laughed, and assured me they had already come to this conclusion long before.

We planted Uncle Claude at Forest Lawn, then repaired to Jack Dempsey's house after Dave Chasen gave us a meal. At Dempsey's, where his beautiful daughters Barbara and Joan had already been sent upstairs, there was an Italian and the wrestler he was managing.

"We have to get rid of this guy," said Pop.

"Willie," said Dempsey, "get rid of these guys. Throw the big fella in the pool."

Dempsey was my godfather and I regarded this as an order. I sneaked up behind the wrestler and gave him a crotch lift over the edge of the pool. When this giant emerged from the water, I recognized him as a killer in the ring. I ran up to Dempsey, who was holding his sides from laughter, and shouted, "You damned coward! Do you know I might have been killed by this guy?" We returned to Chasen's and drank until our elbows wore out. As I put him to bed, Pop said:

"We have a good time, don't we, son? But remember; even today shall eventually become a long time ago."

When Pop finally got down to writing the Jimmy Walker book, he dug himself in temporarily at the Desert Inn at Palm Springs to get away from intrusions.

Shortly after he returned home, Mother awakened one night, crying in pain. I was sleeping in my old bedroom next to my parents, Beverly having gone off on a visit for a few days with her mother.

Pop, a light sleeper, was at her side at once. "What's the matter?"

"All of a sudden," said Mother, "I can't feel anything . . . anything below my hips. . . ."

"Maybe it will pass," said Pop.

Now I entered their bedroom to find Pop kneeling at Mother's bedside.

"Maybe it will pass," said Mother.

It did not pass. Mother tried to arise from her bed, but realized she was paralyzed.

Within an hour after Pop called Harry Brand the next morning, the best available neurosurgeon contacted the house. He was Dr. Ruppert Raney. Following exhaustive studies at St. Vincent's Hospital, Dr. Raney said that Mother had suffered a back injury as a girl and that adhesions had finally blocked the nerves to make her paralyzed from the waist down. Surgery was suggested.

When Mother underwent the extensive spinal operation, Pop took a room next to hers. He stayed in the hospital for several days until she was out of danger. Dr. Raney told Pop the operation was a success in that Mother's life had been saved. His prognosis regarding her chances of ever walking again was doubtful. He told Pop in confidence that it would be a miracle if she did walk.

Now Pop began to use Mother's illness to his own advantage. That is to say, he used it as an excuse to keep people from annoying him while digging in to do the Walker book.

That was the beginning of a series of family illnesses.

When my wife and I arrived home one evening shortly after the birth of our daughter Claudia, our baby sitter told us my son Will was complaining of a stiff neck. Dr. Webster Marxer diagnosed the child's ailment as polio. We were in the midst of the 1948 epidemic. Beverly and I delivered Will to General Hospital and waited all night until an overworked intern emerged to say that our son had the classic symptoms of the disease.

We drove home and tried to pray.

Two days later, Beverly came down with polio.

She hovered between life and death for several days.

During this time, the tall figure of Dr. Barney Kully, one of Pop's closest friends, stood by outside Beverly's hospital room in case he might have to perform a tracheotomy.

After Beverly passed the crisis, Dr. Kully took a hotel room near the hospital where he isolated himself for fourteen days to be certain he had not contracted the disease.

One time Dr. Kully asked Pop why he did not go back to writing for the movie studios, "just to make some money for the family." (Many were under the impression that Pop was not too well off financially because he was not a natty dresser, and he drove an inexpensive five-year-old car.) "Can't you just knock off one or two scripts to make expenses?" Barney said.

Pop sighed, then said, "Barney, would you like to go through the rest of your medical career circumcising rabbits?"

The big house in Brentwood began to seem empty, since only Pop, Mother, Mumsie, and three servants remained. Jane had gone to New York and landed a job as columnist on *The American Weekly*. So Mother sold the house and, discharging the servants, they took a second-floor apartment on Sunset Boulevard. "You'll never be happy with this place," said sister Jane. Mumsie, a lady in her eighties now, jumped up to sit on the kitchen sink, and declared, "I like it." Pop wrote a check for eighteen months rent in advance. He set up a workroom to complete the Walker book. But within three months he began to complain about the noise and not having a garden to tend.

So Mother went out again, having regained the ability to walk, and found a suitable home two hills west of the Barrington place. They moved in, leaving well over $5000 in un-recoupable rent money.

This time, 1948–49, seemed to be Pop's most despondent period. Mother's and Beverly's illnesses made him sad because he was unable to do much about the situation. He had put off the proposed publication date of the Walker book once again, and the letters he received from his publisher were not too cheerful. Before he had submitted any part of his manuscript, *Life* magazine offered Pop $40,000 for the first serial rights prior to the release of the hardcover book, but he turned down the offer.

Pop had a habit of writing lengthy notes to himself as sort of a philosophical logbook, some of them bitterly pessimistic. It seems that "foxy grandpa," as we now called him, fully expected the Walker book to be a flop. In one such note:

My fondest hope is that I appear soon again as a resounding failure. I have had about fifteen recorded failures, each one followed by a "success." The reason for the respective successes was that, during any period of seeming failure, a blessed disdain on the part of fair-weather friends permitted me to reassemble my forces and concentrate on my own work . . .

. . . Any mere flash of notoriety, or what the world calls success, immediately invites torrents of unwanted congratulations, unsought duties, unearned obligations, telephone calls, tedious correspondence, and all the rest. The only happy man is the downright tramp, the untouchable one, with the fortunate aura about him of always seeming on the point of asking for a dime, wishing only a cup of coffee.

I have worked as hard for my present failure [the Walker book] as most men strive for success. My only fear is that some ghastly piece of good fortune will rise to spoil this dream of tranquility and productiveness. Now I have deliberately sought to unframe my gaudy landscape and throw it into the cellar, just as the veteran baseball manager Connie Mack scrapped one or more of his pennant-winning teams at the time of their greatest performances.

All this is meant in a most kindly and destructive way, and not born of the ferments of cynicism nor the anguish of defeat . . .

. . . I just received a long letter from a convict in a Louisiana prison. *God,* how I envy him! He has privacy, reasonably good food, a place to sleep, nobody envying him (except me), *and there isn't an in-law in the place*. No one asks his politics, nor do they care what party he belongs to. No one criticizes his clothing, nor does he need to buy any. Collectors cannot reach him. The income tax is non-existent. There are no landlords. Alimony? Domestic naggings? Criticism by lofty world-lings? All these things pass him by. He is free to think, even if literally not free to do—thus he lives in a special kind of steel heaven. The warden has all the headaches. This man enjoys socialized medicine, or better still is denied the medication which kills most persons. He knows how to be free by reason of the fact that he has been jailed. Cervantes did his best work in stir, as did John Bunyan, Paul Verlaine, O. Henry, Oscar Wilde, and many others. I think I shall collect the writings of all the men who wrote classics during prison terms, and put out a five-foot shelf called *The Jail-Bird Classics*.

Pop completed the Walker book, titled it *Beau James,* then took Mother for a walk around the house and garden. This was a formality they always observed, even though he had to rouse her from her bed to do it. He would always walk into the bedroom, or wherever she was, whatever the time, and say, "Well, honey, I finished the book."

When I finished reading the *Beau James* manuscript aloud to Pop, I asked if this man was not a villain at various times in his political life, adding that this villainy did not seem to poke its head out of the pages of this book.

"I think that authors make a great mistake when they delineate villains and, as authors, sneer at them, ridicule them, or belabor them," he answered. "When the author writes his villain, he should write him from the villain's point of view; that is, a bad man who thinks he is right and that his bad deeds are the only possible ones for him.

"The author should never call his villain a son-of-a-bitch editorially. To be sure, he shows him as one, and the reader readily forms his own opinion. But the author must never step out of the character he is portraying to shout, 'There goes the bastard of the world,' or 'There goes the Savior.'"

As *Beau James* began to climb the best seller list, Pop's journalism teacher, Jim Lockhart, died suddenly in his little room near the Veterans' Hospital at Sawtelle, a few miles from Pop's house. Jim died a victim of asphyxiation, caused by a leaky gas heater.

Through the years, Pop insisted that his frugal teacher take a little money from him now and then. Lockhart used to object loudly, but Pop was Pop, and not to be denied. It was a great surprise when my father discovered, after reading his will that Lockhart had been independently wealthy.

Years later, when *The Rocky Mountain Herald* asked Pop to write something about Lockhart, my father let Denverites know just what a great teacher Lockhart had been. When trying as best he could to recall the names of the men in Lockhart's class, Pop wrote:

My memory is getting almost as bad as Emerson's in his latter days. You will remember that Howells speaks of that sad fading of the faculties, and tells of how he saw Emerson standing at the bier of Longfellow, and saying in effect: "We have buried a wonderfully sweet and philosophical man. *And I regret at this moment that I cannot recall his name.*"

Pop and brother Gene had lunch with Westbrook Pegler in Tucson, Arizona, the day one of Peg's more vituperous syndicated columns hit the Hearst newspapers. The blast was aimed at Pop. Peg wrote in part:

Gene Fowler has been my friend for nearly thirty years. I can think of no more inappropriate man to write a moral appraisal of Jimmy Walker which probably will become the final story of a sad and squandered life. Fowler is a weep-easy whose stock exclamation at our latest evening together a few months ago was, "Oh, a great guy. I love him." He loved that night a roster of the most dissolute bums of our time in New York.

Beau James, The Life and Times of Jimmy Walker, is the tribute of a mawkish fellow with a strain of cynicism, who surely understands, but will not admit, that the personal tragedy of his flippant little friend is not to be compared with the catastrophe to 130,000,000 Americans, indeed, to civilization, on much wider ranges now that we are the world agents of "democracy."

In this column, Peg went on to mention names and episodes Pop had obviously not included in *Beau James*. He categorically tore various underworld characters apart, particularly those who had been acquainted with Jimmy Walker. Some eight-hundred words later, Peg concluded, still full of the old steam which made him a controversial journalist:

Fowler is so emotional that his opinion of Walker is worthless. Yet his emotionalism—God help us—is the very trait that controls many of our political decisions and pollutes our opinions on such practical and solemn problems as labor legislation, *"civil rights,"* rent control, taxes and foreign relations.

I liked Walker personally, but I doubt that he could understand that a man could condemn his behavior and yet have a warm heart for him. Similarly, I find Fowler (with whom and his family I and mine have spent so many happy times) unfaithful to his deepest morals in raising the record of Jimmy's errors only to excuse them. Forgiveness is one thing, but condonation is another!

The research, a pretentious new word for reporting, which went into this book is great journalism. The prankish, irresponsible Fowler never seemed to me to be a thorough reporter when he was on the street, but I must have been deceived. This book is no rewrite of clippings, but a revival of the era of wonderful nonsense itself, and I know that Gene did his work between heart attacks and under a burden of personal anxieties and sorrow that would have made another man chuck it. Other reporters and students of journalism will find it a great example.

When Mother read this column, and she read Peg religiously, she became spitting mad. She called Peg on the phone, only to reach him at a Tucson restaurant dining amiably with Pop and my brother.

Her opening words were: "Peg, how far can friendship go?"

The wire services picked up the story, and before the next edition, an expected feud was being hinted at all over the country. The story was made because, as I mentioned earlier, Pop was visiting Peg at his Tucson home when the column was published.

Jim Murray, who had recently gone over to work for *Time* magazine, contacted me at my home. I gave him Peg's phone number and added, "Look, Jim. Pop is Peg's friend. To allay any misunderstanding, I'll call him and take down the first formal statement about this thing. Then I'll call you back." I fed Pop's statement back to Murray for *Time:*

Westbrook Pegler is an extremely honest and able reporter. His article on me in no way affects our personal friendship. If we are to have free speech and free expression as we so widely announce everywhere, I think this should apply to Pegler as well as any other citizen, including myself. I am having dinner with Mr. Pegler tonight at his home, but will eat nothing except coconuts and the inside of French bread which is not baked on the premises.

I sometimes think that Mr. Pegler goes too far when he throws rocks at ghosts but in this instance, so far as I am concerned, I am still alive and kicking, faintly. As for Jimmy Walker, I did not try to excuse him in my book. Rather I endeavored to explain him in relation to the time that produced him. There is a fine but definite distinction to be made here. Nor am I a moralist loaded down with profound truths and messages for my comparatively small public. Before I could be one, provided I chose to set myself up as an arbiter, I would first have to improve my own way of living. I believe in Biblical teachings although I do not practice all the precepts contained in Holy Writ. One of the things that I always have tried to do is to live up to the admonition of the Scriptures and I quote, *"Judge not, that ye be not judged."*

When he returned from Tucson, I asked Pop what was going on. "Why this solemn viewpoint?"

He said simply, "You are a Catholic, son [my family and I had been converted to the Catholic religion a year earlier], therefore, I tell you now that after these long years, I am taking instruction to become one myself." He added, "Now with the exception of Father Duane Theobald in Denver, only you and your mother and I know about this. I would be happy if you did not mention this to anyone."

"You mean you approached Mother about your becoming a Catholic?" I asked.

"I went to Mother," Pop said, "and asked, 'Do you mind if I

become a Catholic?' She nearly laughed, but with a respectful tone. She said, 'I have no objections at all, dear . . . You've been a Catholic for nearly thirty-five years anyway. . . .' "

The advent of his conversion was first reported in the *Denver Catholic Register*. It occurred this way: Pop mailed a formal letter to the rector of Denver Cathedral in May of 1950 requesting that he might have the privilege of being baptized there within the next few weeks. A date was set, June 5, when the assistant pastor, Father Theobald, would officiate. The *Register* wrote Pop to ask more about the particulars. Pop, unaware that his decision would cause such a stir, swiftly wrote back:

During the past two years or more, I have been in close converse in respect to this spiritual matter with the Rev. Duane Theobald of the Cathedral of the Immaculate Conception. Now, after several months of instruction by this earnest and most helpful young priest, I have been adjudged ready to receive the privilege and the honor of entering into the faith of my choice.

. . . For years I have wanted to be received into the True Church. My decision was not a sudden, emotional event. Also, I did not wish to be a "deathbed Catholic." I am now sixty, and perhaps I can work in a small way to earn my right to be a son of that Church. My sins have been many, of course, for I have been surrounded in my profession as a newspaperman, editor, and author by worldly companions and touched by worldly things. But never once, notwithstanding my trespasses, have I wavered one instant in my belief in God, His Son, the Holy Ghost. That feeling of faith always has been with me. And now I repent of all my transgressions, and would have my sins forgiven and be ready to enter the hereafter as a Catholic, purged of sins and permitted atonement for them. Part of my reluctance to have myself publicized was due to my feeling that converts sometimes are overzealous in proclaiming their conversion. You who have been born, fortunately, as Catholics, can only surmise the great joys that come to one who has found peace after a life of dark groping for that salvation. It is this very ecstasy that sometimes causes the happy convert to proclaim his newfound status to the world, and thus, unwittingly, he is apt to draw censure from worldlings who look upon him as a braggart and even a nuisance. This I desire to avoid, and would seek to be a devout Catholic, to strive for the achievement of good works, but to be modest about it all.

I am indeed grateful that I shall be baptized in the Cathedral, the stones of which I saw rise from the prairie, and in the sacred building which my revered friend, Father Mac, did so much to establish, God rest his soul. This is a priceless experience, and I want to receive my First Communion in that memorable Cathedral, and achieve grace and the peace that comes to one who is penitent and humble before God. With sincere good wishes. Pray for me.

Gene Fowler.

Many began to write to Pop regarding his conversion. He answered only those of priests and the hundreds which came from those who wished to embrace this faith themselves. Writing to Father O'Brien of Notre Dame, Pop sent a fourteen-page letter regarding his conversion. He reported in part:

I have an aversion to praising my wife in public print, or making fulsome dedications of books to her, partly because she would dislike such show, and partly because I think I would seem silly or hen-pecked in the process. But I must say that she posed no difficulty here nor when my younger son Will and his wife and three children were baptized as Catholics some three years before my own conversion. That event had nothing to do with my own subsequent action, and indeed Will was quite unaware of my leanings.

At the time of his conversion, Will asked me the customary question: "Have you any objections?"

To which I replied: "Only one. If either of your sons becomes a priest, please do not expect me to address him as "Father."

Shortly after Pop had become a Catholic, Westbrook Pegler called him to offer his congratulations. During the telephonic conversation, Peg said that Pop would have to excuse him for groaning sporadically. "You see, Gene," Peg said, "I broke my toe, and it's very painful."

Pop broke out into laughter as Peg asked what was so funny about a broken toe. "I'm sorry, Peg," said Pop, "but you'll have to give up kicking Roosevelt's tombstone!"

Chapter Twenty

*THE COLD WAR HAS PLACED
MAN'S MIND IN A DEEP FREEZE.*

GENE FOWLER

During the latter part of June 1950, Pop traveled to Las Vegas to be with Jimmy Durante, who, with Eddie Jackson, was headlining a show at Wilbur Clark's Desert Inn. Pop took along a tape recorder to interview Lou Clayton, Jackson and Durante while gathering material for the biography he would call *Schnozzola.*

"The tape recorder," Pop said, "offered me one hundred per cent recall of dialogue. And it added a new flavor—a greater use of direct quotes."

When it became certain that Lou Clayton would not recover from a disease of the pancreas, Pop began a daily diary, which he first dictated directly to Agnes Bane, then later put on tape. The journal, when completed, was 72,000 words long. At the end of the six months, Pop made the following entries in pen:

Sept. 6, Afternoon—

Have returned from hospital. Went there with J.D. and Eddie Jackson. A gray day, to see a gray man. I had not anticipated seeing Clayton ever again, but at Durante's request I went into the room. Clayton roused, recognized us in turn. He slips into a semi-conscious state, taking, as it were, cat-naps of death. Then he comes to, is exceedingly aware for a few moments of even the small details of the scene. He observed a piece of cigar leaf on Jim's lap. He still clings to what he used to call "the niceties" of behavior . . .

Today he told the doctor with a smile, "Well, we fought a good fight, and we lost it."

Clayton died on Rosh Hashana, the beginning of Jewish New Year, "which," Pop was told, "is regarded as a good omen. All pious Jews wish to die on that holiday." Clayton's death at the beginning of the holiday delayed his entombment until three o'clock, Friday, September 15. He was buried in a crypt at Home of Peace, a Jewish cemetery near Whittier in East Los Angeles. It is opposite Calvary Cemetery, the Catholic ground where John Barrymore's body is in a crypt. Georgie Jessel delivered the eulogy for the Friars Club and the Jewish Actors Guild. He quoted George M. Cohan, who had said "there never was a bad man who made a good song-and-dance-man."

I went back and wrote the story for the *Herald & Express,* whose City Editor Agness Underwood had hired me only a few days earlier. Agness was the first woman metropolitan newspaper city editor in the United States, and today is still one of the best of them all.

Pop was back in hard-working form. He spent little time in his garden. In 1951, after *Collier's* magazine had printed it, Pop having lost his prejudice against magazine publication in favor of ready cash, in serial form, Viking Press published *Schnozzola.* Pop dedicated the book to the jolly, corpulent restauranteur, Bernard "Toots" Shor. On the page following the dedication was a quote from Jimmy Durante: "I don't want nobody to put me on a pedasill."

Richard "Red" Skelton had become more dependent upon Pop. My father was the only man he now trusted. Red and his wife Georgia, accompanied by Mother, Pop, Mr. and Mrs. Bö Roos, Mr. and Mrs. Dave Rose and Announcer Rod O'Connor, headed for Europe and then to London, where Red would headline at the famed Palladium. Before they reached London, after visiting Rome, three engines of the airliner in which the party was riding gave out while flying over the Swiss Alps. Pop tried to reach me in Los Angeles at the *Herald,* "But," he later wrote, "we were out in the 'sticks,' and my knowledge of the French language is almost as limited as is my knowledge of women."

It seems the flight had originated in Khartoum, where not only the police were on strike, but there had also been a Communist riot. When the Skeltons, the Fowlers and the Roos family boarded at Rome, a passenger told Pop the plane had a flat tire upon landing. Now, over the Alps, when three engines ceased to function, it was suspected that sugar had been placed in the gas tanks.

The American Legion Chaplain, Reverend Father Edward Carney, also a passenger, sent up his best prayers. Rod O'Connor and Pop, the only other Catholic members of the party, also did some fast bead-work. Pop said the pilot was "as cool as a Hearst editor two days after the funeral" as he jettisoned three-thousand gallons of gasoline to lessen the chances of an explosion on landing.

Skelton happened to be in a front seat beside Father Carney, and was facing the rest of the passengers. He cracked jokes and otherwise distracted his fellow passengers. "It was like the brave show put on by Eddie Foy, Sr., many years ago," Pop later told me, "when the Iroquois Theatre raged with flames in Chicago."

Skelton went into his pantomime of a man blowing at a feather just before the plane made an emergency landing in a field of clover, just missing a flock of grazing sheep. Skelton then said to the still petrified passengers, "Now, ladies and gentlemen, you may all return to the habits you gave up just twenty minutes ago."

Father Carney turned to Pop and said, "We almost had a reunion in Heaven."

Pop replied, "That's what I was afraid of most, for my grandmother would have given me Hell for having become a Catholic!"

On July 1, 1951, Pop wrote to me from London:

After eight weeks of a successful engagement at the Palladium, Danny Kaye failed to introduce Red Skelton to the audience. This was regarded as a most ill-advised slur by one fellow American and fellow star on another . . . Kaye was well aware that Red was seated in one of the Royal boxes with his party. The other performers glanced up from time to time at Skelton, as did members of the orchestra. But Kaye gave him never a look or any other sign of recognition . . . For the evening performance, Skelton got out of bed and wearily went *again* to the Palladium, as he understood that, according to custom, he would be introduced from the box. Skelton did not feel up to going, but several Londoners of importance advised him that absence from this duty, even because of indisposition, would be construed as a grave breach of manners. So Skelton went to the theatre. What happened?

Again he was ignored. Although Red met the situation like a manly, generous fellow he always is, it was quite apparent that he was mystified by this uncouth treatment.

Kaye soon afterwards wrote a note of apology. In it he said, in effect, that in the emotional flurry of his farewell performance he forgot to introduce Red. Forget? He did not forget to share a bow with the cast members, the orchestra, the cleaning woman and all others. Is Skelton so small and unknown to Kaye that he cannot be seen in a Royal box *twice* on the same day?

Kaye is something of a hero over here, and has been a big hit. But no man is bigger than himself. And whenever one of our actors or other big shots gets so carried away with personal glory as to lose the graces of generosity and courtesy, then such a man reveals himself as somewhat less in spiritual stature than Abraham Lincoln, shall we say? Perhaps Kaye was carried away by the moment of farewell in the presence of his temporary idolators. Possibly he got absent-minded while perhaps remembering the nods of heads bearing coronets. Even so, it should be forcibly brought to his attention that Fame is but a small candle glow, and that a breath can put it out forever. You can wager all you have that George M. Cohan never was guilty of a *faux pas* such as Kaye's. Nor did John Barrymore ever slight a fellow star. Nor will you ever find Jimmy Durante afraid to share a bow, even though Jim may get the name wrong . . .

Kaye's actions of yesterday and last night have removed some of the lustre that has rubbed off on him during his fraternization with Kings.

Skelton will open tomorrow night, and he will go over. But, succeed or not, he never will be found wanting in respect to his fellow workers of all kinds. For example, he has been peddling copies of the Durante story all over town. A champion is a champion. . . .

On July 19, Pop and Mother celebrated their thirty-fifth wedding anniversary in Dublin. This was all too brief a visit for Pop, who felt instantly at home the moment he set foot upon "this dear ground." He said that there was no posing among these warm people, adding that there was an eloquent decency about them. He received a real welcome. The Abbey Theatre had recently burned down, but the players carried on. Pop and Mother attended the second and third nights in a makeshift small place, seeing Sean

O'Casey's *Juno and the Paycock* and *The Plough and the Stars*. When Pop departed, the players presented him with a large ash from the Theatre's proscenium arch and their prompt book for *Juno and the Paycock*.

On returning home from abroad, Pop was ready to tackle another book. When he said he was going to write about Sadakichi Hartmann, I was the first to say this was folly. "Once a newspaper interviewer asked me," said Pop, " 'What of all your experiences and impressions have struck you most forcibly?'

" 'The thing that amazes me most of all,' I answered, 'is how little improvement or change there has been in the design of the garden hose nozzle.' "

"What the hell has that got to do with Sadakichi Hartmann?" I asked.

"Simple," said Pop. "There has been just about as much improvement on man . . . so . . . I am going to write about Hartmann . . . Although a faker, he is a true artist in his fakery. I am *also* a true artist, else I would not have the courage to take on this which shall perhaps be my last book. And a true artist wishes to see his subject under adverse conditions; to see what he would do when carrying a bag of groceries and his pants suddenly fall down. The remotely known Hartmann fills my requirements. . . ."

"But he's nothing more than an old man," I said.

"Old men do not enjoy being put into drydock, so I will do this book."

"But how can it hold the reader's interest?" I asked.

He winked. "I shall decorate the story with such characters as Barrymore, Fields, and John Decker."

"I'd rather see you retire," I complained.

"A high-spirited man's greatest drawback in growing old," Pop responded, "is that it takes him such a long time to do it. When he can no longer hide from himself the facts of the insidious decline, facts which have been known to everyone for years past, he should quit reading the obituary columns in the daily newspapers and turn all the mirrors to the wall. Such a man never should retire, for by so doing he is signing his own death warrant. An old writer should keep on writing, taking care not to tell the same story twice,

and withstanding the fear that he will die before his tale is told."
Then he added, "I am so tired, and my teeth are loose, but I shall
continue writing what I wish to write until I die."

During the collecting of notes for this book he would eventually
call *Minutes of the Last Meeting,* Pop suffered a heart attack which
put him in the hospital for two weeks. He had been working vigor-
ously on his hillside garden when the attack came. He was, in fact,
moving two-hundred- and three-hundred-pound rock boulders.

When Dr. Frank Nolan allowed my father to return to his desk,
Pop felt well enough to make an appearance on Durante's television
show. When he saw himself on the kinescope print, he said, "I
look like a constipated banker; and no doubt will drive thousands
of innocent morons back to the picture houses."

By now it seemed many others were against Pop's writing *Minutes of the Last Meeting,* so the entire family, including myself now,
swung over to my father's outlook just from family solidarity. Pop
wrote me regarding his high dive into a literary pool with a questionable amount of water to slow his plunge:

Sadakichi is a charlatan, a master sponger, a sack of thankless bones.
This misbegotten half-German, half-Japanese has been prancing about
the ateliers of two continents for half a century, insulting his betters,
drinking on the cuff, dancing obscenely, reciting erotic poems with the
manners of an old satyr in a convent. Be well warned: if you waste a
book on this crochety mountebank, you will have been roller skating
on his own purgatory, and the book will die the death of a dog. Thus
encouraged, I at last sit on a beach of the South Seas [a manner of
speech], forget that my bills are growing beyond all reason, and think
of Sadakichi Hartmann. I recall his asthmatic mumblings, his wrinkled,
long face of parchment pallor (he has the appearance of a stale lady
finger), the gray chrysanthemum thatch of his high skull, the home-
made truss lashed to his thin loins. I have already begun to write of
this man, and the book shall become a success.

When *Minutes of the Last Meeting* was published in 1954, it
turned out to be a success. Pop dedicated it to Pascal Covici with
the words: "Veteran friend and incurable confidant."

The last surprise birthday party we were to give Pop took place
that year. Just as the old man was about to retire for the evening

—he was sitting on the veranda with Mother, Gene, Jane, and her husband Paul Morrison—the crowd assembled and broke in on Pop.

Among them were Jimmy Durante, Eddie Jackson, Red Skelton, Thomas Mitchell, Jack Dempsey, George Putnam, Vincent X. Flaherty, Ned Cronin, Mickey Walker, Dave Chasen, and Leo McCarey. Pop had not had a drink for two years, but he would have a few that night. Putnam, the host, dissuaded Pop from running a foot race with Mickey Walker, who was years my father's junior and a sober citizen of long standing.

The following morning, as Pop was suffering his next to last hangover, a representative of the Ralph Edwards television show, *This Is Your Life,* telephoned me to ask if Pop might be a subject for that program. Before I began to talk this person out of the idea, I was asked, "Does Mr. Fowler still drink?"

"Hell yes," I said. "And as a matter of fact, I wouldn't trust him on your program if I were you."

When I told Pop about this conversation some time later, he said, "That's the trouble with some people. An author sits in his lonely office for two solid years. One night he decides to blow off steam. He travels to the nearest public saloon, gets tipsy and whistles at an old maid as she crosses from the dining room to the rest room. When she returns to her table, she tells her friends that she has been insulted. The author is recognized by one of the party who says, 'Why! That's so-and-so! I hear he's an incurable alcoholic!' And so it goes, my son."

My father started his final book a short time later that year. The working title was *Till Kingdom Come,* but Mother gave him the title *Skyline . . .* It was intended to be a thousand page volume, a reporter's reminiscence of the 1920s.

Pop was a charmingly ribald man, prone to toss out a collection of hardrock miner's four-letter words, but he did not like what he termed "smut" in the published word. He delighted in the works of Rabelais, Balzac, and Voltaire, although the monumental works of these three great authors are hardly reading prescribed by the Catholic Church. "They were inventive," Pop said, "and not like the smut writers of today who just like to put four-letter words on paper. Certainly the masters of the past have been realistic without constantly pounding home the fact that we sweat, evacuate, and are, in effect, walking septic tanks." He thundered, "Man seeks to be lifted above the sewage level, which is entirely important to health, but hardly as inspirational as contemplation of a Grecian urn or the gleam in a loved one's eyes."

One of our young author friends once asked Pop if he would review his latest book for a local newspaper. The author was unaware of Pop's dislike of four-letter words or the description of the sex act in a published book, and this one was replete with them.

Our friend must have been rather shocked when he received the following from the old man:

. . . The sad thing about any sincerely written book (as yours most assuredly is) is that, once it appears between hard covers, it no longer belongs to its creator. It is his only so long as he and it are conspiring at the desk . . .

Pop went on in detail to compliment this author on the lucid way in which he developed his main characters. Then he continued:

If you will permit me to say it, there were two or three scenes in your book which made me feel "dated" and hopelessly out of step with modern fiction. I refer to a few of the incidents which involve your character L—— and her didoes in the pursuit of that which we used to call "Nookie." I am so partisan to your powers of lyricism, and your patently deep mind as to think that you may, in your future works, not find it necessary to go into the actual bedroom rodeos in their bald details, from the saddling-up to the stroke-by-stroke bucking (I am glad I did not make a typo here) and sunfishing and squiggling. I am mindful that I am now in a minority in saying this, but I would like to state my case briefly. I am not speaking from a moral height (for, as everyone knows, I have been around for some time, and in all biological fields except the homosexual). But as an old codger, roguish, robust, life-loving and death-defying, I simply find that the younger writers sometimes go beyond the margins of license in making photographic exposures of that which Rabelais used to call "the two-backed beast." I tire of the acclaimed genius of Mr. James Jones *et al.* in their pages-upon-pages of nudes at work. It is very necessary and of dramatic value at times to bring in the nuptial flight of the queen bee and the tragic drone, and even to show the male vitals dragged from their roots and flung to the sky. BUT not *ALL* the time. *Life in the privy is not all of Life!*

. . . I remember a time when I stepped overboard (it would be considered mild and ordinary now in the writing world) in my first novel. I received two letters which impressed me—and most certainly did not offend me, because they were written by two wonderful friends: Ring Lardner and Elmer Davis. Both these gentlemen took me to task for some phrases which were descriptive of the love-locks of amatory wrestlers . . .

You know I never hesitate to get a bit ribald when the occasion arises (perhaps too often) but I try to *imply* the thing, not to *photograph* it . . .

. . . You have so many fine assets which are denied to the lesser writers, who must shock to be noticed, that I for one believe you should not put any shadow on your authentic abilities by writing with the fly open. . . .

While on the subject of his fellow writers, Pop told me at this time, "Some months ago, Ernest Hemingway wrote an article in *Esquire* magazine about Ring Lardner. I do not recall much about the article, except that I thought it disparaging, and detected in it a slight bit of envy. Hemingway has been acclaimed the most masterful fellow at handling dialogue. His clipped sentences have placed his devotees in a condition of incurable ecstasy. [Now that both Pop and Hemingway are both dead, the following quotes may now be most fair.]

"Now Mr. Hemingway is indeed one of our foremost writers, but I find many of his sentences, in effect, in the Third Grade readers of my own boyhood, and I do not recall any of my comrades having swooned with delight upon reading same.

"He undoubtedly will have a more considerable fame than Lardner, and perhaps justly so, but when we speak of the dialogue of athletes, particularly of baseball players and fighters, I can assure you as an old sports writer that Lardner is unsurpassed."

Soon after this, Pop wrote me a letter airing more of his views on current literature and its fashionable bleakness:

I was reading the Book Review section of *The New York Times*.

One of the literary critics, whose name I forget, extolled five of the apostles of doom who had predicted the age of despair which seems to have fallen upon our land. And in this article, the author indicated, by implication if not by exact statement, that we ought not to like life as it is lived, nor should we love the world; and also that the world is "gone" and that our most popular writers, clever as they are, seem to revel in the belief that there is no hope.

I say: "To hell with them!" I am still, in my somewhat advanced years, an optimist. I cannot believe in my heart that we are lost. I think that the men who run the world, the ones who operate the nations, perhaps, are lost or inefficient or lackadaisical to say the least. But life itself is not lost. And what in God's name are we living for if we do not have hope and if we do not have faith?

So many bleak thoughts, well-meant perhaps—but I think ill-advised —have sprung from cry-baby examinations of minorities. Well, the greatest of all minorities is this: *the living*. The dead are the majority. Shall we struggle against the dead?

When we look at the endless conflicts of one man against another, one creed or race against another, what are we to think of those who raise such a hullabaloo about the Protestant, the Catholic, the Jew, or the Arabian?

I look about me and ask: Has nature changed much through the centuries? Has the tree changed? Has the bird that I see changed? Has man himself changed in essence?

Man has changed only in his thinking. He thinks perhaps this thing is bad, and this thing good, fixing arbitrary values. But I ask this: Is the mountain a Jew? Is the ocean a Catholic? Is the shore and the land beyond it a Protestant? Is the sky Islamic?

What in the world are we doing, making these small-minded partitions, these divisions of Life, when Life is one thing and over all? Cannot we live intelligently in peace and think of life as a desirable thing? And of death as an eventuality? And not speak or write—as do these clever men of literary fashion—of life as not being worth the living?

Pop had taken complete stock of his memories. While putting together notes, millions of words of notes, for *Skyline*, he was, as Arthur Robinson told me, reliving his favorite decade, the twenties. Each morning and night when he walked down the seventeen steps to the room in which he worked, he was actually going back into the past, to relive it, to experience again the happy times he had when he and Mother were young, when everything was so different, and more fun.

But for his visits with cronies Jack Dempsey, Thomas Mitchell, Red Skelton, Ben Hecht, Lucius Beebe, Hedda Hopper, Paul J. Howard, and others, and his phone calls each day with Harry Brand, Pop had practically gone into monkish seclusion.

Cecil Smith of the Los Angeles *Times,* because he was a newspaperman, was granted an interview with Pop, who told him:

"I can never see myself as a literary man. I'm a newspaperman who writes books . . . Everybody's so touchy, they've taken the fun out of life . . . Sometimes, I think my writing sounds like I walked out of the room and left the typewriter running . . . [Quoting a glib critic:] This guy wrote about one of my books and said it was the best badly written book he'd ever read . . . Isn't that great?"

Shortly after Cecil Smith's interview, incinerators were banned in Los Angeles because they contributed to the smog. The day before the edict came into effect, Pop called me on the telephone to come over.

"I have a certain trash burning in mind, son," he said.

When I arrived, Pop had properly built up a bed of coals with an overglow of hotter yellow flames. "I did this with the clippings from my lemon tree . . . The one everyone said I couldn't grow down there in the shade."

Pop had me carry a corrugated box of about two cubic feet up from his work room. It was stuffed full with canceled checks. One, on top, had been for $500. These canceled checks represented loans to his friends throughout the years, say from 1922 to 1954. The reader would be astonished to know some of the names of those who since have become wealthy. Taking an average of the first thirty checks of each of sixty bundles I went through, it was my estimate that Pop had given away at least a half million dollars to his friends. It was Pop's fond dream to start an organized home for old newspapermen. What he did not realize during this burning was that he had actually provided a "home" for these men all the time.

I threw the box into the large brick incinerator. Pop left the iron door open and poked the charred paper slivers with a metal rod to be sure all the checks would burn. He said, "Not a word of this to your Mother."

"What makes you think Mother doesn't know?" I asked.

"I know she knows," said Pop, "but she doesn't know that *I* know."

"You're getting old, Pop," I said as I hugged him.

He laughed as he turned over the last of the burning checks and said, "I know that too, son."

As Pop chuckled—and I wanted to weep for the lost money I might have inherited to live out my days comfortably as a bum—a beat-up orange, white, and red cat stalked into the back yard and lay down at Pop's feet. Pop petted him and said, "My God, son. He reminds me of my old fighter friend Frank Moran after fifteen tough rounds."

This beat-up character of a cat tried to purr. He had only one front tooth. "Good night, son," said Pop. "I have a companion more in need than you."

When I drove away, Mother saw me off. "How about that cat?" I asked.

"You know Pop," said Mother. "If it's breathing, it'll be healthier than that lemon tree in no time."

Chapter Twenty-One

AFTER SIX WEEKS, A LUXURY
BECOMES A NECESSITY.

GENE FOWLER

Pop entered the hospital in November of 1955 for a glandular operation, packing along at least a thousand pages of notes and manuscript for *Skyline*. It was as though he expected to be a patient for months instead of ten days. On the eve of the operation, I allowed him to believe he was alone, only because the doctor suggested that he enjoy a good night's sleep before the operation. During the time Pop was awaiting the opiates to carry him into limbo, he wrote me a four-page letter. Shortly after he fell asleep, I walked into his room and took the letter. I read:

I expect to come out of this bind for two reasons: first, I love my Agnes and my children. Second, I am afraid of so many little things, as well as of high places, snakes, and lightning; but of life never afraid, and of mankind never timorous . . .

. . . Not that I am brave—I am proud. Proud to live. Too proud to die —without a rousing resistance. So the will to live is with me, and I hope and believe that God is with me, too.

I am at peace with God—and the fine priest, Father Norton (I think that is the young chaplain's name) has comforted me no end by telling me that which I have always wanted to believe is true: that for us to think that our sins are too grave for God to forgive, is to insult our Creator by saying or thinking that we poor mortals can do *anything*, however bad, that is greater than His infinite mercy. So do the right as best you can, and *believe!*

I have asked Mother not to come until I am on the mend. She has gone through so many trials (never once complaining) that I wish to spare her as much as possible.

He rambled, treading the brink of sleep as he wrote:

Wish I had been more thoughtful of Agnes in the years gone. But no need to put one's head or heart between the jaws of that Beast called the Past.

God love you and keep you, and let us have a few years more of a great relationship that squares all the troubles that come from the quarter where the ill-winds are whelped.

Pop came through the operation in good shape. When he opened his eyes, I was standing over him. He said, "Bill? I'm glad you're here. Am *I?*" I had promised him to be there when he awakened.

"Most assuredly, Pop," I said.

Pop chuckled, "I feel like a gelded lily." Then he slept.

When Polly Adler, the retired madam, who was visiting Paris at the time, was apprised of Pop's most personal male operation, she sent him a cablegram to the effect that the French Tricolor was "at half-mast!"

During the fourth night, after I had gone home to rest, but remained up to play penny-ante poker with George and Susie Clarke, Pop reached me on the phone. He seemed in panic. He told me he had fired his night nurse and asked that I come to the hospital immediately to assure him he was on the mend. Dr. Carl Rusche had already informed him that his disease was not of a malignant nature, but Pop wanted someone in the family near him.

I tried to lessen the pressure by saying, "George Clarke has me for nearly two dollars, and I have three queens against him."

Pop did not appreciate this, so I ran to my car. I was at the hospital in less than twenty minutes. I hired a new nurse to take the case, one more sympathetic than the previous one. Pop refused sedatives, and asked only that he speak with his son until he fell asleep.

A month later, Pop wrote to his literary representative, Willis Kingsley Wing:

Am back at work (part time) and am doing my own typing (and it looks it!). In a month or so I probably shall have thirty, or perhaps forty-thousand words to let you see. I am none too sanguine about a magazine market for this book, notwithstanding your remarkable ability to sell our prose. I cannot tailor the material to conform with the very understandable requirements of magazine matter. And there would be no point in my so doing when I could manage the same thing for movie sales and get ten times as much money for it (if I ever finish the work). So I must be content to concentrate on a book, and let the words fall where they may.

Pop was such a pessimist that he earnestly believed that when he became sixty-five some ancient edict would be invoked and Social Security benefits would automatically lapse. But the miracle did come to pass. He got his first "old age" check on schedule.

About this time Pop wrote a few lines to his ginger-coated cat, Frank Moran. He wrote, while working on the ending to his *Sky-line:* ". . . I should like to have you know that I always have had a pet beside me whenever I set to work on a book. I find that pets do not offer any criticism of me or of my work at a time when I am most vulnerable to snide intrusions. Would you like to be my mascot now? In many ways you remind me of the scars and scratches I incurred while trying to fulfill a vow I made years ago: 'To keep my spirit unbroken till kingdom come.' "

When playwright Charles MacArthur died in 1956, I heard Pop say while working in his hillside garden: "I couldn't believe Charlie was sixty. He was an eternal youth. Helen Hayes had written to me only a few weeks ago that Charlie was on the mend. Then this." Pop did not attend the funeral, for he was on the West Coast and Charlie was being laid away to rest in New York.

"I'll never forget," Pop told me, "when I was absolutely without money many years ago, and Mother and I were visiting Charlie and Ben at Hecht's Nyack house. I was broke, and when we left, Charlie gave Mother an envelope, warning her not to open it because, he said, there was 'something dirty' written there." As

Mother drove the car over the Queensboro Bridge, Pop opened the envelope. In it was a check for $1000. Attached to it was a note which read: *"This is a little something to tide you over. And if you ever try to pay it back, you son-of-a-bitch, I'll disown you!"* The next day in the mail, came another letter. It was from Ben. Hecht matched Charlie's $1000.

So many of his friends had gone now that Pop began to dread being the front left man on the casket. Passed on already were John Barrymore, Alexander Woollcott, Herbart Bayard Swope, Damon Runyon, John Decker, W. C. Fields, W. R. Hearst, Lee Casey, Jimmy Walker, Ashton Stevens, David Belasco, Fannie Brice, Heywood Broun, Arthur Brisbane, Roland Young, George M. Cohan, Jim Corbett, Sam Langford, Sadakichi Hartmann, Grantland Rice, only to name a few. "The dead are the many," Pop told me, "and the living are the few. I grow weary."

Those left included Ben Hecht, Jack Dempsey, Robert Hillyer, H. Allen Smith, Harry Brand, Lucius Beebe, Leo McCarey, Raoul Walsh, Joe Filkas, Lowell Thomas, Westbrook Pegler, "Bugs" Baer, and Pop's "adopted sons" Red Skelton and George Putnam, the latter a top Los Angeles television news commentator.

Now Pop bogged down on the writing of *Skyline*. He visited his workroom each morning before the sun rose, just to be around the millions of words in notes he had written about the '20s. For years he had holed up there to write. Lucius Beebe called it "a caboose," and that it was. Actually, it jutted over his great rock garden like a Spanish galleon's stern, minus the rococo carvings. It was of redwood siding on the outside, only about six by nine feet in size. When I built it, I had no plans. There were six walls, and none had the dimensions of the other. It was cantilevered for the front third over a garden drain Pop had put in himself. The entrance had a sliding door which disappeared into the wall, and it blended into the relaxed design of Pop's garden. A red bougainvillaea grew over the roof like a shock of Red Skelton's hair. Most important, it afforded a magnificent view of the gully below and the hill beyond.

My brother, Gene, supplied me with a rare type of ironwood, specially cut and laminated, from the Fiji Islands. Gene designed a desk which was built into the view wall and covered three angles.

Gene also designed bookshelves which held their own weight along one side and above the entrance door. Pop's Italian carpenter friend, John d'Amato, and Gene built them.

There were kept the original manuscripts of all Pop's books, plus the play, *The Great Magoo,* and the nearly completed screenplay *Farika,* on both of which Ben Hecht was his collaborator.

About the room were many mementoes, most of which are now gone. Above the built-in desk is a leaded-glass colored window, featuring two nuns, designed by Rockwell Kent, which will go to my brother. Below that, and directly over the desk are three niches which no longer contain various religious objects. Here about are pictures of Gene Fowler's children, Father Mac, Father Herbert Rogers, Father Duane Theobald, George Putnam, and a penny weight-guessing machine picture card of Red Skelton.

To the right still hang the hats of Red Skelton, Jimmy Durante, Jack Dempsey, W. C. Fields, and Gene's and my service caps. Then there is a picture of Pegler and Eleanor Roosevelt sitting in happy repose. The autograph below reads: "When we were young, Peg." The hats surround an oil painting in primitive style by the "toy bulldog" of boxing fame, Mickey Walker. It depicts a bulldog sitting in the middle of a room where a copy of *A Solo in Tom-Toms* lies on a desk. Next to the desk is a miniature Gladstone bag which used to carry the boxing gloves of Jack Dempsey before he became heavyweight boxing champion of the world. Then there is the prompt book of *Juno and the Paycock.* The sofa which graced the back end of the room is now gone. Over this used to hang the death sketch of John Barrymore which John Decker executed. Decker did two similar sketches, one of which he sold to Norman Kerry and the other to Earl Carroll. There might have been more, but the original is on manila wrapping paper.

Above where the death sketch hung was W. C. Fields' famed crooked pool cue, the prop which first brought him to the public's eye. Uncle Claude had left this to Pop in his will. Mother gave the cue to Red Skelton.

And there is another precious possession: a six-volume copy of *Good Night, Sweet Prince* in Braille which Mother intends to give to the Braille Institute in Los Angeles. Pop prized this above all.

There is a rare museum piece miniature ancient suit of armor

Ben Hecht gave Pop nearly thirty years ago, a four-wood golf club which Kitty Rice sent Pop after Grantland Rice died. On the left side, and above several boxed notes on the Barrymore and Walker books, are silk hats which belonged to these two men. And, naturally, there is a huge blue ostrich-feathered hat owned by his close friend Hedda Hopper. The decal color window, which New York Mayor William O'Dwyer sent Pop from the Tombs Prison chapel when it was dismantled, now hangs in my workroom.

An Italian hand-carved crucifix, below which was a first class relic (the bones) of St. Stephan, the saint after whom Pop had been baptized, now hangs in the room where I work.

Among these mementoes, Pop had carried on his remembrance of the past. He actually completed only two books, *Schnozzola* and *Minutes of the Last Meeting,* in this room. As for *Skyline,* he re-lived it more than he wrote it. But Pop continued on, as if his tome would be at least one thousand pages longer. I shared his belief that he would never live to finish this work.

Pop left home twice in his last years, both times late in 1957.

Dr. Paul Dudley White, the noted heart specialist, then President Dwight D. Eisenhower's physician, was attempting to record on paper the heart beat of the great gray whale. Dr. Frank Nolan was also attempting this feat, but under more difficult circumstances. Dr. White had selected the inland waters of Baja California, where the gray whale travels south to satisfy his mating urges. Dr. Nolan preferred to work the seas where the Japanese Current thrusts itself between Catalina Island and the mainland. A harpoon was devised which would enter the whale's fat-insulated body, then a seltzer-bottle capsule would drive a tranquilizer into the behemoth's system. After this, it was planned that Dr. Nolan would take two small harpoons with anodes and cathodes attached to an electrocardiograph, thrust them into the barnacled skin, and thus receive a reading of the monster's heart beat.

When Frank Nolan told him of the proposed venture, Pop said: "I've *got* to see this!"

Brother Gene and I went along with two camera crews. We put up in a Long Beach hotel the night before we were to board a Coast Guard cutter and seek the whales. Pop was the first up. He ordered coffee, then we all left for the cutter.

By 7 A.M. we were off the coast of Catalina Island and the sea was ripe with gray whales. Pop, a truly fine sea captain, notwithstanding the trip on which Durante became sick many years ago, directed the ship's captain to a grouping of four of the whales. The ship's chief petty officer hit home with the tranquilizer, but the result was not what we had expected. When the one-hundred-foot cutter drew alongside the whale, which was actually as huge as the ship, and the shot was administered, this beautiful mammal, with king-sized barnacles on his back, objected. He twirled in the sea, then threw off the barbless harpoon. Frank Nolan had his two electrocardiograph weapons in hand. He aimed, but when he viewed the size of the creature and what it might do to the ship, he retreated like a confused matador who was unsure of the placement of his *banderillas*. The tranquilized bull thrashed northward in the opposite direction from that in which he had been traveling for months to be serviced by some unsuspecting cow in the shallows off Baja California.

Pop directed the chase for the bull, but without luck. The ship's screw could not turn that fast. "If we proved anything during this scientific trip which was inter-spliced with huge passion," said Pop, "it's that there is *one* whale in the ocean which doesn't know north from south, nor, perhaps, girl from boy!"

As we journeyed toward the mainland, I looked up at Pop on the bridge. He was a happy captain. He looked great up there on the bridge, giving orders. He should have been the skipper of a freighter all his life, I thought.

Pop's last trip was with Jack Dempsey who asked him to travel to San Francisco for a grocer's convention. When Pop told me he would go, he remarked that "Dempsey is thirty pounds overweight; I'm only about ten above the required limit."

Recounting this last trip with his boyhood friend, Pop said: "When Jack and I are together, we don't spend too much time talking about fights or fighters. That's all part of Jack's public life . . . As a rule, I think we shouldn't know our public men behind the scenes because they put on their reputations as one would a cloak and nobody wants to believe anything other than the exterior of any so-called hero or public figure . . . Such people wear a mask, the personal legend, and they don't usually depart from it

. . . But with great old friends who know too much about each other to lie, it's different . . . We don't always talk all the time. In fact, Dempsey is pretty tired in private when nobody is looking at him, and he snoozes some. . . ."

Pop said a trip like this tired him somewhat, and that no one but Dempsey could draw him to a strange hotel room where the bed pillows were soft. "I'm used to hard pillows," he said; "like Jacob, I like to wrestle with angels."

There was to be a prize fight that night between Hurricane Jackson and Eddie Machen. "I thought that Jack was to be present for the fight in the course of his duties," Pop observed, "and I was delighted when Jack said, 'No.'"

"These guys are bums," said Dempsey when they reached the hotel.

"Well," Pop said, "what heavyweights today aren't bums?"

Dempsey nodded.

The two removed their shoes, then turned on television. The station they turned to was showing a film about the local zoo. Pop told me, "We came upon a very meaningful thing. An old bison had been king of the herd. He owned some nine cows. He was being attacked by a younger bull, challenging ownership. When we tuned in, the fight had been going on for about a half hour. We watched the tail end of the fight in silence; the last round, you might call it. The young bull was in the background. He had won the fight and seemed somewhat proud and happy as a few cows gathered 'round him. And the magnificent old bison was being attacked by the remaining cows. I have a dim memory of reading about this kind of thing in nature books. I suppose the females do attack feeble, or senile, or impotent husbands for the sake of a stronger race.

"At any rate," Pop continued, "the poor old bastard was standing there, his feet planted rather solidly and his great shaggy head, slowly, slowly, bowing while the keepers were prodding off the cows with pitchforks. And I might say these cows really wanted to get at the old boy.

"We watched intently after the cows had been cleared by several men who looked like various Neptunes with their tridents . . . Jack and I were still not speaking . . . It was rather gripping . . . And

I believe the various lessons of the scene came home to both of us . . . Slowly, the head of the dethroned bison lowered in a posture of magnificent dejection, and then, in contrast to the slowly lowering head, the body gave a quick whip-over and the buffalo was dead.

"I looked at Jack, and his face was set in an expression of awareness. A sorrow, I thought, came to his eyes.

"Jack said, 'That's the way it goes. We all are defeated at some time or another.'

" 'Yes,' I said, 'in anything we do, we have to meet defeat.'

"Jack said, 'And the dames, too. They turn on you, don't they?'

"I said, 'They quite often do. I suppose that's nature.' "

Pop told me it seemed to him that this bison's defeat in physical combat could apply not only to life, but to Jack in particular. "He often looked like that bison," Pop concluded.

Pop returned home tired. When I saw him, I noticed the luster of his eyes was somewhat dulled. When Mother saw him to bed, she turned to me and said, "You really have to have something to back up Pop's kind of unbridled nature. Few men have it."

Now Pop's friend Ned Cronin, sports columnist on the Los Angeles *Times,* suddenly died. Pop was at Cronin's house when the litter arrived and Cronin was carried away to the hospital to breathe his last. In one of his final columns Cronin wrote about a new friendship which had been struck up between Fowler and a recently retired English teacher hired by the University of Southern California, who made our language and its teachings interesting once again through the medium of television, Dr. Frank Baxter. Cronin wrote:

There is a professor of English out at Southern California known as Dr. What's-his-name, who was the Willie Shoemaker of his day until he got himself unhorsed at the Battle of Hastings and was sidetracked into the field of classroom enlightenment.

The most entertaining of all intellectuals, the good doctor had lunch out at 20th Century-Fox one day with two of his admirers, namely Gene Fowler and me. We tossed Harry Brand to see who picked up the tab. Tossed him clean through the window, in fact, and when he regained consciousness he learned he had just been nailed for the bill.

According to Cronin, Dr. Baxter sent Pop a picture of himself in a Roman toga, but I have yet to see it. Dr. Baxter wrote to Cronin:

Many thanks for sending along the magnificent epistle from the Abominable Snowman of Brentwood. I am, of course, more than a little hurt about the descriptions you and Fowler give of my beautiful burnoose.

This chaste garment was handed down to me from ancient Roman relatives who were regular free loaders at the feasts of Petronius Arbiter. One of my ancestors wore it when he was covering the courthouse beat for the Rome Picayune Times Papyrus on the very day that Julius Caesar was scratched.

I regret that two gentlemen, previously well considered by me, should mock me in my moment of imperial grandeur. I had thought of consulting my attorney, but after rereading your letters I decided instead to go to my chaplain!

Pop was getting little work done on *Skyline*. He worried his impatient publishers. He had now been working five years on the same manuscript, and there was a sizable advance outstanding. To get himself mentally in shape for resuming work, Pop called me up to accept an invitation which my friend Bob Williams offered, a Catholic retreat, fifty hours of silence. Pop, Bob Williams, his own father, and I reached the old Rindge estate on a finger of a small mountain which overlooks the sea and the Malibu colony—a peninsula of sand sprinkled with the big houses of the movie colony. Before this time, my mother-in-law, Bess Blanchard, a realtor, held rights to the exclusive selling and buying of houses here where old-timers of the movie world who had overextended themselves sold to the newer names of the cinema world. It always seemed to me that the houses were actually trading people, rather than the other way around.

The Franciscans conduct this retreat. We were silent all the time as we absorbed religious teachings and good, simple food. Pop and I were in separate cells, but during the first night, he could not sleep for the coughing and snoring and groaning of a fellow retreatant on the other side. Pop slipped me a note. It read: "Is he breaking silence . . . . or *shattering* it?"

Pop returned to his garden after the retreat. He seemed peaceful once again, and wrote me:

I like to garden for the reasons set down by Bacon:
The exercise it affords, then the out of doors when the sun sets. The sense of accomplishing a labor of love, for the hope of seeing life come from the earth, but most of all I like it because it is a bank of devouring, parent justice, with no governmental snoops to oversee the non-profit overture.

In March of 1959, Pop's friend, Secretary of Labor James P. Mitchell, was much taken by what my father had arranged in his garden. It was a plateau raised up so that flagstone could be laid there and a hole sunk for Mother's umbrella against the hot sun. Pop put a wall around the small place, only about four-by-four feet. He called it "the smallest park in the world." Fred A. Seaton, then Secretary of the Interior, wrote Pop a letter saying:

. . . Should you be interested, I would hope a mutually convenient time could be arranged for yourself, Secretary Mitchell, and me to meet at your home and undertake the ceremony which this project obviously so richly deserves.

Pop named the sanctuary over his garden St. Agnes National Park.

Men about to leave each other for good usually know it. Pop's old friend, former city editor of the New York *Herald Tribune*, Stanley Walker did. His final words to Pop were, "Carry on, punch sharply with the left, and alert me when you think I need alerting."

Pop, in many ways, was like a good book, and he lived his life the way a good book is read: You never really wish to finish it, although you race through the volume until you reach the last page. He was nearly seventy. Seventy is a fine long life to live . . . except, that is, to a man who is sixty-nine. Late in 1959 he wrote me:

Cigarets are said to cause lung cancer in people who smoke them; cranberries cause cancer in rats. Cigarets have not been stripped from the shelves and banned in the markets; cranberries *have* [he was speaking of that cranberry fiasco during the last administration when the red fruit in cans was labeled dangerous for human consumption, investigated, then quickly put back on the shelves]. It is good to find our rats protected—S.P.C.A. biddies can sleep undisturbed.

How he lampooned the Republican administration now, although he was a Republican! He went on to say:

As 1959 starts to get the death rattle, we have another problem facing us—how to keep selling "furriners" more gadgets than they can sell us! We have been successful in educating them to buy on the cuff, but the ninnies buy their own stuff that way instead of ours. In the early 1940s Germany blasted hell out of much of Europe, then we joined the party and blasted hell out of Germany, Italy and Japan.

Comes the dawn of peace—no! just the cessation of blasting—and we overwhelmed ourselves with remorse and dumped in dollars (good ones then, too); we educated those "furriners" to make all kinds of gadgets, and we gave 'em new, modern plants for the scrap heap we had made, and now look at the ungrateful glommers! They are selling too damn much stuff in our markets, and reaching right into Fort Knox for our gold. And our people, on the cuff, are touring Europe madly in droves, apparently only for the satisfaction of being overcharged and sneered at. There is nothing that Americans like better than to set themselves up as better clay than "furriners" and to lay themselves open to gypping and insults. And here comes 1960 with travel agencies booked solid for more of the same. Ah, well! We live without learning! On with the big splurge!

At our next meeting, I decided there were a few important questions I wished Pop to answer. "What about birth control?" I asked him. "This is a perpetual question asked of Catholics by non-Catholics, and I don't seem to have an adequate answer."

Pop said, "Birth control information for backward people threatens Peace, Prosperity, People, and the Pulpit. The romp in bed is in danger of censorship. We are not told who loses if there are fewer infants to die in babyhood, or to grow to a maturity that never is to be adequately nourished . . . Query—who loses? Certainly not the child that never was. . . ."

"Don't you think," I asked, "that if man keeps on practicing his favorite pastime with such fervor there soon will be standing room only?"

"I am too old now to bother or discuss that," said Pop.

"Well, then," I continued, "let's talk about the dollar."

"The stock market goes up and up—almost as fast as the dollar gets eroded," he said. "In order to get market speedup to that of dollar erosion we have to consume more goods on the cuff. Someday equilibrium will be reached—maybe Congress can boost things with more spending. Then we really can hit the toboggan for the best little old slide ever. There is a fly in this ointment, but people don't see him yet. The fly is the fact that there is no tow lift to go back for another slide. But—so what!"

"What do you mean, 'so what'?" I asked. "That's a hell of a summation."

"To me," Pop said, "the expression 'so what' is the epitome and acme of philosophy. The Russians have beaten us to the moon. So what! We failed to put a monkey in orbit. So what! It will rain like hell in ten minutes. So what! Stocks made a new high today. So what! It's all there. So what!

"The year 1960 is at hand and it is going to be tougher than ever. So what? So let's have a Merry Christmas—you and me—and anyone else like-minded!"

Pop and I had our last tipple together the day Mother met me at the front door and said, "Pop's cat just died, and I don't know how to tell him." I said I'd do it.

I found Pop in his tan bathing trunks, wrestling with a huge boulder in his precipitous hillside garden. He saw me and called out, "If I move this damned Gibraltar, I can give that scrawny lemon tree Paul Howard said couldn't grow where it's growing an extra ten minutes of sunlight."

I did not offer to help him move the three-hundred-pound boulder. I am not the lazy type, but Pop was a man with pride. As he tussled with the stubborn stone, I marveled at the muscle tone of this man who was nearly seventy years old. The sweat poured from beneath the wispy white hair that had forever been combed as a pompadour. The deltoids which made his shoulders unusually broad were beaded with sweat as the sun reflected the power still contained in this tanned body.

"He's fighting that damned rock," I said to myself, "like he fights life—with all he has—everything."

As he put the stone into its new place and gathered and packed the dirt around so that at the next rain it would not be dislodged, he said, "I'll be with you in a minute, son . . . My cat, Frank Moran, is very sick, and I'm worried. . . ."

"Plenty of time, Pop," I said. Then I thought: I'll give it right out to him, the way he wants it.

"See my new rose?" he said, as he started up the precarious alpine slope of his garden. "The one with a tinge of blue in it. Absolutely wonderful. I planted it in a bad spot, but it's just put out a bud." He sat on the boulder and pointed to a semi-shaded place. "Look at it. Isn't it beautiful?"

"Now that's really something," I said. "It does seem to have a bit of blue in it."

"Paul Howard calls it 'Sterling Silver,'" said Pop.

"You'd better get up here before you catch cold," I said. "Mother told me Frank just died, and she was afraid to tell you."

Pop looked at me, almost lost for a moment, then took in several deep breaths as he started up the hill to the patio. "I figured that. I don't know why. Always expecting the worst, I guess." He was up to me now, and leaped over the four-foot wall at the top of the hill. "There's some Scotch in my workroom closet," he said. "Break it out and bring down some ice and water while I take a shower. I smell like an old goat. I'll be right down."

When Pop appeared in his workroom, which was littered with thousands of pages of notes on *Skyline,* I had a cold, tall drink of Scotch and water awaiting him. He took a draught, then sat down. He spoke not a word of his cat's death. Rather he complained that the Bureau of Internal Revenue had recently sent him a letter alleging that there were discrepancies in earned income against what he had been paid in Social Security old age benefits, and demanding an answer.

"I blew my top," he told me. "I phoned them and informed

their unlucky representative, Mr. Johnson, that there had been *six* grammatical errors in their demanding letter, and although I didn't expect a William Faulkner or a John Steinbeck to write it, they should at least have achieved third-grade English if they demanded absolute perfection from me as a bookkeeper and mathematician."

Pop further told me that Mr. Johnson of the Bureau had visited him that day; the whole thing was now straightened out, and he did not owe the government money after all. To show good faith, Mr. Johnson wrote a letter for Pop to keep everything clear. The gentleman asked: "Now do you understand what to put down next year?"

"Less than ever," Pop had said.

"Then I'll be back next year," said Mr. Johnson, "and write it for you."

Pop finished his drink, and said, "The government should publicize nice guys like Johnson. But then, I suppose Uncle Sam would remain in the red if this was done. I'm going to miss that old one-toothed cat of mine."

I mixed another drink, and we talked until dawn.

Pop shed a few Irish tears for his cat before he went to bed. He always put a great blob of Vaseline into his mouth so that his throat would not become parched during his usual night of tossing. As I said good night to him, I wondered at his stamina.

On March 8, 1960, Pop became seventy. It was a quiet birthday. George Putnam mentioned it on his television news show. Old friends called on the phone, and Pop was happy to visit with his family and be quiet.

His granddaughter, Martha, wife of UCLA geology student John Warme, had presented him with his first great-grandchild, a girl, named Susan Lynn. Pop spent much of his time visiting with Martha and her newborn. Being a great-grandfather was to Pop like winning the Congressional Medal of Honor. He bore this status proudly. The new child's picture now occupied the first window in his wallet.

Three weeks later, Thomas Mitchell became a great-grandfather, and the two formed an exclusive club for great-grandfathers. Only two members.

Pop and his group of friends were now down to a very few. He and Mitchell visited with each other most. When Dempsey was in town the three got together, sometimes with George Putnam or Paul Howard, always with Harry Brand. There was also Roseñdo Ramirez, his gardener. Whenever Pop lapsed into a melancholy mood, Harry Brand was the one who usually was first to sense it and trumped up a luncheon of some sort. In June of 1960, Pop met writer John Lee Mahin at a children's dance recital at which my brother's daughter, Kim, was appearing.

"I hear you're going to write for television," Pop said to John.

"I was," said Mahin, "until I went back East to meet these people. Now, I'm getting out of it as quickly as possible. They're a bit dense for me."

Pop laughed, then commented, "Yes. I hear they get TV writers from the Yellow Pages of the phone book now."

Pop had written to his old friend, newspaperman Arthur Robinson, that he was stuck on page 386 of his projected book on the '20s and that he had only passed through the year 1919. Robinson wrote back, "If you are stuck, Gene, write your very last chapter. Then write *up* to *it*."

Pop started on the last chapter. His tome was never to be completed, perhaps because, as he told me many times, "When I finish the book, son, I think I will die."

He completed a draft of the last chapter on July 2, 1960. On that day he visited all of the family he could find, driving more than fifty miles, then traveled home to be alone with Mother. And, as it turned out, with death.

As the friends began to congregate shortly after Pop died, Mother was the last to go out on the patio where he rested; where he had been looking at his garden. I closed the small door off the dining room and peeked through at my father for the last time as Mother bent down gently and kissed him. "I want your lips to be the last to touch mine," Pop had told Mother.

Chapter Twenty-Two

THE LIFE OF A FOOL IS
WORSE THAN DEATH.

GENE FOWLER

July 3, 1960

It was strange that I found time for six hours' sleep. I had driven my brother home earlier. Halfway to Beverly Hills, the usual impolite Southern California auto brushed past us and the passenger on the right side shouted an obscenity in our direction.

I exploded and pursued the car, honking my horn until the vehicle turned a sharp corner and skidded to a halt at the curb ahead of us. It suddenly occurred to me that I would not like to appear at my father's Rosary with a black eye or a broken nose. I felt like a gladiator who had reached the end of his combat days. In my younger years I could have taken both the fellows on with a dazzling display of a technique I had learned first from my father and later practiced in various barrooms. But now I am older, wiser, and have had too many draws, not to mention a few losses. I remembered, as I got out of the car, Pop's words: "If you haven't been knocked on your ass, you can't say you've ever really been in a fight."

I made the proper challenge to one of the young men, squared off, shouted that I had just lost my father a few hours earlier, and that I really did not give a damn what happened.

The young driver's fists relaxed. He offered his hand to me. This was the oldest trick in the book. I was awaiting the next move.

Then the driver said, "I know how you feel, pal. I lost my own father four years ago."

We shook hands. . . .

I mentioned I had six hours' sleep. Actually this sleep was interrupted by the telephone ringing several times. I scarcely recall talking to thoughtless drunks who wished to unburden their foggy minds, thinking they were affording me a great comfort.

I arrived at Mother's house about noon. Harry Brand was there with George Putnam and the rest of the family. Sybil Brand had prepared a cold cut buffet for those who would be dropping in to pay their respects. Jim Murray, now sports columnist of the Los Angeles *Times,* and his wife Gerry were there. Tommy Mitchell was back again. Father Herbert Rogers, Pop's boyhood chum John Pierce, Dave Chasen and his wife Maude, Jimmy Durante, Leo McCarey, Dr. Barney Kully and Audrey, Pop's gardener Roseñdo Ramirez, and many others showed up.

Red Skelton called me by telephone. He was starring at a night club in Las Vegas, but said he would do his last show and hop a plane for Los Angeles to be in time for the 9 A.M. service at St. Martin's on Wednesday. He promised that his wife, Georgia, would be there.

A telegram came from another friend which read:

DEAR WILL—I'LL BE THERE WEDNESDAY MORNING WITH SORROW IN MY HEART FOR THE LOSS OF YOUR FATHER AND MY BEST FRIEND. JACK DEMPSEY

We spoke of getting Pop's will, but it was locked up in a safe-deposit vault over the long weekend. The cemeteries were closed, too, and we were not able to bury Pop until Wednesday.

Jane, Gene, and I decided who the active pallbearers would be: Harry Brand, Jack Dempsey, Jimmy Durante, Randolph Hearst, Ben Hecht, L. D. Hotchkiss, Barney Kully, Leo McCarey, Thomas Mitchell, Dr. Frank Nolan, Westbrook Pegler, George Putnam, Roseñdo Ramirez, and Red Skelton.

At 4 o'clock in the afternoon, I sat on the chaise longue on which Pop had died just twenty-four hours earlier. Beverly came and sat beside me. Seeing my watch at four, straight up, gave me a sort of sick electric feeling. This was the first direct experience which started me to withdraw from the numbness, the shock nature seems to protect us with during these times of extreme stress. All at once, I began to hear and understand what friends sitting about me on the patio were saying. I took my watch off and put it in my pocket, then joined in the relaxed conversation.

By Monday, which was Independence Day, the long vigil had begun to tell on us all. We got Mother to bed early, then I went home as the children were waiting for me to set off their fireworks. Previously on Fourth of Julys, I had stolen most of the fun from the children by lighting the larger and more interesting-looking explosives myself. Tonight, they conducted the pyrotechnics by themselves. Claudia was overwhelmed by my generosity, as was our fourth child, Jenny, now just five years old.

Next day Beverly and I called for Mother so we might pick out Pop's grave site. We headed south on the San Diego freeway toward Holy Cross Cemetery in Inglewood. Mother said, "We must find a spot where I won't have to walk too far. My legs aren't what they used to be."

A poker-faced salesman escorted us to his automobile. On the way, a lady whose car was stalled on a difficult grade asked me to assist her. I tried to push the car, but could not budge it. I called to three loitering, uniformed attendants: "Is it possible, without having another Resurrection, that a body might be helped *out* of this joint?" The young men sprang to action.

We chose a site on a gentle hill near a young tree which I hope will be an old tree when I am buried there. The salesman placed metal markers that looked like out-of-bounds markers on a golf course at the head of four graves in a horizontal row. He pointed to the one which would receive Pop tomorrow. The remaining three will wait for Mother, Beverly, and me.

We stopped at the drive-in where Pop had so often ordered two pieces of lemon pie and coffee. Because Mother had already lost eight pounds during the past four days, we convinced her she should eat a hamburger. I had a milk shake to quiet a returning duodenal ulcer.

We went to the bank, where Mother took Pop's last will and testament from the safe-deposit vault. The lady who showed us into the vault was named Miss Bourbon. Pop would have appreciated that name.

At the Brentwood home, Mother gathered Jane, Gene, and me into the bedroom. Jane and I sat on Mother's bed. Gene and Mother chose hard chairs. Mother opened the will and glanced briefly at the first of the six-page holograph document, then said, "It's dated November 15, 1955. Who wants to read it?" Gene read the will:

Inasmuch as I, Gene Fowler, Sr., have become increasingly mindful these last two years that the Grim Reaper has sharp elbows, and is nudging me, I desire now to make my Last Will and Testament. This is it. I hereby revoke any and all other documents of its kind heretofore made by me in the days when material goods were appreciably more sizable, but my spiritual assets immeasurably less valuable, than they are now. As of today there is nothing wrong with my brain or my mind, in the clinical or the legal sense, although I wish that I had made a more earnest effort to improve both brain and intellect in the areas of knowledge and of good will to my fellow man. I dislike few men, and can say in God's presence that I hate no one. Life has been good to me.

(1)

I need not apologize to my heirs for the fact that I have given such small attention to the material prizes of this World. I do desire, however, to thank my wife, *Agnes Fowler,* and my three children, *Gene, Jr., Jane Fowler Morrison,* and *Will Fowler,* and all my friends for their loyal forbearance and deep understanding of my attempt, at a great loss of financial opportunities for their and my benefit, to achieve my life-long aspiration to write for my own soul's satisfaction instead of for the possible applause of the larger audience. There comes a time in the life of every artist when he must choose between the objective of mon-eyed ease and/or the sure prospect of lonely struggle and sacrifice and lack of recognition until he grows very old or is dead. The latter choice was mine, and my only regret is that I am unable to insure the financial protection of my beloved wife *Agnes* if she survive me.

(2)

It is with these sober thoughts that I make the following provisions in this, my Last Will and Testament: [Numbered paragraphs 2 to 7 directed that all his earthly goods and properties be given to Mother. The last paragraph read:] To my many dear friends I leave a large share of my love and gratitude. And to my children and their children I express the hope that, when they remember me, they do so with a smile, and never a tear. May God bless you in every way, and keep you and our Great Country forever free and in the right.

Two black limousines picked us up for the Rosary at St. Martin of Tours. Scores of richly colored flower sprays and wreaths decorated the entrance to the church, in which about five hundred people were waiting. The moment Gene and I helped Mother up the steps and into the entranceway, the young Father Theobald, attired in black vestments, blessed the polished walnut casket directly in front of us.

I saw the family to its cars afterwards, then walked back into St. Martin's to see that Pop's body would remain overnight near a side altar. Beverly had requested earlier that the coffin remain open during the night for reasons of her own. "Even open it for just one minute," she said. "Pop had claustrophobia, you know."

Later at Mother's house, some old friends phoned from Ireland to suggest that we have a wake. The connection was poor, so I spoke as loudly as possible and said, "It wasn't planned this way, but I believe we have been having one for the past four days!"

The theatrical trade newspaper, the *Hollywood Reporter*, published a front-page paragraph naming the pallbearers for Pop's funeral. The story was impeccably correct, but the sub-headline exhibited a glaring typographical error. It read GENE FOWLER BALLBEARERS. Mother claimed that the fellow who set the type had been a close friend, adding, "He had to be."

The following day, a long-time friend, piano virtuoso Ray Turner, picked up my family at our Encino home. He remained with us after the black cars had called once again to deliver the family to the church. Bishop Timothy Manning was present to conduct the last rites.

Father Ed Carney, the Celebrant, shook the rafters in eulogy with his deep voice.

Although L. D. Hotchkiss, retired managing editor of the Los Angeles *Times*, and Dr. Barney Kully were active pallbearers, their state of health did not permit them to help carry the casket.

Ben Hecht's printed recollection of the funeral a few days later best portrays Pop's character and attitude while he himself was attending the last rites for a dear friend. He wrote:

Our Fowler was a reverent and antic man. He loved deeply but with amusement. This quality was most evident in him as a pallbearer.

He never wept at the planting of a friend. His salute to mortality was always a burst of merry and tender anecdote starring the newly buried one. His pain was always a private matter.

I had been to many funerals with Gene. I remembered them all as I sat in the Los Angeles church staring at Gene's coffin—eight of us with white carnations in our buttonholes, waiting to tote the mighty Fowler to another hole in the ground. It was hard keeping in mind that Gene had changed places—left our midst for the flower-decked walnut box in front of us. Nor had he, entirely. For his point of view was alive among us, and his soft chuckle for the oddities of funeral solemnities still sounded.

"Well, well," said Gene during the church service, "I see that you boys have utilized my demise for a night of heavy drinking. Brother McCarey looks as if he'll not last the sermon through. I offer eight to five I look in better shape than he does. I see that Brother Mitchell is teetering in the pew. Sitting silent for two hours is always a dreadful strain on Tommy. I recall at Barrymore's obsequies he outwitted the parson by going into a coma. A rumor swept the mourners that we were burying the wrong man.

"All right, boys. The Reverend Father will wind down after another bird call. You may all rise, and follow me. Careful, Brother Dempsey, your footwork isn't what it used to be. It's only a short haul to the hearse, Brother Skelton. Try and make it without distracting the mourners with one of your world-famed pratfalls. Not that I'd mind, gentlemen, but my good Agnes was always a little critical of undignified behavior. And justly so—mark you. And what could be more undignified than a bouncing cadaver?"

Looking back from the first mourner's car on the San Diego freeway, I noticed a half mile of automobiles. The caravan with headlights glowing seemed like a stream of fireflies. Father Theobald gave the final blessing at graveside.

While George Putnam delivered a short layman's eulogy, a

hummingbird with bright yellow plumage zoomed in close to view the family sitting on folding bridge chairs. It made a tight turn, looked over the yellow roses and flowers from Pop's garden on the casket, then made a great circle and passed on into the sky.

Hecht went on to write, as though Pop were still speaking:

"Well, here we are again, gentlemen, gathered at one of my favorite spots—a cemetery. A beautiful day, a beautiful scene. But don't let me oversell you, boys. I picked this pretty yard myself because it's on a small hill and thus a few feet nearer to God. Remember when we called on Brother W. C. Fields during his last days and found him in his garden, pouring gin into himself and holding, of all things, a Bible in his hand? And I said, 'Mr. Fields, what are you doing with that Bible?' To which he answered, 'Looking for loopholes.'

"I may have found one.

"Well, grab hold the handles, boys, here we go on the last of my travels. And, please, as a favor, try not to trip on the way to my final resting place. I see Brother Dempsey has squashed his finger in the casket handle. And Brother Skelton is stumbling about as if he were playing Blind Man's Bluff. And Brother Mitchell's hernia is taking his mind off his work. But, praise the Lord, Brother McCarey is calling firmly, 'Let's not muck it up, boys!' A pal to the end. Well done, gentlemen. Everyone still on his feet and my casket going neatly into its pit like a golf ball on a perfect putt.

"Thanks, Brother Pegler and Brother Hecht. I'll put in a fair word for all of you.

"Not a bad funeral—except, if I may be allowed a small boast, Pallbearers aren't what they used to be. Good night, ye sinners all—God love you."

After the services, we traveled to Mother's house where Dave Chasen had prepared a fine meal, the chief dish of which Jimmy Durante insisted was *"Lagoo."* Friends talked quietly. There were some I could hear say, "I remember the time when Gene and I . . ." Then there was laughter which promised that things would be swinging full force within a few hours.

I did not say goodbye to anyone as I left through the front entrance unnoticed. I was heading home to feel alone for the first time in my life.

Outside, I noticed that Pop had finally won Mother over by removing that stringy rose bush in the shaded parkway bed.

Then I looked to the other side of the entryway and saw a brown milk bottle with a note thrust halfway down its throat. Inquisitive, I plucked the note from the milk bottle. There were only two words penciled on it. They read:

Nothing today.